Making the Global Econom

Marco Magnani

Making the Global Economy Work for Everyone

Lessons of Sustainability from
the Tech Revolution and the Pandemic

palgrave
macmillan

Marco Magnani
LUISS Guido Carli
Rome, Italy

ISBN 978-3-030-92083-8   ISBN 978-3-030-92084-5   (eBook)
https://doi.org/10.1007/978-3-030-92084-5

To my mom,
for her tireless and unconditional support,
in the making of this book and much more....

To Dave, Linda, Suzie and Mike,
who have generously welcomed me,
opening their home and their hearts,
providing an essential contribution to my personal development

Be fruitful and multiply and
fill the earth and subdue it,
and have dominion over the
fish of the sea
and over the birds of the heavens
and over every living thing
that moves on the earth. [...]
The Lord God took man
and put him in the garden of Eden
to work it and keep it.

> (*Genesis* 1:28; 2:15 ESV)

Man puts an end to darkness
and searches out to the farthest limit
the ore in gloom and deep darkness. [...]
Man puts his hand to the flinty rock
and overturns mountains by the roots.
He cuts out channels in the rocks,
and his eye sees every precious thing.
He dams up the streams so that they do not trickle,
and the thing that is hidden he brings out to light.
But where shall wisdom be found?
And where is the place of understanding?

> (*Job* 28:3; 9–12 ESV)

Consider well your seed
that gave you birth:
you were not made to live as brutes,
but to follow virtue and knowledge.

> (Dante, *Divine Comedy*,
> Inferno, XXVI, 118–120)

Acknowledgements

There are many people I have to thank for their help in making this book.

I thank friends and colleagues for the many comments, insights and suggestions. Among them Philippe Aghion, Ugo Amaldi, Giuliano Amato, Carlo Bernardi, Andrea Bianchi, Giovanni and Lorenzo Bonotto, Rossana Borretti, Alberto Broggi, Massimo Cacciari, Antonio Calabrò, Marco Cantamessa, Giuseppe Casagrande, Mimmo Castelli, Bruno Ceretto, Livietta Ceotto, Michele Ceotto, Daniele Checchi, Franco Chiarini, Piero Cipollone, Federico Colonna, Richard Cooper, Giovanni Cucci, Gian Paolo Dallara, Ferruccio De Bortoli, Luca De Francesco, Domenico De Masi, Marco De Masi, Antonio De Vuono, Mario Enrico Delpini, Massimo Egidi, Sergio Fabbrini, Maurizio Ferrera, Giovanni Maria Flick, Grazia Francescato, Daniele Franco, Sandro Gambuzza, Marco Gardini, Espedito Gasparo, Kristalina Georgieva, Francesco Giavazzi, Enrico Giovannini, Bruce Greenwald, Gilberto Guidi, Tarja Kaarina Halonen, Bengt Holmström, Glenn Hubbard, Pietro Ichino, Renzo Iorio, Philip Kotler, Hans-Helmut Kotz, Luciano Larivera, Riccardo Lattanzi, Vincenzo Lenucci, Luca Lucentini, Giorgio Ricci Maccarini, Carlo Emilio Maggi, Mauro Magatti, Riccardo Magnani, Walter Magnoni, Kishore Mahbubani, Micaela Marcon, Mauro Maré, Davide Masi, William Mebane, Maurizio Melis, Roberto Menotti, Marcello Messori, Roger Myerson, Francesca Montagna, Nicola Monti, Massimo Mucchetti, Joseph Nye, Attilio Oliva, Fabrizio Onida, Marco Orofino, Horacio Pagani, Pietro Panepinto, Luca Parmitano, Antonello Pasini, Cristina Pensa, Tommaso Piffer, Luca Pizzamiglio,

Francesco Profumo, Giovanni Quaglia, Martin Reeves, Alessandro Roselli, Alfonso Rubinacci, Dominick Salvatore, Anna Scalfi, Stefano Scarpetta, Augusto Schianchi, Pietro Sebastiani, Amartya Sen, Maro Sesana, Robert Shiller, Alp Simsek, Michael Spence, Joseph Stigliz, Larry Summers, Anna Maria Tarantola, Fabrizio Traù, Guido Traficante, Alfio Torrisi, Robert Zoellick, Matteo Maria Zuppi. I am particularly grateful to Andrea Cane, Angelo Ciancarella and Maurizio Gili for their sincere friendship and precious advice.

Special thanks to Giuseppina Tomasello, a brilliant young economist, without whose collaboration the content of the book would not be so precise and documented, and to Fosco Riani, one of the brightest among my former students and currently a successful manager, without whom the English edition would contain many inaccuracies. Those that may still be present are my total responsibility.

I would like to thank Gian Luca Pulvirenti, managing director of DeAgostini Libri, and Mattia de Bernardis, publisher of UTET, for their role in the publication of the book in Italian and the production of the second edition. A special thanks to Maria Luisa Borsarelli, De Agostini Libri Foreign Rights Manager, for the tireless effort and commitment in the process of transferring publishing rights. Finally, I would like to express my gratitude to the publisher Palgrave Macmillan, particularly to Executive Editors Tula Weis and Ellie Duncan and Editorial Assistant Srishti Gupta for their trust and support. I am grateful to the entire publisher team for the work of editing, proofreading and the other tasks necessary to the finalization of this volume.

Milan
December 2021

Praise for *Making the Global Economy Work for Everyone*

"Due to our extraordinary innovations, for the first time in history machines are replacing not only our muscles and hands, but also our minds. Are we heading towards growing but desperately jobless economies? Marco Magnani does not exclude it, yet he proudly indicates a division of labor by which the soft skills of humans, from creativity to all the dimensions of emotional intelligence, will not be replaceable. Shepherds we were - he writes - shepherds we will remain. Even with robots."

—**Giuliano Amato**, *Vice President of the Constitutional Court, former Prime Minister of Italy*

"We look at the future with hopes and fears. We feel great responsibility and have many unanswered questions. In this book, Marco Magnani analyzes some of the key challenges of our times, stimulates reflection and suggests new paths to explore. A must-read."

—**Mario Delpini**, *Archbishop of Milan*

"Making the global economy work for everyone might seem an impossible mission. The route to a just and truly sustainable future is impervious and strewn with pitfalls. Yet Magnani's compelling and thoughtful roadmap dispels many lingering fears and provides sound hopes that a balance can be found between economic growth and protection of the environment, avoiding a human vs. machine conflict and making innovation a constructive key factor to face the perilous journey beyond the Pillars of Hercules!"

—**Grazia Francescato**, *Environmental leader, former President of Italian Green Party and member of Italian Parliament, former President of WWF Italy*

"Magnani guides us through the fascinating territories of a future shaped by a new nexus between innovation and growth – at best, one of a technology-driven jobless growth, at worse one where the tie between technological progress and economic expansion is strongly severed. He offers a sharp insight on the challenges and responsibilities ahead of us to smooth out the potential disruptive effects on world prosperity."

—**Daniele Franco**, *Minister of Economy and Finance of Italy, former Senior Deputy Governor of the Bank of Italy*

"The COVID-19 crisis has brought humanity unprecedented hardships and, perhaps more than other crises before it, it has served as a catalyst to innovate and an opportunity to transform to build a better world. In his insightful and thought-provoking book, Making the Global Economy Work for Everyone, Marco Magnani helps us imagine that better world. He puts innovation in historical perspective, and shows how we can 'put human beings at the centre' to harness 'socially balanced and sustainable' innovation for the well-being and betterment of us all."

—**Kristalina Georgieva**, *Managing Director of the International Monetary Fund*

"Marco Magnani's book is a welcome reflection of those risks and opportunities that lie in economy and technology in a post-pandemic world. It is very necessary to continue this discussion."

—**Tarja Kaarina Halonen**, *President of Finland 2000–2012*

"The flip side of innovation and its potential is disruption and its discontents. Waves of innovation have brought gains around the world. In this important book, Marco Magnani reminds us that the current pace of technological change and innovation raises difficult questions of sustainability and broadly sharing prosperity's fruits to bolster support for innovation and disruption. Business leaders and policy makers will want to read the book's insights on how to navigate these questions. Otherwise, as Magnani notes, 'this time might be different' in ways that leave us worse off."

—**Glenn Hubbard**, *Russell L. Carson Professor of Economics and Finance, Columbia University. Chair of the U.S. Council of Economic Advisers for President George W. Bush*

"Finally, a book helping us to think intelligently about our exciting but also worrisome future. Innovation propels economic growth that in turn provides jobs for all. But innovation also destroys jobs. Machines and robots replace workers. AI and algorithms replace professionals. Unconstrained economic growth can ruin the planet. Marco Magnani helps us understand how we can navigate through these challenges."

—**Philip Kotler**, *S. C. Johnson Distinguished Professor of International Marketing at the J. L. Kellogg School of Management*

"Contributing to making "human beings shareholders of development" is the ambition of Marco Magnani's highly readable and immensely instructive book. As a precondition to achieving this objective, he addresses all the issues – immensely accelerated technological change, ever deeper integration of markets, unsustainable demands on resources, depletion of nature's capital – which create fundamental uncertainty, haunting ever larger swaths of people. Magnani's response to those deep concerns is to engage his readers in an enlightening debate, with the purpose of fostering their capacity to judge – and suggesting applicable ways to keep our societies on an inclusive and prosperous course."

—**Hans-Helmut Kotz**, *Resident Fellow, Center for European Studies, Harvard University, former member of the Executive Board of Deutsche Bundesbank*

"What next? This is the all embracing question beyond the pandemic. In his powerful book Marco Magnani does not hesitate to deal with the most critical issue of current transition: is technological innovation an opportunity or a threat? By offering a wide ranging and stimulating analysis of the main forces at work, the book is an essential tool to understand and go through the 'interesting' - and challenging - times we live in."

—**Mauro Magatti**, *ARC Centre for the Anthropology of Religion and Generative Studies Dept. of Sociology, Università Cattolica del Sacro Cuore, Milan*

"Our zeitgeist exudes pessimism. Marco Magnani bravely makes a case for cautious optimism in the face of the many daunting global challenges we face. His measured wisdom merits deep reflection."

—**Kishore Mahbubani**, *Founding Dean of the Lee Kuan Yew School of Public Policy, National University of Singapore and the author of "Has China Won"?*

"In this brilliant book, Marco Magnani explains why we can have a better future if we ride technology placing man at the center and aiming at sustainability."

—**Nicola Monti**, *Ceo of Edison group*

"I have seen with my own eyes, both in orbit and on Earth, the catastrophic effects of climate change: Marco Magnani reminds us the planet does not belong to us, but its future is in our hands."

—**Luca Parmitano**, *Astronaut*

"Will robots replace man in most tasks and destroy millions of jobs? Will AI overtake humans' intelligence? Or will the technology revolution stall in the face of social constraints? In this book, Marco Magnani responds to the concerns triggered by the rise of machines with an in-depth analysis of how technology is changing society, business, and labor, identifying threats and opportunities. Magnani also puts forward some important policy proposals aimed at ensuring that everyone can benefit from the digital economy."

—**Martin Reeves**, *Senior Partner of Boston Consulting Group in San Francisco and Chairman of the BCG Henderson Institute*

"Magnani's book deals with one of the most important and serious challenges facing the world today—how to harness the new technologies to work for everyone by increasing labor productivity and incomes, even of low-skilled workers, in both advanced and emerging economies. The challenge is great because the new technologies are truly revolutionary and are being adopted very rapidly with the pandemic. This is a splendid book for everyone interested in economic growth and income inequalities."

—**Dominick Salvatore**, *Fordham University, New York*

"We are witnessing an acceleration of the digital transformation that will now be coupled with the green transition. This book by Marco Magnani provides an excellent roadbook on how to grasp the many opportunities these changes bring about, but also address the challenges and risk of growing divides."

—**Stefano Scarpetta**, *Director, Employment, Labour and Social Affairs, OECD*

"ESG issues are of crucial importance for investors and business people today. Marco Magnani's book has the merit of focusing on the social sustainability of the technological revolution. I believe this to be the decisive factor: there can be no economic growth without social growth, meaning quality employment, new skills, and integration of people and technology. We need to put to work all our best qualities of human beings: creativity, empathy and vision will be our key resources. And the technological revolution will be our ally."

—**Marco Sesana**, *Country Manager & Ceo of Generali Italia and Global Business Lines and member of the Advisory Board of the International Center of Finance at Yale School of Management*

"Technology and what it means for how we live is as fundamental as any question facing humanity. Marco Magnani's challenging book is a terrifically thoughtful exposition of the issues. Agree or disagree, Magnani's arguments are worth the consideration of anyone who wants to be thoughtful on this vitally important topic."

—**Larry Summers**, *Charles W. Eliot Professor and President Emeritus at Harvard. Secretary of the Treasury for President Clinton and the Director of the National Economic Council for President Obama*

"In this fascinating book, economist Marco Magnani clearly grasps the strong connection between environmental and social sustainability and explains the importance of pursuing growth in justice, which lies at the heart of the Economy of Francis."

—**Cardinal Matteo Maria Zuppi**, *Archbishop of Bologna*

Introduction

This Time Might Be Different

Throughout history, innovation—be it technical, scientific, technological, organizational, commercial, financial—has brought about disruptive changes in the economy and in society, often upsetting established balances. However, in the long term, innovation has always had a positive impact on both growth and employment.

On the one hand, the virtuous link between innovation and growth has generally helped overcome demographic constraints and resource scarcity, allowing new opportunities to be seized. On the other hand, growth has acted as a transmission belt between innovation and employment: innovation has allowed the economy to expand, which has translated into new jobs. Of course, in every industrial revolution the economic benefits emerged after some time, due to the necessary adaptations to new technologies, organizational models and working methods. Moreover, the ones benefiting from innovation were generally not the same entrepreneurs and workers who had lost traditional activities and professions. Nevertheless, the final balance—both in terms growth and employment—has always been largely positive.

Will it be the same in the future? Is the current growth model sustainable in the long term? And will it be sufficient to achieve a "development that meets the needs of the present generation without compromising the ability of future generations to meet their own needs"[1]? Will the wave of innovations that characterizes our time, especially the technological ones, be able to generate an increase in the economy and in employment? When and with what economic and social costs will a new point of equilibrium be reached?

The answers to these questions are not obvious. History may repeat itself, once again providing a positive solution. However, there are elements that lead us not to exclude that this time things may be different from the past.

Many times over the course of history, fears have emerged that economic growth might encounter insurmountable obstacles, such as demographic explosion, scarcity of food and depletion of energy resources. However, geographical and scientific discoveries, inventions and innovations, have always made it possible to overcome these constraints and continue the trajectory of development.

Sometimes the enlargement of the economy took time and in the short term innovations slowed down growth. After a transition period, however, the size of the economy increased and employment benefited. The transportation sector provides a good example of these dynamics. In 1933, the *U.S. Bureau of Census* noted that the Great Depression of 1929 had been affected by the spread of automobiles, due to the reduction of one-third of the horse population in a few years and the consequent crisis of horse-related activities and services. The new means of transport made those who provided services for horses superfluous and caused the collapse of oat production (horses' main "fuel"). However, the success of cars triggered the need for new services, such as mechanics and gasoline. After some time, a completely new range of activities arose, such as the production of vehicles and spare parts, refining and distribution of fuel, car insurance and other services.

Another example is the double transition that technical and organizational innovations brought about in advanced economies last century. From 1900 to 2010, agricultural employment in the United States of America fell from 36% to less than 2% of the labour force (in Italy from 66 to 4%). Similarly, the number of those employed in manufacturing has fallen since World War II from 30 to 10%. In both cases, industry output, the size of the economy and per capita wealth have increased significantly. And so have the labour force and overall employment.

Fears of resource depletion have been recurrent. In the short term, innovations have led to the sacrifice of some sectors and related jobs. In the longer term, however, the innovations themselves have been decisive in overcoming growth constraints, expanding the economy and creating new jobs.

---

[1] Definition of sustainable development by the UN Commission on Environment and Development in the Brundtland Report *Our Common Future* (1987).

Increased productivity has also allowed average wages to rise. As a result, new jobs created by innovation have always been higher in quantity and better in quality than those lost as a result of progress.

What follows is a journey through the history of how major innovations have affected the economy and an attempt at understanding what the consequences of the ongoing technological revolution might be for growth, sustainability and labour.

Chapter 1 provides some historical context and shows how innovation has always been the driving force behind extraordinary increases in agricultural productivity and food supply, the exploitation of new natural resources and the development of alternative energy sources. Innovation has also contributed to the development of trade, industrial revolutions, the organization of labour and the growth of finance.

Innovation has always been part of the history of mankind, but we are currently living in the most innovative period of all time. The consequences are difficult to predict. Chapter 2 describes twelve potentially revolutionary innovations and analyses the opportunities and threats that each one poses for the economy and business, but also for the quality of human life, society, politics and ethics. Chapter 3 summarizes the possible implications for employment, in terms of jobs destroyed, downsized or greatly changed, but it also identifies new professions. The innovations reviewed in depth are: advanced robotics (including drones), driverless cars, 3D printing and additive manufacturing, Internet of Things, *big data*, quantum computing, *cloud* storage and computer cloud, artificial intelligence (with *machine* and *deep learning*), augmented and virtual reality, blockchain, nanotechnology and nanomaterials, and biotechnology. The research extends to the great potential of improvements in energy storage, genome engineering, micro- and nano-sensors, neurobionics, *space economy* and 5G infrastructure. Moreover, the close connection between several of these innovations on the one hand further accelerates their development and diffusion, and on the other allows new and unexpected applications. The case of artificial intelligence is emblematic, because it expands and accelerates—among other things—the development of robotics, nanotechnology, materials science and human genome *editing*.

What will be the impact of these innovations on growth and employment?

In the most optimistic view, history will repeat itself. Once again, innovation will make it possible to overcome the constraints of sustainability and open new cycles of development, increasing productivity and expanding the economy, with positive consequences for employment as well. In this scenario, the main critical issue is the management of the transition period.

But this time things may be different than in the past. Mainly for two reasons. First, as explained in Chapter 4, it is not so obvious that innovation will continue to generate economic growth. Some argue that there is a risk of secular stagnation, due to a structural slowdown in either the growth of potential output or in aggregate demand. According to others, the virtuous link between innovation and growth is facing a crisis due to much stronger constraints than in the past. Today, not only demographic, food and energy sustainability are threatened, but ecological-environmental, health care, social and political-institutional sustainability are also facing challenges.

In both scenarios—the more optimistic one with history repeating itself and the more prudent one introducing the challenge of new growth constrains—the traditional growth model of liberal capitalism is under extraordinary pressure. And from many quarters there are calls for its "scrapping" or at least its "adjustment". Among the proposed alternatives—in addition to consciously choosing the path of degrowth (happy or not)—innovative suggestions emerge from the *blue economy*, civil economy, circular economy, *sharing economy*, convivialism and *commons* movements.

The second reason why this time might be different is that, even if there is growth, it might no longer act—as it did in the past—as a transmission belt between innovation and work. Chapter 5 explains how new technologies are paving the way for jobless growth, as human labour is largely replaced by machines. In this case, overall wealth increases but huge redistribution problems emerge.

The issue of the relationship between technological change and employment—which was also raised in the past by Ricardo, Marx, Keynes and Meade—is once again highly topical. It is not the first time in history that technological innovations have revolutionized the labour market. The loss of certain professions will continue to be matched by the emergence of new ones. However, this time the transition phase could be particularly difficult and the final balance on employment uncertain. There is even the possibility of a scenario in which new jobs are fewer than those lost and the average value placed on work is lower. Several signals point in this direction, suggesting a possible relevant difference with the past.

First of all, the frequency with which disruptive innovations are introduced is unprecedented. In the past, after a period of adjustment, a major innovation produced a new balance in the labour market that lasted a few generations. Think of the industrial revolutions. Today, each generation experiences several radical innovations in the course of its working life and is increasingly anxious about constant change.[2]

Other unprecedented elements are the penetration rate and pervasiveness of current innovations. Think of computing capacity and its relative costs. As highlighted by a McKinsey study (2013), in 1975 the fastest computer cost 5 million dollars, while today with a few hundred dollars one can buy a smartphone with similar computing power. This trend is favoured by technology itself, globalization and the succession of continuous improvements, the speed of which has made Moore's Law obsolete.[3] Today's technological innovations also present a very strong "combinatorial effect" as they feed off each other by accelerating progress and expanding fields of application.

Another novelty with respect to the past is that physical automation is increasingly accompanied by cognitive automation. Not only are machines and robots replacing human hands but artificial intelligence is also replacing many intellectual tasks. As a result, for the first time highly skilled jobs requiring medium to high levels of education are at risk. The spread of technological innovations is also creating an unprecedented dichotomy in the labour market—widening the gap between those who know how to use them and those who do not—resulting in income polarization. This also contributes to a frequent existing *mismatch* between the skills required by firms and those offered by workers. In addition, the substantial investments needed to develop and introduce new technologies mean that capital investment is paid for much more than labour. Finally, the combination of technology and globalization encourages international labour mobility, especially of new creative and high value-added jobs. This in turn exponentially increases competition between territories to attract new employment. All of these trends, which were already underway, have been accelerated by the recent pandemic.

The relationship between technology and labour is the focus of Chapter 6. Excluding the possibility of a Luddite strategy to hinder and slow down the spread of machines, which history has proven to be impractical, several alternatives are analysed in their theoretical and practical implications. One possibility is to delegate work to machines—in whole or in part—and increase leisure time for humans. This implies rethinking the function of

---

[2] An original measure of the level of anxiety about the future of work can be found by typing "future of work" into Google: the number of searches, for the English language alone, is almost 5 billion!

[3] In 1965, Gordon Moore, the future co-founder of Intel, predicted that computing power and complexity of microcircuits—measured by the density of transistors in a microchip—would double every year (an estimate later extended to eighteen months), while the cost would fall in the same period by 50%. Until now, the empirical validity of the prediction had been impressively confirmed.

work itself and the way of life of individuals. It also requires the introduction of important redistribution mechanisms, such as universal basic income, social dividend, guaranteed minimum income and negative income tax. An alternative is that the state, regardless of the level of automation, guarantees everyone a job.

There is also a third path: accepting the challenge of intelligent coexistence between humans and machines. In this scenario, humans do not surrender to the rise of machines and therefore refuse to accept high rates of unemployment in exchange for compensation that replaces traditional income from work. But neither are they content with a "job guarantee" possibly useless and unproductive.

Intelligent coexistence between humans and machines can be pursued on two levels, which are not alternative to each other. At the macroeconomic level, through the division of labour between humans and machines. Here, the rise of machines becomes an opportunity to invest massively in labour-intensive activities—such as education, cultural heritage, health care and personal services—leaving to technology those that require high capital intensity, such as most manufacturing. At the more microlevel of the individual profession, intelligent coexistence means close collaboration between humans and machines. The idea is to harness innovations to improve human job performance. Technology provides an opportunity for workers to focus on those tasks within each profession that generate added value. Those based on characteristics that are difficult to automate such as critical and creative thinking, problem solving and decision making, empathy and other dimensions of emotional intelligence, relational, social and communicative attitudes (the so-called "*soft skills*").

Regardless of which scenario prevails from the complex interweaving of innovation-growth-employment, the transition will be long, difficult and it will impact all sectors. It is impossible for individuals, companies and territories not to be affected. Moreover, any *policy* decision requires significant financial resources, which according to some should come from taxation of unsustainable behaviour (e.g., *green tax*) and of machines that replace workers (e.g., *robot tax*), or from the recovery of tax avoidance facilitated by technology itself, especially from digital platforms (e.g. *web tax* or *digital tax*).

The challenge is to integrate technological progress into the economy and in society as quickly and smoothly as possible, incorporating the main objectives of sustainability into the current growth model, seizing the new opportunities for economic and employment development, and ensuring that everyone can participate in and benefit from them.

Can we do that?

In Chapters 7 and 8, we will try to indicate some navigation routes to make this otherwise worrying and very hard journey sustainable and exciting. Navigation routes that take into account the lessons offered by some of the epoch-making changes we are experiencing, such as globalization, the tech revolution, financial crisis and economic downturns, the threat posed by climate change, and the pandemic. Let us imagine that we are taking part in the most dangerous and ambitious expedition in history. Even those who start their travels well equipped may not be able to overcome the Pillars of Hercules this time. But it will be an intriguing and thrilling experience. At times, it may even be exhilarating.

This is how it has always been: from the myth of Prometheus to Noah's Ark, from Christopher Columbus' three caravels to the Space Shuttle missions, up to the endless wars that have punctuated (and still punctuate) the path of mankind, there are those who get burned, those who get injured and those who perish. But in the end, new horizons open up, new worlds are discovered, opportunities emerge that were previously unimaginable.

This time might be different. No one knows exactly to what extent, when and how. But it is difficult to harbour doubts about the positive outcome. On two conditions. The first is that man remembers that the Garden of Eden has been entrusted to him so that he can cultivate and safeguard it. The same care must be reserved for the planet and its resources, preserving them for future generations. The second condition is that, in his relationship with machines, man rediscovers and fully exercises his own ability to lead, fulfilling his age-old function of "shepherd". Shepherding robots means using them to improve one's own life while maintaining centrality and pre-eminence.[4]

So, let's set off on our journey. With the curiosity and fears of those who navigate in uncharted waters, but also with the passion and optimism of those who aspire to go beyond the Pillars of Hercules. The end goal is improving people's lives, leveraging robots and machines despite their formidable and unjustifiably frightful rise, to make the global economy work for everyone.

---

[4] Philosopher Luciano Floridi (2019) of Oxford University points out that for millennia man has managed animals, animated forces with some form of intelligence such as herds and flocks.

Contents

About the Author

Marco Magnani has been living between the United States and Italy for more than 30 years.

He currently teaches International Economics and Monetary & Financial Economics at Luiss University in Rome. He also lectures at Alta Scuola Politecnica (top students of Politecnico of Milan and Turin), Luiss School of Government and Luiss Business School. He has been a Senior Research Fellow at the Harvard Kennedy School and a Visiting Fellow at the School of Advanced International Studies of Johns Hopkins University in Washington, DC.

Magnani worked for nearly 20 years in investment banking in New York at JPMorgan and in Milan at Mediobanca. In 2010, he was appointed Young Global Leader of the World Economic Forum of Davos. He is on the Board of Directors of the Center for American Studies, a fellow of IAI-Institute of International Affairs and a member The Aspen Institute, Chatham House, and The Economic Club of New York. He currently sits, as independent, on the Board of Directors and Advisory Boards of several companies.

Magnani holds a degree in Economics from the University of Rome "La Sapienza" and an MBA in Finance from Columbia University. He has completed programs in leadership and public policies at the Harvard Kennedy School, at the Jackson Institute for Global Affairs at Yale University and at the Lee Kuan Yew School of Public Policy in Singapore.

Magnani writes for *IlSole24Ore* and *AffarInternazionali*. He is the author of *Sette Anni di Vacche Sobrie* (Utet, 2013), *Creating Economic Growth. Lessons for Europe* (Palgrave Macmillan, 2014), *Terra e Buoi dei Paesi Tuoi* (Utet, 2016), *Fatti non foste a viver come robot* (Utet, 2020), *L'Onda Perfetta* (Luiss University Press, 2020).

1

Innovation: Engine of Economic Growth (and Employment)

Throughout history, innovation—be it technical, scientific, technological, organizational, commercial or financial—has brought about disruptive changes in the economy and in society, often upsetting established balances. However, there has always been a strong positive correlation between innovation and economic growth,[1] with significant gains also for employment.

In agriculture, the introduction of new production tools and techniques has made it possible to exponentially grow output levels employing a fraction of labour. The same happened with mining and energy resources. Trade, a key driver of growth, has also benefitted from multiple technical and financial innovations.

Inventions such as the steam engine in the late eighteenth century and the dynamo and electricity in the mid-nineteenth century produced the First and Second Industrial Revolutions, expanding the economy and increasing productivity. Similarly, the introduction of the computer in the 1950s, the

---

[1] Innovation plays a central role in all the main economic growth theories. According to the classical and neo-classical schools, technological progress is an exogenous variable of the growth model, generally the result of inventions or discoveries. For the new growth theory, on the other hand, it is an endogenous variable, and therefore, the economy can continue to grow even without external shocks but solely by using and improving available factors, including existing technology. This happens thanks to the accumulation of knowledge and human capital, which is considered a fundamental factor of production. Edmund Phelps (2013) introduces the concept of "indigenous innovation", which comes from the rise of "modern values" such as dynamism, passion, desire to create, explore and face challenges. According to Phelps, it is this type of innovation that has generated in the countries that were leading the industrial revolutions a gigantic increase in well-being ("mass flourishing"), which goes beyond the growth of gross domestic product because it includes personal growth, self-realization and professional gratification.

© The Author(s), under exclusive license to Springer Nature Switzerland AG 2022
M. Magnani, *Making the Global Economy Work for Everyone*,
https://doi.org/10.1007/978-3-030-92084-5_1

personal computer in the 1980s and the rise of the internet since the 1990s have multiplied the productivity of intellectual labour and created new activities, with positive effects on the economy as a whole. The sequence of innovations in science, organization and finance has stimulated growth in all sectors.

One of the greatest organizational innovations has been the division of labour. For Adam Smith (1776), it is one of the sources of the wealth of nations. Frederick Taylor (1911) and Henry Ford introduced it into factories, paving the way for organized mass production. From the craftsman who made each product alone, we moved on to a coordinated series of workers, each performing a specific task. Organizational innovation is also an important source of growth because, as John Kenneth Galbraith points out, "it dispenses with the need for genius". "The real accomplishment of modern science and technology", Galbraith explains in *The New Industrial State* (1967), "consists in taking ordinary men, informing them narrowly and deeply and then, through appropriate organization, arranging to have their knowledge combined with that of other specialized but equally ordinary men". And this is good for the economy because "the resulting performance, though less inspiring, is far more predictable".

Finally, the development of finance has accompanied the growth of the economy over time, facilitating payments and boosting trade, channelling savings into productive investment, and enabling risk diversification and hedging. Financial innovation has often been decisive in making possible technological change itself. The evolution of financial tools and techniques has allowed inventions to become innovations, ideas to be translated into processes, products and services. This has facilitated and accelerated the positive impact of technology on growth.

It should be noted here that an invention does not necessarily result in an innovation. For the great Austrian economist Joseph Schumpeter (1942), an invention does not always involve the introduction of a new process, product or service onto the market, whereas an innovation has economic consequences. Therefore, innovation is the application or the commercialization of a discovery or invention.[2]

---

[2] The invention of the first automobiles at the end of the nineteenth century was technically revolutionary. However, the transport market was not overturned by it because the high price of vehicles did not allow their wide distribution and, as a consequence, the traditional operators of the sector—horse-drawn carriages—were not replaced in the short term. On the other hand, Ford's introduction in 1908 of the Model T—not an invention but only an improvement of the product—had disruptive consequences because its low price allowed mass distribution.

Cowboys Versus Astronauts

"Anyone who believes exponential growth can go on forever in a finite world is either a madman or an economist". The quote is from Kenneth Boulding (1941), an English economist and poet whose work focuses on the environment, conflict resolution and cooperation. The fear that economic growth will encounter severe constraints—such that even innovation will not be able to overcome—is not something new.

Those who believe in unlimited growth have always been opposed by those who believe growth has constraints: the cowboy's vision of the world has always been countered by that of the astronaut.

The cowboy is driven by the optimism of those who, pushing towards the Far West with a pioneering spirit, have always found land to conquer, bisons to hunt and resources to exploit. The cowboy believes that there are no limits to the possibility of increasing one's own well-being, other than that of freedom and the individual ability to pursue one's own goals. Ronald Reagan, President of the United States of America from 1981 to 1989, in the inaugural speech for his second term in office, recalled that "there are no limits to growth and human progress when men and women are free to follow their dreams".

On the contrary, the behaviour of the astronaut is characterized by the prudence of those who, engaged in dangerous missions in space, must carefully manage the available resources in order to survive. The astronaut is very sensitive to the issues of scarcity and sustainability, which are considered serious constraints to economic growth. In the astronaut's metaphor, Earth is an enclosed space—vast but not infinite—just like a space station. According to Boulding, until now nature has managed to cope with continuous economic expansion because planet Earth is very large, but it is urgent to change direction.

There is also another point of view according to which the real risk is not the exhaustion of natural resources but the inability to redistribute them. In this perspective, the limitation is the relations among human beings. Because, as a quote attributed to Mahatma Gandhi very well summarizes "Earth provides enough to satisfy every man's needs, but not every man's greed".

Malthus and the Constraints on Economic Growth

In *An Essay on the Principle of Population* of 1798, English economist and demographer Thomas Malthus pointed out that economic growth has two constraints that are difficult to overcome: scarcity of natural resources and demographic development. Studying the demography of the colonies of the British Empire, in particular of India, Malthus had noticed that while agricultural production grew in arithmetic progression, population increased in geometric progression, therefore much faster. The combination of these two factors constituted a natural limit to economic development. Hence, the Anglican reverend's proposal to cut some poverty subsidies in order to deal with overpopulation.[3]

It is well known that Malthusian fears have been disproved by history. Discoveries—geographical, scientific and of raw materials—and inventions have always led to increases in productivity that were sufficient to face shortages of resources and demographic growth. At the end of the eighteenth century, technological innovation enabled the First Industrial Revolution which, through the development of productivity and the enlargement of the economy, demonstrated that these limits could be overcome. The same happened with the Second Industrial Revolution.

The debate on constraints to economic growth is not new. Recurring concerns about growth stalling have always been overcome, largely due to innovation. This is true in all sectors.

From Nomadism to Sedentism: Innovation and the Neolithic Revolution

Perhaps the earliest examples of how innovation facilitated economic growth, through increases in food production, date back to the Stone Age.[4] In the Mesolithic Period, humans led a nomadic lifestyle, feeding on hunting. The constraints to growth were represented by the supply of animals and man's ability to hunt them regularly and in sufficient quantities. A revolutionary

---

[3] Malthus was against the cash subsidies provided by the "poor laws" while he was in favour of workhouses, places where poor people were guaranteed food and lodging.

[4] The Stone Age spans from the appearance of the first hominids, about 2.5 million years ago, to the forging of metals in 8000–5000 BC, and it is traditionally divided into the Paleolithic, Mesolithic and Neolithic periods.

innovation of the time was the use of controlled forest burning which, by encouraging the growth of young vegetation, attracted game.

In the Neolithic period, technical innovations in stone working—which led, among other things, to the production of axes, hatchets and sickles—facilitated the development of agriculture and animal husbandry and contributed to the transition from a nomadic to a sedentary lifestyle. Agricultural activity increased the productivity of foodstuffs, thus promoting further demographic and economic advancement.

The Neolithic revolution marked the birth of agriculture as intentional sowing and domestication of plants.[5] Humans from predators become producers. This allowed for the storing of food surpluses which in turn ensured food security for long periods. The possibility of feeding also social groups not dedicated to hunting or agriculture led to a new organization of society and laid the foundations for the first specialization of labour, a great source of economic growth.

The debate over the causes of the Neolithic revolution is wide-ranging, and innovation is only one of many hypotheses. Scholarly explanations range from sudden climate change to demographic development, from pressures from the natural environment to human social, organizational and cultural evolution. According to American anthropologist and archaeologist Robert Braidwood (1948), neolithization is largely the natural result of human evolution: increased technical skills made it possible to obtain increasing amounts of food.[6]

It is certainly difficult to clearly establish in which direction the link between innovation and sedentism is oriented, as well as the link between sedentism, increased agricultural production and population growth. In other words, is it innovation that leads to sedentism, which gives rise to agriculture, that in turn allows for population increases? Or is it demographic expansion

---

[5] It is not clear what triggered, relatively synchronously at the end of the last ice age, the Neolithic revolution in three different places, very distant and not communicating with each other. Indeed, the domestication of wheat is said to have occurred 10,500 years ago in eastern Turkey, the first cultivation of rice 10,000 years ago in south-eastern China, and that of maize 9,000 years ago in Mexico.

[6] In the 1950s, Braidwood entered the debate on the causes of the Neolithic revolution and opposed those who—especially Australian archaeologist Vere Gordon Childe (1928) with his "theory of oases"—considered climate change the determining factor. Childe places the Neolithic revolution near the end of the last ice age, when a climatic crisis forced humans and animals to gather near the springs. Within these oases, the lack of food would have led to the adoption of productive techniques. Braidwood, on the other hand, considers the climatic factor irrelevant—also because such a change would precede domestication by two or three millennia—and privileges the cultural factor of a maturation of knowledge and technology. Most current studies attribute a decisive role to culture as a factor of change.

that forces humans to seek new livelihoods in agriculture, driving sedentism and innovation? It is difficult to give an answer as these are most likely interconnected processes which developed over the course of the centuries.

In any case, even for those who espouse the thesis of climate change or other exogenous factors that would have led to sedentism, it is difficult to deny the important role played by innovation in facilitating humans transition to an economy based on agriculture and animal husbandry. Innovation was therefore at least a necessary condition for this transition.

From the Plough to Genetic Engineering: Innovations and Growth in Agriculture

Throughout history, inventions and innovations have revolutionized agriculture, allowing extraordinary increases in productivity and facilitating growth, both demographic and economic.

A great example is the plough, invented by the Sumerians around 3500 BC. The introduction of iron is also very important, around the twelfth century B.C. in the Middle East with the Hittites and later in Italy with the Etruscans. Its use allowed the manufacturing of new tools, such as the scythe, and increased the effectiveness of other tools already in use, such as the spade, the hoe and the plough.

The many refinements of the plough over time are good examples of incremental innovations, fundamental in making farmers' work more efficient and improving the productivity of the land. So much so that many historians link the widespread diffusion of new types of ploughs to the flourishing of civilization in the period between the early and late Middle Ages. The first ploughs were very simple and consist of a vertical wooden stick that cleaved the ground, pulled first by men and later by draught animals. Over time the plough was equipped with some important accessories: the coulter (the blade that cuts deep into the ground, cutting it vertically in the direction of the plough), the asymmetrical ploughshare or vomer (a second blade, with an inclined cut, capable of cutting the ground horizontally), the mouldboard, which lifts and turns over the soil, improving tillage, aeration and fertility. Another example of important incremental innovation in agriculture is the introduction, in the Middle Ages, of a new system to harness draught animals that allowed for greater weight-carrying capacity. The shoulder collar, which does not press on the animal's neck and therefore does not hinder its breathing, increased the pulling power up to eight times.

A great impact on agriculture also came from the many innovations in water management. From the ramified system of aqueducts built by the Romans to the use of hydraulic or wind-powered mills to grind, squeeze and operate bellows, which became widespread starting in the eleventh century, to the drip irrigation technique that saves water by slowly administering it to the root zone of plants through small pipes—making it particularly useful in arid areas.

At the beginning of the twentieth century in Europe, the mechanization of agriculture began with the progressive diffusion of tractors, threshers and dryers. Today, the new frontier of innovation are robots, satellites, drones, sensors, automated and intelligent agricultural machines connected with each other. The spread of digital technology allows the development of precision agriculture: targeted interventions that take into account the actual crop needs and the biochemical and physical characteristics of the soil. This prevents wasting of seeds, water and fertilizers, with considerable cost savings and productivity enhancements. In addition, the creation of digital twins—virtual copies of activities, processes and agricultural products—facilitates activities of management, helps improve decisions, reduces environmental impact and increases yields.

There are also many non-technological innovations which have disruptive effects. An example is the introduction in Europe, between the sixteenth and eighteenth centuries, of the cultivation of plants originating in the New World, including corn, potatoes, tomatoes and beans. A more recent example is genetic engineering applied in agriculture and animal husbandry.

In modern history, continuous innovations have allowed unthinkable improvements in agriculture productivity per hectare and per worker. Between 1948 and 2011, the U.S. agricultural output more than doubled, with an average annual growth of 1.49%. With little growth in total measured use of agricultural inputs, the extraordinary performance of the U.S. farm sector was driven mainly by increases in total factor productivity[7] (U.S. Department of Agriculture, 2015).

---

[7] Total factor productivity (TFP) is one of the most informative measures of agricultural productivity: it takes into account all of the land, labor, capital and material resources employed in farm production and compares them with the total amount of crop and livestock output.

From the Wheel to the Blockchain: Innovations and Growth in Trade

The development of trade has always been driven by innovations, primarily technical and financial ones.

The list of technical innovations that have revolutionized trade is a long one. In land transport, they range from the invention of the wheel to the construction of the railway, from steam trains and ships to the internal combustion engine. Many innovations in shipbuilding favoured the development of maritime transport; in particular, at the end of the fifteenth century, various changes enabled the first Atlantic crossings and the subsequent opening of commercial routes between Europe and the New World. Single-masted ships, inadequate for long distances, were replaced by multi-masted ships that absorb the strain evenly. A few large sails, difficult to steer, were replaced by a greater number of smaller sails, both square and lateen, which reduced the risk of heeling. Moreover, the hulls were much stronger, both because seasoned oak wood was used and because, instead of planks lying side by side, they were superimposed in horizontal layers, increasing their ability to withstand impact. Air transport increased the speed and flexibility of international trade. Drones could bring about the next revolution in local distribution of goods.

Financial innovations have also been key to the development of trade. With the introduction of currency, bartering declined and trade flourished.

The use of currency has three fundamental advantages. First, it reduces transaction costs: in a barter economy, several exchanges are needed before acquiring the desired goods, while with currency only one transaction is needed. Second, it reduces storage costs: with barter it is necessary to store the goods used from time to time for exchanges. This can be difficult or costly given that in ancient times the means of exchange were often perishable goods like animals and grains. Finally, transfer costs are lower: transferring money, even when coined in precious and heavy metals, is less expensive than moving flocks or transporting crops. With electronic money, transfer costs become almost zero.

Another milestone for the development of trade was the introduction of the letter of exchange. This financial innovation sped up the movement of capital from one marketplace to another, facilitating exchanges and making them more secure. Introduced in the mid-eighteenth century, the letter of exchange was a document by which a banker who has received a payment from a client ordered another banker operating in a different marketplace to pay the beneficiary. It was the first rudimentary form of bill of exchange or promissory note. Instead of facing a tiring and dangerous journey with large amounts of money, Tuscan merchants travelling to Flanders to buy fabrics could make a deposit before leaving at a bank in Florence in exchange for a receipt that they would hand over in payment for the goods. The seller presented the receipt at a branch or correspondent of the Tuscan bank in Bruges and received the payment in cash. Alternatively, he could use the receipt to make purchases himself, "endorsing" it to a third party.

The letter of exchange is an innovation attributed to Italian merchants and bankers. So are double-entry bookkeeping and insurance, which also transformed trade and overall economic activity. More recent innovations include the electronic transfer of funds, which facilitates long-distance trade; financial derivatives, which allow management of the volatility of underlying commodity prices; and blockchain technology, which could become in the future the primary channel for fast, secure and certified payments.

Steam Engine, Electricity, Computers and the Internet: Industrial Revolutions and Economic Growth

Technical inventions, scientific discoveries, technological and organizational innovations have always been fundamental to the economy, specifically to industrial activities. Industrial revolutions mark periods of formidable productivity gains due to the spread of new technologies.

The First Industrial Revolution developed between 1760 and 1830, primarily in England, and is characterized by the introduction of the flying spooler, multiple spinning machine, mechanical hydraulic loom and, above all, the steam engine. The latter, invented and perfected by James Watts between 1765 and 1781, allowed the development of the first large textile factories with mechanical production in the late eighteen century. In a short time, Manchester became the most important textile centre in the world. Moreover, the new source of energy allowed the construction of bigger iron machines, stimulating the development of the metallurgical industry, whose main centres were cities near important coal deposits such as Birmingham, Leeds, Sheffield, Cardiff, Newcastle and Whitehaven. A dense rail network rapidly developed throughout the region and the port of Liverpool became central to the shipping of goods.

The Second Industrial Revolution started in 1870 and was about the introduction of electricity, chemical and pharmaceutical products, steel and oil. In particular, it was the dynamo—a device invented by Antonio Pacinotti in 1860 capable of transforming mechanical energy into electricity—and its coupling to the hydraulic turbine (which took place in 1870), that led to the commercial production of electricity. The applications of electricity—from the light bulb invented by Thomas Edison in 1879 to the patents on the alternating current electric system and motor registered by Nikola Tesla in the following years—allowed an impressive development of industry in the second half of the nineteenth century. With the invention of the light bulb and electric lighting, the revolution spread from factories to cities.[8] The Second Industrial Revolution touched all sectors, lasted until just before the start of World War I and had a particularly relevant impact in England, Germany and the United States.

The Third Industrial Revolution was linked to developments in electronics and computing, from the introduction of the first computers in the early 1950s to the launch of the personal computer in the early 1980s. It is interesting to note that, although information technology between the 1970s and the 1980s developed significantly, productivity in the 1980s and early 1990s grew by only a few percentage points. The concept was first described by Nobel Prize-winning economist Robert Solow (1987) who jokingly pointed out that the age of computers was visible everywhere except in productivity statistics (the "Solow paradox"). Productivity increases only came later on, probably helped in part by globalization. In other words, it took some time for technological innovations to have a major impact on productivity and growth.

The Fourth Industrial Revolution began with the emergence of the internet in the 1990s. Today, digitalization is disrupting all sectors of the economy and profoundly transforming jobs and professional skills. In the new digital economy, the diffusion of knowledge is essential to stimulate the development of innovation and economic growth.[9] In the Triple Helix model of Henry Etzkowitz and Loet Leydesdorff (1998), the key to fostering the diffusion of knowledge is to develop a dense system of relationships and close collaboration between the three key players in innovation processes: businesses, government and local administrations, universities and research centres.

---

[8] Thomas Edison is considered the father of the incandescent light bulb. However, it is believed that German Heinrich Göbel and Italian Alessandro Cruto preceded him in inventing it, although with less success in marketing it.

[9] In recent decades, fundamental contributions on the subject have come from, among others, Paul Romer, Robert Lucas, Daron Acemoğlu, Philippe Aghion and Bengt Holmström.

Financial Innovation, the Transmission Belt Between Technological Change and Economic Growth

Financial systems provide several essential services, such as channelling savings into investments, allocating capital, facilitating transactions and allowing risk management. An efficient provision of these services directs capital flows to the most promising firms, promoting economic growth. Financial innovation—with the creation of new securities, markets and institutions—can improve financial services and, in turn, accelerate growth.

In addition to being a source of funds and services for various economic activities, financial innovation has often been decisive in enabling techno-logical change, which in turn is a driver of growth. There is no shortage of examples.

The oceanic expeditions and great commercial voyages of the seventeenth and eighteenth centuries required significant long-term capital injections. Traditional investors were reluctant to make this type of investment because it precluded access to liquidity and produced returns only after long periods. The emergence of securities markets addressed the issue as it allowed investors with liquidity needs to sell claims on the future profitability of shipping.

Rail network development in the nineteenth century struggled to obtain financial support from the traditional capital providers of the time, namely banks and private investors. Although potentially profitable, indeed, railways were technologically complex and spanned large geographical areas. These obstacles were overcome by the emergence of investment banks capable of evaluating and monitoring the profitability of railway companies. In the late nineteenth century, John Pierpont Morgan played a crucial role in the devel-opment of the U.S. railroad network, both as a direct lender and as an issuer of railroad companies' securities.

A more current example is that of start-ups. The traditional financial system—commercial banks and financial markets—has difficulty valuing them. For several reasons: they generally do not generate sufficient cash flows to cover loan payments, are run by tech experts with little managerial expe-rience and are based on complex technologies. Innovation has led to the emergence of venture capital firms, equipped with tech-savvy staff who are able to understand new technologies but at the same time to make projections of future revenues and profits. The benefits are widespread because the ability to provide long-term financing for the most promising start-ups encourages the development of new technologies, which often improve quality of life and make the economy grow.

The story of biotechnology in the twenty-first century is a natural continuation of the virtuous circle between financial innovation, technological change and economic growth. Neither the banking system nor venture capital are able to effectively price this sector, which requires a mix of biology, genetics, chemistry, engineering and biorobotics skills. Moreover, supporting these activities requires very significant injections of capital and detailed knowledge of legislation. The innovation in this sector comes from collaboration between financial operators and large pharmaceutical companies: the former provide capital and market knowledge, and the latter contribute scientific know-how, legal expertise and connections with distribution networks. Collaboration between the two sectors makes it possible to identify and support the most promising biotech companies.

Financial innovation also gave rise to microfinance, the most important component of which is microcredit: the provision of loans to customers considered unviable by traditional financial institutions. This tool makes a significant contribution to the fight against poverty and to economic growth, both in emerging countries and in advanced economies, because it sustains consumption and supports small activities of artisans, traders and farmers. Crowdfunding also allows large groups of people to work together to pursue—through loans, capital contributions or donations—economic or non-profit initiatives, even with small sums. Crowdfunding is a bottom-up financing mechanism that allows to achieve two goals at the same time: collecting resources for a specific cause and mobilizing a large number of people who share that cause. A dual objective that is difficult to achieve with traditional financial instruments.

These examples show that financial and technological innovations are closely linked and often evolve together. Financial innovation is crucial for sustained economic growth. For Adam Smith (1776), it is essential for improving the wealth of nations. Indeed, the very essence of economic growth involves greater specialization and the use of more sophisticated technologies. However, as is evident from the examples above, increased technological complexity makes it more difficult for the existing financial system to evaluate new ventures and manage their risks. In other words, economic progress itself makes any existing financial system obsolete. As a result, without adequate innovation in finance, the quality of its services decreases while also slowing economic growth.

According to Nobel economist Joseph Stiglitz (2010), part of the cause of the 2008 crisis was the failure of recent financial innovations to bear fruit, as they often tended to be an end in themselves. As a consequence, they rarely triggered growth in the real economy. According to Stiglitz, the last great financial innovation capable of generating economic growth was the automatic teller machine (ATM).

Disruptive and Sustaining Innovation

Innovations are often classified based on the impact they have on the economic environment. American economist Clayton Christensen (1995) distinguishes between *disruptive* and *sustaining* innovation.

According to Christensen, *disruptive innovation* is the process by which a small company with scarce resources manages to create a new market, successfully challenging the existing leaders. Such innovations are more easily achieved by small businesses for several reasons, including corporate values and culture, cost structure, flexibility and speed of decision-making. Moreover, small businesses usually focus on markets that are considered too small by market leaders.

Disruptive innovations typically arise from simple products and services that—at least initially—have low profit margins and cover new or limited market segments that large companies have little interest in. Well-known examples are Zipcar and Netflix, which built their success by focusing on the then-new and niche markets of car rental by the hour and online video sales, respectively.

Sustaining innovations instead support (and thus maintain) current customers in existing markets by enhancing the products and services already offered. Generally, such innovations are developed and introduced by large companies enjoying leadership positions. This is the case with many incremental innovations in mobile phones and consumer electronics.

An example that helps understand the difference between disruptive and sustaining innovations comes from the asset management industry. In 1975, Charles Schwab launched the discount broker service, which allowed people to buy and sell securities online paying limited commissions. The service covered a new market segment that was initially niche and low-margin, and that was not coveted by traditional asset managers. Today, Schwab is an online trading giant. According to Christensen, this is a case of disruptive innovation. In contrast, in 1987, Merrill Lynch introduced the Cash Management Account: a combination of a checking account, securities account, debit card and line of credit guaranteed by available securities. A typical sustaining innovation aimed at improving the service provided to existing customers.

Christensen's argument is interesting but his definitions are reductive. Indeed, according to his criteria, innovations introduced by companies such as Uber or Airbnb should not be considered disruptive because they have not created new markets nor have they introduced low-margin services. Indeed, Uber and Airbnb are both operating in variants of existing markets, respectively the taxi service and the hotel service sectors, and are both enjoying healthy margins.

Radical and Incremental Innovation

Going beyond Christensen's framework, it seems to us that any innovation capable of creating new markets and value chains, or disrupting existing ones, displacing dominant companies and products, should be considered radical or disruptive.

It is no coincidence that the concept of disruption evokes that of destruction. The transformation brought by radical innovations is so intense that Schumpeter (1942) calls it "creative destruction". The expression alludes to the violent selective process that follows innovation, in which some companies disappear, others are born, and still others grow stronger. In a free, capitalist society, innovation can have such an intense impact on some industries that the firms in those sectors are forced to evolve, or else become extinct. An example used by Schumpeter (1991) in *The Economics and Sociology of Capitalism* is the construction of the railroad through the Midwest of the United States. According to the Austrian economist, on the one hand, the Illinois Central railroad created many opportunities for growth—such as the construction of infrastructure and the foundation of many towns along the route—but on the other hand, the industrialization that followed was a death sentence for traditional agriculture in the West of the country.

The difference between *radical* and *incremental* innovation is that the former shakes up and replaces an existing business paradigm, upsetting production, technical, economic and social dynamics and balances; the latter updates, improves and brings new features to an already established paradigm but does not radically change the dynamics of an industry, nor does it require a change in consumer behaviour. Incremental innovation is often used by companies to maintain an existing technological advantage over competitors.

It should be noted, however, that some innovations that are initially incremental, because they simply enhance a product or service, become so successful that they create a huge overcapacity in an existing market. The consequence is that the market is turned upside down, companies and products that were dominant until then are displaced, and a new value chain is created. Even in these cases we can speak of radical innovation. There are many examples. Uber creates value by significantly increasing taxi supply, just as Airbnb does for accommodations, WhatsApp for telecommunications operators, Wikipedia for the paper (and paid) encyclopaedias, MOOCs (Massive Open Online Courses) for traditional university courses and Waze for car navigators.

Over the course of history, many innovations that improved an existing product or service have upset the market and are therefore to be considered radical. Think of steamships replacing sailboats, high-speed trains competing with short flights, smartphones challenging traditional telephones, personal computers and cameras. Likewise, consider the impact of digital technology on photography, music, cinema and TV. In all these cases, innovations that were initially incremental, while not creating new markets, have disarrayed and destabilized existing ones and created value.

* * *

Although often disrupting established balances, innovation has always been a formidable engine of economic growth throughout history. In the past, the virtuous link between innovation and growth has made it possible to overcome demographic constraints and the scarcity of food and energy resources, indeed enabling new growth opportunities with consequent increases in employment.

Will it be the same in the future?

Bibliography

K. Boulding, *Economic Analysis,* Harper and Brothers, New York 1941.

J. L. Bower, C. M. Christenssen, *Disruptive Technologies: Catching the Wave*, "Harvard Business Review", January-February, 1995.

R. Braidwood, *Prehistoric Men,* Chicago Natural History Museum, Chicago 1948.

C. Casalone, *Una ricerca etica condivisa nell'era digitale*, "La Civiltà Cattolica", no. 4075, 4 April 2020.

FAO, *The future of food and agriculture. Alternative paths to 2050*, Rome 2018.

J. K. Galbraith, *The New Industrial State*, Houghton Mifflin Company, Boston 1967.

V. Gordon Childe, *The Most Ancient Near East: The Oriental Prelude to European Prehistory*, Paul Keagan, London 1928.

M. Krishnan, J. Mischke, J. Remes, *Is the Solow Paradox Back?* McKinsey Quarterly, 4 June 2018.

D. Landes, *The Unbound Prometheus*, Cambridge University Press, New York 1969.

R. Levine, *Financial Innovation Boosts Economic Growth*. A Debate with Joseph Stiglitz, The Economist, February-March 2010.

L. Leydesdorff, H. Etzkowitz, *Triple Helix of Innovation*, "Science and Public Policy", 1998.

T. Malthus, *An Essay on the Principle of Population*, J. Johnson, London 1798.

M. Magnani, *Sette Anni di Vacche Sobrie. Sfide e opportunità di crescita per sopravvivere alla crisi*, UTET, 2014.

E. S. Phelps, *Mass Flourishing: How Grassroots Innovation Created Jobs, Challenge, and Change*, Princeton University Press, Princeton 2013.

J. Schumpeter, *Capitalism, Socialism, and Democracy*, Harper Bros., New York 1942.

J. Schumpeter, *The Economics and Sociology of Capitalism*, Princeton University Press, Princeton 1991.

A. Smith, *An Inquiry into the Nature and Causes of the Wealth of Nations*, William Strahan, Thomas Cadell, London 1776.

R. Solow, "We'd Better Watch Out", *New York Times Book Review*, July 12, 1987, page 36.

F. W. Taylor, *The Principles of Scientific Management*, Harper & Brother, New York 1911.

S. L. Wang et al., *Agricultural Productivity Growth in the United States: Measurement, Trends, and Drivers*, U.S. Department of Agriculture, 2015.

2

The Technological Revolution: The Rise of Machines

We are living in the most innovative period in all of human history.

On the one hand, the technological and scientific revolution opens up unprecedented opportunities: accelerating human progress, improving the quality of life and overcoming many constraints. From an economic point of view, technology and science can increase productivity and expand the economy generating wealth, relieve humans from heavy and dangerous activities, and increase labour flexibility. On the other hand, some technologies can be used for criminal activities, terrorism, sabotage, restriction of personal freedoms, repression or other ethically controversial objectives. The risks also affect the sustainability of economic growth, the fabric of society and the future of labour, humanity as a whole and its role.

Simply witnessing technological development as a mere spectator is not possible. New technologies influence the way we live, think, produce and work. Beyond the technical aspects, they introduce new mental, cultural and strategic models. The wave of innovation affects everyone. To ride this wave instead of being overwhelmed by it, one must grasp the main innovations and understand how they work and are connected to one another. Today more than ever, as William Brian Arthur (2009) of Stanford University says, "technology is too important to be left to the specialists".

© The Author(s), under exclusive license to Springer Nature
Switzerland AG 2022
M. Magnani, *Making the Global Economy Work for Everyone*,
https://doi.org/10.1007/978-3-030-92084-5_2

Advanced Robotics

What Is It?

The term robot comes from *robota*, which means "heavy labour" in Czech and "forced labour" or "servitude" in Old Slavic. According to the Robot Institute of America (1979), a robot is a "reprogrammable, multifunctional manipulator designed to move material, parts, tools, or specialized devices, through variable programmed motions for the performance of a variety of tasks". Robotics is an interdisciplinary science involving different types of knowledge: mechanics, biology, computer science, linguistics, psychology and automation. The many applications can be divided into *service robotics*—which includes *professional* and *personal* applications—and *industrial robotics*.

The sector is growing rapidly. The purchase of industrial robots alone in the world has tripled in the last ten years. Reasons for this growth are price reductions, better ergonomics and greater flexibility, and the growing possibility of integration with traditional production systems. The largest robot manufacturers in the world are China, Japan, South Korea, United States and Germany, which together account for over 70% of new installations.[1]

The Big Change: Threats and Opportunities

Traditionally, robots were designed and manufactured as rigid structures, with controlled positions suitable to perform automated actions and almost totally devoid of interaction with human operators. Today, advanced robotic systems boast two important features: first, they are no longer either fixed or movable, but rather autonomous vehicles; second, they are able to interact with humans, respecting high safety standards. This aspect is so relevant that it has defined a particular class of machines: *collaborative robotics*. Co-bots are able to cooperate with humans in carrying out industrial and service operations. Unlike traditional robots, which are born pre-programmed, collaborative robots are often equipped with artificial intelligence (AI) and therefore able to learn from humans. Moreover, as they are generally simple to use and small in size, they have the potential for rapid deployment even in small businesses.

---

[1] Italy is well positioned in advanced robotics research and development due to institutes such as the IIT, Italian Institute of Technology, in Genoa, the Sant'Anna School of Advanced Studies in Pisa and the Polytechnics of Turin and Milan.

As far as *service robots* for *professional use* are concerned, the main applications are in logistics and distribution, defence and security, monitoring and maintenance, surgery and medical rehabilitation, and agriculture.

In logistics, the spread of robots is largely a consequence of the success of e-commerce. Autonomous Guided Vehicles (AGV), which are able to move autonomously within a circumscribed area, are becoming more and more popular for moving goods within warehouses. AGVs and Unmanned Aerial Vehicles (UAV), or drones, are also used for automated delivery of products directly to homes or distribution centres.

Just as purchasing methods have been disrupted by the internet, delivery methods may be revolutionized by autonomous vehicles and drones: a McKinsey report (2016) predicts that 78% of items will be delivered in this way in the future (with traditional deliveries at 20% and bicycle couriers at 2%).

Today, deliveries by autonomous vehicles—especially drones—are still largely limited in densely populated urban areas due to operational and regulatory issues. To overcome these obstacles, urban warehouses—places that can be easily reached by automated vehicles and from where customers pick up purchased products—are spreading rapidly. In 2021, there were 110 Amazon Prime Now distribution centres in the United States (185 around the world). In the past couple of years, Google Wing was licensed for commercial transportation in the United States and UPS launched a drone service to deliver samples for medical examinations. Walmart, a leader in traditional retail, is also embracing drone delivery. In China, where regulation is less restrictive, e-commerce groups Alibaba and JD have invested billions in unmanned vehicles and have long employed a fleet of drones.

Conceived and developed in the military field, AGV and UAV are now also adopted for civilian purposes. The military use them in combat[2] but also in intelligence, surveillance and reconnaissance operations. Law enforcement agencies use them with the same goals in anti-drug and anti-crime operations. The United States and Mexico use drones to control the flow of illegal immigration. The Italian Army uses them to monitor illegal activities in the "*terra dei fuochi*" in Campania.[3] INPS (National Institute for Italian Social security) could employ them to track down and monitor the many irregular seasonal workers in agriculture.

---

[2] In 2014, General Robert Cone, leader of the U.S. Army Training and Doctrine Command, predicted that by 2030 about a quarter of soldiers would be replaced by robots and combat drones. However, in the raids against Osama bin Laden (May 2011) and Abu Bakr al-Baghdadi (October 2019), the use of two Belgian Malinois shepherd dogs—named Cairo and Conan—was preferred to robots!

[3] The "Land of Fires" consists of a clearly defined geographical area in Campania, Italy, poisoned by thousands of tons of toxic material and waste illegally buried beneath roads and land.

In the field of security, quadruped AGVs are important. Thanks to their greater stability compared to bipeds, they are used to access dangerous areas, such as nuclear power plants (e.g. Fukushima in March 2011) or sites on fire, to operate in areas affected by natural disasters or to intervene in risky situations, such as defusing bombs or preventing attacks. These robots are usually designed for search, rescue and disaster management. In such situations, UAVs are also very useful. During the disastrous fire of Notre-Dame Cathedral in Paris in April 2019, images captured by drones allowed firefighters to deploy fire extinguishers effectively. There are also many applications to replace humans in dangerous occupational tasks. Australian mining groups Fortescue Metals Group and BHP Billiton use fleets of drones to gather information inside mines, monitor dangerous areas and prepare for explosions.

UAVs are often used for environmental and architectural monitoring. The tasks include guarding from above green or urban areas that cannot be reached by land, analysing pollutants in the atmosphere, studying wildlife, verifying architectural structures, detecting heat dispersion in buildings and taking films and photographs. The maintenance of infrastructures, such as electrical and telecommunications networks, is more efficient with drones because they can carry out interventions even in remote geographical areas, without the need for technicians. For marine infrastructures, Boeing has created the underwater robot *Echo Voyager*.

In the agricultural sector, field robots are very common: AGVs, such as autonomous tractors, herbicide machines, automatic harvesters and UAVs, dedicated to seeding, pest control and data collection on the state of crops. Traditional service robots are also widespread, primarily used in repetitive operations such as milking, harvesting fruit and vegetables, and packaging. Drones are essential in precision agriculture: by taking aerial photographs and collecting data with sensors, they help farmers assess soil and crop health and take tailored actions.

Service robotics has a wide range of applications in the medical sector. In 2017, there were nearly 700 thousand surgical procedures executed with the assistance of robotic systems in the United States. The robot does not perform the surgery but assists the surgeon. The combination of the two allows a level of performance that would be unattainable to humans alone. Think of laparoscopic surgeries performed through a single hole, or of microsurgery on tissues smaller than a millimetre.

In rehabilitation, particularly in the orthopaedic field, robots allow the development of customized therapies, with benefits for the patient, physio-therapist and insurance companies. A spin-off of the Sant'Anna School of

Advanced Studies in Pisa has created *Alex*, a robot that aids the rehabilitation of patients who suffered a stroke. Rehabilitation can also be aided by exoskeletons, wearable armours able to support the patient's body and replace motor skills. A segment with great prospects in healthcare is biorobotics, which develops robots inspired by nature.

The trend of demographic ageing is a great stimulus to developing and enhancing machines that help fragile people, such as robot guides for the blind, humanoids for elderly care and robotic walkers. These machines are generally equipped with voice recognition capabilities and in the future will also perceive human movements and gestures. The ability of social robots to interact is growing thanks to the progress in AI. For example, *Paro*, a seal-like machine made in Japan, is used in pet therapy for dementia patients. *Sophia*, an android that performs customer service, therapy and education roles, is able to converse, imitate human gestures and facial expressions.[4]

These are all examples of *service robots* for *personal use*. In this segment, the major applications are for cleaning, gardening, home service and personal care. Think of robot vacuum cleaners, lawn mowers, toy robots for children and entertainment, humanoids for personal care, and even robotic pets.[5] These robots' interfaces are usually simple because they have to interact with inexperienced users.

Industrial robots have three essential features: they operate exclusively in industrial environments, they are programmable and they relate to their physical surroundings, for example by interacting with other production devices. The sectors that use them the most are automotive and electronics, followed by metalworking, machinery, plastics and rubber. Their use in manufacturing improves product quality (by reducing defects), increases productivity (by shortening cycle times), reduces fixed personnel costs and allows work in environments that are hostile to humans.

Industrial robotics includes traditional automation (i.e. entirely automated production processes), integrated robotics (i.e. robots inserted in specific points of the production line) and the already mentioned collaborative robots. The use of industrial robots ranges from classic handling, assembly, packaging, measuring and inspection activities to a wider range of less conventional applications such as casting, painting and welding. Collaborative robots are able to perform complex tasks together with humans, without any separation barriers and in total safety. Examples are *Yumi* by ABB, a

---

[4] In 2017, *Sophia* was granted the Saudi citizenship after passing difficult language tests. It was the first robot with legal status.

[5] In addition to pet robots made to entertain humans, there are also robots whose purpose is to entertain pets!

double-armed robot used in various sectors usually to assemble small parts, or *Aura* by Comau, which can operate in collaborative or non-collaborative mode as needed. The most advanced research is focusing on the development of increasingly flexible co-bots, capable of adapting to small-scale productions that are typical of craftsmanship. The manufacturing sector will increasingly leverage exoskeletons, a sort of artificial musculature that supports, compensates and helps the worker in difficult positions, limiting fatigue and improving performance. A good example is *Mate* by Comau, which is worn like a vest and weighs only three kilos.

Driverless Car

What Is It?

Driverless cars are the most well-known application among self-driving vehicles.

The Society for Automotive Engineering identifies five levels of driving autonomy. The first two are already on the market, the third is in the prototype stage, and the last two are still under study. The last three levels have significant regulatory implications.

The first level is "assisted driving": a car with a navigator, where the system never takes full control of the vehicle. The second level is "semi-autonomous driving": an assistance system that keeps the car in the right lane and at the appropriate safety distance, allowing the driver to temporarily rest their limbs while maintaining a high level of attention. An example is the Tesla. The third level is "highly automated driving": the driver may take their eyes off the road because the vehicle steers, brakes and accelerates autonomously. The fourth level is "fully automated driving": the car handles complex situations without the intervention of the driver, who is in the driving position but can take care of other things. Autonomy occurs in limited areas and situations, such as certain geographical areas or precise weather conditions. The fifth level is "autonomous driving": the car has no steering wheel and no driver and is connected with surrounding infrastructures and other vehicles.

The Big Change: Threats and Opportunities

The push to invest in driverless vehicles came from big tech companies, particularly Google, which started driverless car testing in 2009 and since 2016 has concentrated activities in its subsidiary Waymo. In 2018, Waymo reached an agreement with FCA (now called Stellantis) to develop a version of the driverless Chrysler Pacifica minivan. Apple has been investing for years in the Titan project, aimed at developing a self-driving electric car. Samsung teamed up with Hyundai, Microsoft with Renault and Nissan, Intel with BMW. Players in this segment are also Amazon, Uber, Nvidia, Airbus, the Russian search engine Yandex and Chinese Baidu. Deeva made by VisLab, a spin-off of the University of Parma directed by Alberto Broggi, is also an interesting example.

Both traditional vehicle manufacturers and technology providers are involved in the development of autonomous and assisted driving. Research and development on self-driving vehicles is transforming the automotive industry, shifting the focus from vehicle design and manufacturing to new forms of mobility. The spread of these vehicles will radically change the entire transportation sector, for both people and goods. Driverless road transport vehicles are already being used for regular, repetitive tasks over short distances with large volumes of goods, for example in connecting production logistics hubs and ports. An example is Volvo Vera, used in the port of Gothenburg. The vehicles can be hooked to a cloud service and a control centre can constantly check exact location, load status, need for assistance and many other parameters.

As for self-driving vehicles for personal use, their deployment will be part of a changing urban transport environment. A transition is underway from a model based on car ownership to one in which mobility is seen as a service. Evidence of this trend is the many forms of shared mobility in urban centres.

The spread of autonomous vehicles is expected to result in fewer collisions and personal injuries, with benefits on public health costs and potentially disruptive consequences for the insurance industry, which will have to shift its focus to technical failure coverage for vehicle manufacturers and technology providers. The impact on people mobility will be huge, including on mobility of old or physically challenged individuals. Competition for air and rail transport will increase. Finally, the spread of autonomous vehicles will also affect infrastructures: roads will have to exchange information with cars and trucks; the need for parking will drastically decrease in traditional locations such as airports, stations and city centres.

3D Printing and Additive Manufacturing

What Is It?

3D printing allows the realization or reproduction of three-dimensional objects—products, components, mechanical parts—starting from a digital model. This is usually developed through a computer-aided technical drawing—the so-called *Computer-Aided Drafting* or CAD—or from an existing object, scanned using special laser equipment. There are already many online libraries of downloadable models for printing objects.

The novelty lies in the use of an additive manufacturing process—previously only used for microelectronic components and thin films—as opposed to the traditional subtractive process. Additive manufacturing involves the perfect superimposition of layers of material—such as clays, polymers and metals—in the form of powder, resins or filaments.

The technology was introduced in 1982 when Chuck Hull invented stereolithography and founded 3D Systems. Since then, 3D printing has evolved rapidly thanks to the introduction of new techniques and materials that can be used as "ink". The sector has four segments, based on type of use and price range: personal printers, professional, design and prototyping, and industrial manufacturing. Professional and industrial printers together account for about 70% of the market and have the highest growth rates.

Skylar Tibbits (2014), a researcher at MIT, recently invented 4D printing with the fourth dimension being time. The output is 3D products printed with "programmable material", therefore capable, at a later date, of modifying themselves autonomously and forming new structures by adapting to particular conditions or external stimuli. Possible applications include pipes that either expand or contract according to the volume of water that passes through them, prostheses that model themselves and adapt to parts of the body, organic material that deforms itself in reaction to contact with blood to heal internal haemorrhages, clothing and jewellery that adapt to the physical structure of the person.

The Big Change: Threats and Opportunities

The spread of 3D printing is set to revolutionize part of the manufacturing sector. It will certainly benefit the production of goods and components of a certain complexity or that require customization. 3D printing makes it possible to create new geometries—such as internal voids, undercuts and complex reticular structures—that would otherwise be impossible to produce with traditional systems. In addition, the possibility of using new materials and the overcoming of traditional design limits allow for a more agile production and greater creativity in design.

A first advantage is the increasing number of degrees of freedom: while a milling cutter and a robot working by subtraction have limits in their movement, an additive process makes possible geometrical shapes that would otherwise be unattainable. A second benefit is the possibility to design the shapes of the final product, without having to think about the subsequent separation from the mould. A third element of flexibility is the change in the distribution of geometries and material: it is no longer necessary to oversize some parts to obtain greater resistance in the production processes or to limit the margins of error.

In product development, 3D printing is used to make prototypes and samples before moving on to mass production. This can be done in-house, quickly and at low cost. And it leaves more freedom to designers, as they can make an initial assessment of the suitability of the project, verify the validity of the assumptions and make any necessary corrections, test functional compliance and strength characteristics of a product.

High flexibility in the production phase means that designers no longer have to first design the parts and then plan how to produce them, setting up an industrialization process. With 3D printing, the two phases coincide, with positive impact on design time and costs. Design to cost—the use of design techniques aimed at optimizing costs—also changes because production costs—which depend on the complexity of the project—are greatly reduced, and therefore, the focus shifts to material costs and production times.

The flexibility of 3D printing also derives from the fact that production can be decentralized: specifications of the prototype can be sent via internet and the final product can be printed at the consumer's site. This is a real revolution, not only in the organization of production but also in the supply chain. It implies a shift from a model of physical shipping—with the need for warehousing, logistics, transport—to one in which only data is sent and the product is produced only in the quantity needed and in the location where it is needed. This can be disruptive for distribution and retail. Products can be made with a high degree of customization, in real time and directly at the store (or at the customer's home). Moreover, flexibility and agility in production allow a reduction in the time needed to bring ideas to market, stimulating continuous product innovation—especially in design—to meet customer needs.

In a sector-by-sector analysis, repetitive, high-volume, simple-architecture manufacturing—such as engineering components—has no advantage in adopting 3D printing, which is characterized by high material costs, low processing speeds and low productivity. In this case, mass production and economies of scale can achieve much lower production costs per unit. On the other hand, the costs of 3D printing are sustainable for productions of greater complexity and customization or for which, given the limited output, large investments in production lines are not convenient.

In the low-volume aerospace industry,[6] 3D printing is used to produce heavy or complex architectural parts on site. The savings in transportation and manufacturing time and costs are significant, with reductions in energy consumption and material waste of up to 75%. Boeing recently received the first certification from the Federal Aviation Administration to print structural aircraft components and expects to save about $3 million per aircraft. In the automotive sector, 3D printing is used to produce chassis prototypes, with a reduction in time-to-test. Italian sport cars maker Dallara Automobili prints about 80% of the components of the models tested in the wind tunnel.

The construction industry is one of the most receptive for this technology. In China, since 2014, Winsun New Materials has built several houses with prefabricated panels printed in 3D using cement mixture and treated industrial waste. In Italy, Pisa-based D-SHAPE has developed a printing technology that turns sand into rock to construct low-cost buildings. In 2018, Ravenna-based WASP presented *Gaia*, the first eco-friendly 3D printed house using natural and waste materials, and in 2021 announced *TECLA* (from the words "Technology" and "Clay"), the first habitat with the same features. In architecture, the possibility of printing models allows the designer to present the client with solutions of considerable visual impact. In the cultural heritage sector, 3D printing makes it possible to create and restore works of art and architectural heritage, reproduce archaeological finds on a small scale, create realistic replicas of sculptures and set up tactile paths for the blind in museums and educational activities in schools.

In fashion, additive manufacturing has two advantages: the designer can modify the creation before moving on to the production phase, and shapes can be obtained that would not be possible with traditional techniques. Maison threeASFOUR, Chromat, Xuberance and Nervous System are among the pioneers in the field. The printing of customized accessories, such as buttons, buckles and studs, is also on the rise.

---

[6] A project of the European Space Agency foresees the construction of a settlement on the Moon with bricks printed in 3D using as "ink" a very fine powder that covers the lunar crust called "regolith".

3D printing has favoured the rise of a new digital craftsmanship, which combines manual tradition and technology. The most widespread applications are in footwear and goldsmithing where products often have unique characteristics. There is no shortage of applications for peculiar hobbies, such as the creation of objects with unconventional shapes that are impossible to find on the market or spare parts that are discontinued. There are also various applications for printing toys at home.

Retailing products with a high degree of customization can also change significantly. Think of glasses and lenses. They can be tailor made in real time and directly at the store. Luxottica is one of the frontrunners in this field. In some sectors, decentralized production can make stores strategic and technologically sophisticated.

Numerous are the applications in the medical field: from printing dentures at the dentist's office to making orthopaedic braces that are lighter and more breathable than traditional casts, to printing bone parts and even organs. In 2014, in Utrecht, a diseased part of a skull was replaced by a 3D printed prosthesis. In 2017, researchers at the EHT in Zurich developed an artificial heart made of silicone and more recently, MIT produced flexible and elastic reticular materials similar to tendons and muscles. In Italy, at the Mayer Hospital in Florence, an ear was reconstructed with 3D technology using the patient's own cartilage as a raw material, while at the Rizzoli Hospital in Bologna, bone parts are printed in titanium. The future is bioprinting, the printing of organs using the cells of different tissues as "ink". Experimental transplants have already been done with flat organs, such as skin, and hollow ones, such as trachea, blood vessels and bladder; more complex are solid organs such as heart, liver and kidney. In surgery, it is possible to prepare an intervention on 3D printed models that perfectly reproduce the interested part, a very useful possibility in facial reconstructions or operations for brain tumours.

Among the main risks of this technology is the possibility to easily print weapons, which are not traceable because they are not registered and have no serial numbers. This is something that has already occurred.

Internet of Things (IoT)

What Is It?

Internet of Things—the term was first used in 1999 by MIT researcher Kevin Ashton—is simply the extension of the internet to objects. Through social networks, the internet has connected people with people; with IoT, it connects people with things and things with other things. Objects become "intelligent" because of their ability to exchange data with each other. The increasingly dense network of objects and devices that interact with the surrounding world allows detection, monitoring and transfer of information, creating great opportunities. For example, with smart products and services capable of communicating data about the individual user, companies can know in detail the needs of each one and adapt their offer accordingly, reaching high levels of personalization. The deployment of 5G infrastructure, which will make thousands of simultaneous connections possible, is an enabling factor for the application of IoT. The size of the market goes hand in hand with the spread of connected objects. By 2025, it is expected that there will be more than 30 billion IoT connections, an average of almost 4 IoT devices per person.

The Big Change: Threats and Opportunities

IoT has many areas of application.

Smart cities represent the introduction of IoT in the management of urban contexts: from urban planning to mobility, from energy efficiency to environmental safety. In the smart city, infrastructures communicate with people, with the aim of improving their quality of life and satisfying their needs: traffic lights turn green when there are no oncoming cars, and dumpsters and trash bins collect data on garbage to reward those who do recycling and penalize offenders.

There can be no smart city without *smart mobility* because mobility is crucial to the quality of life in cities. The most visible applications are smart cars, connected cars and smart bikes, which allow an efficient and shared use of vehicles. Applications in public transport are growing, making it possible to inform passengers about delays, adjust the speed of vehicles to save fuel and improve traffic management. Copenhagen's driverless metro, thanks to its "reactive timetable", sends more trains to stations with peak users, for example at the end of sporting events or concerts.

Similarly, there can be no smart city without *smart buildings*. Smart buildings primarily respond to the need for efficient energy consumption. This implies the creation of buildings that interact with both the external and internal environment, for example by using data on brightness, temperature and weather conditions to manage the use of light and heating. Each smart building can serve the city by sharing data on weather, air quality and energy consumption. There are also intelligent infrastructures, capable of reacting to contexts and needs: tunnels that light up only when cars pass and bridges that transmit data on structural strength.

Inside the building increasingly popular are smart home and domotics, or home automation. For example, the intersection of information on habits and preferences of the inhabitants with weather forecasts or other external data automatically operates various domestic devices, such as heating, air conditioning, appliances, shutters and alarm systems.

The most widespread applications of environmental and territorial sensors are in *smart agriculture*. In precision farming, the collection of data from the ground (soil moisture, effectiveness of nutrients, pathogen pressure) and from weather applications can help improve productivity and avoid waste of seeds, water, fertilizers and manure. Thanks to sensors and algorithms, Californian almond growers are dosing irrigation and fertilizer with savings of up to 20%. A sensor for livestock introduced by the English company Smartbell is placed around the neck of animals to monitor their movements, indicate the ideal moment for reproduction and predict the possibility of lameness.

An area of broad application for IoT is *smart manufacturing*. "Industrie 4.0" in Germany and "Advanced Manufacturing Partnership" in the United States are industrial policy programs aimed at digitizing manufacturing. In the digital factory, the application of sensors to machinery collects data with different objectives: standardizing the quality of products; monitoring the wear and tear of specific parts and conducting predictive maintenance, thus avoiding costly interruptions in the production cycle; keeping track of every production variable (time, downtime, waste) to increase efficiency and reduce costs; using some data to improve product industrialization (i.e. to better design products in the future).

Especially in the business-to-business sector, there is an increase in the number of machinery manufacturers who use sensors and algorithms to remotely monitor the operation of what is installed at the customer's premises, signalling anomalies and suggesting maintenance. This is the case of the bottling systems made by GAI in Cuneo, the intelligent looms made by Camozzi in Brescia and the packaging lines made by IMA in Bologna. The consequence is the growth of the "servitization" phenomenon, consisting in the shift of manufacturing companies towards the provision of services, such as machine monitoring and maintenance, and data management and sales. Thanks to the wide range of machines installed, GE is a leader in this field.

In addition to machinery and equipment, IoT can be embedded in manufactured parts or pieces, allowing companies to track them throughout their lifecycle. Automakers can monitor the wear and tear of vehicle parts, suggesting to customers the timing of overhauls and replacement. In some cases, the change of settings can be made remotely: it is the case of Tesla that raised the suspension of cars by acting on the software. Similar applications can be found in home appliances and consumer electronics.

In logistics, IoT generates efficiency and savings. UPS, Fedex, DHL and other firms in the sector monitor every aspect of transport and delivery, improve routes, promptly carry out maintenance on vehicles and manage downtime. Amazon uses a controversial "electronic bracelet" to monitor the performance of employees and help them quickly find products within the warehouse.

In retail, IoT applications are spreading rapidly. In Amazon Go stores, a network of sensors identifies customers as they enter, recommends purchases and reminds them of promotions, records their choices from the shelves and automatically handles their payments. A Japanese department store uses sensor-gathered information on customer flows and characteristics in order to optimize the composition of its sales team. Ralph Lauren uses an interactive fitting room with a smart mirror that recognizes clothes, displays information about the garment and collects data about the customer behaviour (from the length of the fitting session to the number of items tried on and purchased) in order to improve marketing and sales. Italy's Almax has developed a mannequin with facial recognition that identifies customers by gender, age and somatic features. The decline in sensor prices and the spread of the internet are increasing IoT applications in consumer products. Like the digital diapers by Procter & Gamble and Google, whose sensors signal when it's time to change the baby's nappy!

IoT can also be helpful in managing human resources. The analysis of parameters such as light, humidity and temperature in workplaces makes it possible to assess the effect of the environment on productivity. These techniques are also used in sports to monitor athletes' body parameters and are finding increasing application in the medical field for remote monitoring of patients and the elderly.

One of the major critical issues of IoT is the total dependence on the internet network infrastructure. Other critical issues are security and privacy. The expansion of IoT is adding to the network numerous potentially insecure devices—such as surveillance cameras, home appliances and electronic devices—that can be easily used by hackers to break into private networks. It is not hard to imagine the possible damage of an attack on algorithms for autonomous driving or managing mobility in a smart city. Network vulnerability represents an important constraint to the spread of IoT.

Big Data

What Is It?

The term "big data" refers to the massive collection of data—in terms of volume, format and variety—the analysis of which requires specific and very complex algorithms and methods. The great potential derives from the possibility of extracting information otherwise unobtainable from small data sets. The quantity and heterogeneity of data, and the need for real-time processing, impose new methods of structuring inputs and require huge storage and computational capabilities.

The extraction of patterns or series from raw data is, instead, entrusted to the so-called data mining techniques, which permit the obtaining of useful information and make scientific or industrial use of it. An example is the sentiment analysis. Starting from a database of product reviews (raw data that cannot be analysed by a machine), an algorithm is able to understand the user's positive or negative evaluation, generating structured data that can be used for analysis with the aim of improving the product. It is therefore important to distinguish between *big data* and *big data analytics* in order not to confuse raw data with analysis and results. Big data is the raw material of the digital universe, the oil of the knowledge economy that has value only if it is extracted and refined.

There are different types of big data analysis. *Descriptive* analysis allows to represent and describe the past and present of certain situations or processes, for example to understand the causes of diseases through the historical analysis of medical records or production inefficiencies through the historical analysis of production flows. *Predictive* analysis enables the design of future development scenarios, such as disease outbreaks or consumer preferences. Based on historical and predictive data, *prescriptive* analysis suggests possible solutions in order to aid decision-making.

Investment in collecting, processing and interpreting big data is growing. It involves all sectors and also governments.

The Big Change: Threats and Opportunities

As illustrated, big data finds a natural and immediate application in the industrial world, also thanks to IoT that enables its collection. However, the wide diffusion of digital technologies has also significantly modified individuals' behaviour, for example purchasing habits, demand of services and use of leisure time. The vast amount of data collected from phones, tablets and computers allows an accurate profiling of consumers, used by companies to customize their offer.

The service sector particularly benefits from these information flows. Several applications are in the sectors of tourism, culture and hospitality, where knowing the habits of the client helps make targeted proposals. The Art Institute of Chicago analyses data collected anonymously from visitors' mobile phones—such as visiting times, routes taken and time spent in front of each work of art—to improve access and displays, develop marketing strategies and choose books and gift items to offer in the museum shop.

Banks and insurance providers use data to estimate the risks associated with each type of customer and, as a result, offer appropriate products and services and better distribute their risk. Some connections are not surprising. Sports car purchases and late utility payments increase a customer's risk profile, while maternity and home ownership decrease it. Interestingly, those who buy felt pads for furniture are considered more reliable in meeting their debts on time. In human resources management, the analysis of data helps to better understand the functioning of operational processes and employees' performance, but also to predict candidates' potential.

In the field of justice, both descriptive and predictive models are used. They are based on historical data on offenders, crimes, places and situations, in order to increase the level of security and predict the probability of occurrence of a crime. In medicine, big data is useful to understand the causes of a pathology but also to try to prevent it. Many applications have been tested in oncology but their use can be extended. In pharmacology, the analysis of big data facilitates the determination of the appropriate dosage, based on the physiological characteristics of each patient. Tailored treatments could also solve a critical issue in clinical trials, 80% of which fail due to some level of mismatch between patient and drug.

A possible criticality of big data is that of bias, or prejudice. First, because the algorithm is a reflection of those who elaborate it, including their biases. Second, because the training phase conditions the output. If, for example, an algorithm is trained to recognize tumour masses only on male clinical cases, it will be less effective for female diagnoses.

The main risks of big data are linked to the possibility of manipulation and misuse that can threaten privacy and alter free competition. Hence the criticism of Amazon, Google, Facebook, Apple. The same "libertarian paternalism" that through the so-called "nudging" techniques allows to direct individuals towards socially desirable behaviours—for example, less energy consumption, payment of taxes, organ donation—can be used to push them towards commercial decisions or political choices.

Analysis of the data made available by social media not only reveals where people go, what they do, what they consume and what they read, but also what they think.[7] That's why politics is increasingly using big data: to develop targeted electoral campaigns in democratic systems and to strengthen regimes in totalitarian ones. Ahead of the 2016 U.S. election, Donald Trump caused a stir by hiring Cambridge Analytica, a firm which acquired information on 220 million Americans, to send customized messages on the basis of their profiles.[8] The British political consulting firm was also involved in the Brexit referendum that took place in June 2016. According to some (Politico, 2018), in both cases the misuse of data contributed to "cheat" results. In a more transparent way, Barack Obama's campaign had also leveraged on big data for the 2012 election, doing extensive data mining and micro-targeting.

In various countries, big data, combined with other technologies, is used for mass surveillance. The news that the Chinese government is using a social *credit system* as an instrument of social control has caused concern. Citizens, institutions and businesses are monitored by a complex evaluation system that triggers rewards and sanctions based on their behaviour. Each is assigned a score determined by a mix of negative elements (unpaid debts, fines, reports) and positive elements (social services, volunteering). Those with a positive rating receive free or guaranteed public services, while those with a negative rating are denied access to bank loans, certain job opportunities, domestic flights and fast trains. The coronavirus pandemic, being regarded as a public health emergency, has further spread the practice of mass surveillance, particularly in Asian.[9] For example, Vietnam has been tracking locals and foreigners through mobile apps; Thai immigration authorities have been using location data of those arriving in the country. Taiwan, South Korea, Singapore and China have been doing extensive use of big data for tracking purposes.

There is clearly a fundamental tension between the capacity of digital technologies to harvest data and the risks that the use (or misuse) of that data can pose to privacy or individual liberty. As pope Francis pointed out his

---

[7] Alessandro Vespignani (2019), a physicist at Northeastern University, considers interventions on social networks a "thermometer of thought" that can enable "the understanding of society as an aggregate".

[8] Targeted messages allow for the efficient allocation of campaign finance because they are sent—via phone, email and social networks—to selected audiences in a customised manner. In Trump's case for example, the favourable stance on gun ownership was offered as a form of *defense* to fearful residents of dangerous neighbourhoods, as a *right* to constitutional purists and as a *tradition* to sport hunting enthusiasts. The same message took on different values depending on the recipients.

[9] In general, while data protection laws in Europe and the United States are driven by the intrinsic right to privacy—therefore, for example, mass tracking of people's movements and contacts using smartphone location data violates the law—many Asian countries have "more pragmatic" legislations. This contrast clearly emerged in the different strategies adopted to fight the COVID-19 outbreak.

address to the plenary assembly of the Pontifical Academy for Life (2020), "this asymmetry, by which a select few know everything about us while we know nothing about them, dulls critical thought and the conscious exercise of freedom".

Quantum Computing

What Is It?

This is an experimental technology for the generation of new computers capable of exploiting the laws of physics and quantum mechanics for data processing, thus exponentially accelerating computational operations.

The quantum computer—inspired at the beginning of the 1980s by Nobel Prize winner for physics Richard Feynman (1982)—is not a simple evolution of the traditional computer but a new way of thinking about calculation. A classical computer faces problems in a sequential manner; a quantum computer solves many problems at once. It's as if, in order to look for a client in a hotel room whose number you can't remember, instead of checking the rooms one by one, there was a mechanism that allowed you to carry out a single search in all the rooms at the same time, with considerable savings in time and energy.

In traditional computers, data are stored one at a time, in the form of a succession of bits (binary digits), the basic units of information. Quantum computers, whose fundamental unit is the quibit (quantumbit), are based on two laws of quantum mechanics: the possibility of existing simultaneously in several different places (superposition principle) and correlation at a distance (*entanglement*). These characteristics make it possible to record several data simultaneously in the memory of the computer and retrieve them quickly at the time of calculation.

A race for computational supremacy has been going on for decades. Some multinationals—such as IBM, Google, Microsoft and Intel—and several governments—especially China, the United States and France—are investing heavily in the development of quantum computing.

The complexity of the technology and the challenge to develop it are well summarized by Feynman, who believed that "if you think you understand quantum physics, you don't understand quantum physics".

The Big Change: Threats and Opportunities

The realization of the quantum computer would stimulate the development of many other technologies. This huge computing capacity would allow for better use of big data, acceleration in AI development, faster deployment of IoT and blockchain, and improved performance of robots and drones.

Quantum computing could revolutionize—directly or indirectly—all sectors: in chemistry and biology, it would make it easier to perform simulations that would otherwise be very complex; similarly, in pharmaceutical research, it would drastically reduce the time and cost of designing new products, it would be easier to make tailor-made drugs, and response times to epidemics would decrease[10]; in astronomy, the analysis of the enormous amount of data collected by space missions would be much faster, meteorology forecasting would be more accurate, and it would become easier to analyse the impact of human behaviour on climate and the ecosystem.

In manufacturing, quantum computing would make it possible to identify, among millions of possibilities, the best material for the construction of automobiles, robots or space stations, and allow optimized traffic management—air, land, sea—through very precise forecasts and calculation of optimal routes. Volkswagen and D-Wave have developed a programme to this end.

The main criticalities are related to technical problems. The characteristics that guarantee rapid calculation are manifested only in the case of total isolation from the external environment, which means it could be necessary to operate at temperatures close to *absolute zero* (equal to $-273.15\ °C$). Another critical issue is related to information security because the quantum computer would be able to violate the current computer security systems.

Cloud Storage and Computing

What Is It?

The computer cloud indicates a place where data are saved. A virtual warehouse from which to draw remotely, thanks to the internet, at the time of need. In addition to archiving and storing data, the cloud is also a platform for providing other services on demand, to people and companies.

---

[10] Quantum computing would have been a very valuable tool in facing the challenge of COVID-19 in 2020 and 2021.

People use it to store their data and to remotely access services. Think of the many applications offered by Dropbox and Google or the content managed on social networks. Companies use it to store and process operational data—for example customer information for banks or production data for manufacturing companies—and to purchase various software and hardware services. In addition, the cloud is often the storage tool used by IoT applications because it allows easy sharing of data and reduces the size of memory used in devices.

The main innovations brought about by the cloud are the network distribution of services, the ability of the infrastructure to increase and decrease performance and functionality according to demand, the reliability and continuity of the service, and the quick delivery of new storage and computing resources. Infrastructures are large data centres that centralize the management of data[11] and make available to users the resources they need—storage capacity, virtual servers, applications, software programs—on a pay-per-use basis. The cloud is therefore stimulating the spread of a new organizational model that allows companies to reduce their own internal IT capacity and functionality to acquire it externally, according to the needs of the moment. On the one side, there is the supplier who offers hardware and software services that can be used at any time, from anywhere and with any device; on the other side, there is the client who can, on demand and paying according to usage, remotely access services without the need to make large initial investments.

The great flexibility offered by the cloud is very useful in the development and testing phase of new products that will not necessarily go into production or for companies that operate in segments with variable demand. On average, companies spend a third of their IT budgets on cloud storage and computing, making it a high-growth and high-margin sector. The market leaders are Amazon, Microsoft and Google.

The Big Change: Threats and Opportunities

The cloud helps companies increase their productivity, first of all by lowering their initial fixed costs and increasing their flexibility in terms of access to services; moreover, the company can focus on its core business, freeing up resources—both human and financial—that were previously dedicated to infrastructure management. It is therefore a fundamental element in the

---

[11] However, the Bologna-based start-up Cubbit is developing a "distributed data centre"—a network of devices in the homes of connected users—that reduces consumption, costs, environmental impact and vulnerability to hackers.

process of advancing an economic system, also because it improves the use of many other technologies.

By increasing flexibility, connectivity, speed and security throughout manufacturing systems, the cloud is the enabling technology for the digital transformation of manufacturing. It benefits large enterprises, which improve communication between sites in different locations, as well as small businesses, which can take advantage of technologies and services that would otherwise be unaffordable. Electronic invoicing is a well-known service often offered through the cloud. In e-commerce, the cloud ensures the operation of an online store by providing the necessary computational resources with reliability and flexibility and requiring a limited investment.

By its very nature, the cloud offers opportunities for growth to start-ups and microenterprises on the supply side as well. They can distribute software products, applications and services widely without having to make large investments in sales and distribution networks. The impressive growth of Zynga, a firm specializing in video games for social platforms, is also due to its use of the cloud.

However, the cloud presents some criticalities. The total dependence on the infrastructure of the internet network can jeopardize continuity and quality of service. There is also the risk of cyber-attacks on sensitive data, for sabotage or industrial espionage. That is why several multinationals use a private cloud, more defensible from external attacks. Finally, the outsourcing of many IT activities on the one hand reduces the costs of companies but, on the other hand, makes them lose control over an important phase of the production process.

Artificial Intelligence, Machine Learning and Deep Learning

What Is It?

Artificial intelligence (AI) is the ability of machines—defined as a combination of hardware and software—to solve problems, perform actions and execute tasks that are typical of human intelligence. These include understanding languages, recognizing images, sounds and patterns, autonomously processing historical data and solving problems. These are all actions relevant to learning and decision-making.

The term *Artificial Intelligence* was introduced in 1956 by Stanford University mathematician John McCarthy, who—together with MIT cognitive scientist Marvin Minsky and Nobel economist Herbert Simon—is counted among the fathers of AI. However, Alan Turing—considered the father of computer science—formalized the concept of algorithm as early as the 1930s. And in the forties and fifties significant progress was made in the creation of neurons and artificial neural networks. In *Computing machinery and intelligence*, a fundamental article for AI published in "Mind" in 1950; Turing introduced a criterion to determine whether a machine is able to think (the Turing test). The first concrete application of AI is in 1952 with an IBM program for the game of checkers that learns from the interaction with humans.

AI requires four different intellectual skills. *Comprehension*, that is recognizing texts, images, tables, videos and voice; *reasoning*, that is connecting the multiple information collected through mathematical algorithms; *learning*, that is learning from experience through the so-called machine learning, which analyses the consequences of historical data and past decisions; *relational ability*, that is interacting with humans through natural language processing.

AI is one of the most potentially disruptive innovations in history due in part to the simultaneous availability of huge amounts of data (big data), large storage capacity (cloud storage), unprecedented computing power and predictive analytics algorithms that transform data into useful information.

Machine learning (ML) is a branch of AI that focuses on the ability of machines to learn through algorithms that, based on the processing of large amounts of data, adapt to situations. By learning from experience, even from mistakes, machines improve performance.

Deep learning (DL) is one of the approaches to machine learning that has taken its cue from the structure of the brain, particularly the interconnectedness of neurons. DL is a learning technique in which artificial neural networks are exposed to vast amounts of data so that they can learn to perform tasks. The most diffused applications of ML and DL are those of *image* and *speech recognition*. The extraction of information by the machines from images or speeches can help medical diagnosis, fraud identification, autonomous driving and customer relationships management.

The Big Change: Threats and Opportunities

Just as the cloud is an enabler for many technologies because it improves the way data is stored and archived, AI is an enabler for the use and exploitation of big data. It is through *data mining* and AI, indeed, that big data becomes a source of information that enables forecasting and decision-making.

There is no shortage of examples. Landing AI™ has developed *machine vision* tools to help manufacturing companies detect microscopic defects in products. *Euclid* is a platform that collects and analyses, thanks to IoT sensors embedded in buildings, factories and production lines, data on internal energy consumption and helps make operational decisions to improve performance. *Nest*, Google's smart thermostat, thanks to ML applications, adapts to inhabitants' habits and preferences. The most advanced cars use video game-like algorithms to learn and modify their behaviour based on that of the driver.

The increasingly popular virtual assistants—such as Amazon's *Alexa*, Google's *Assistant* and *Now*, Apple's *Siri*, Microsoft's *Cortana*, Samsung's *Bixby*, Nokia's *Viki* —use AI algorithms to recognize language but also to learn, over time, the habits and preferences of users. The world of customer assistance has been revolutionized by chatbots—software designed to simulate written and verbal conversation with a human being—whose performance improves with use. The real challenge for these systems is to be able to increasingly understand the natural language of humans, to the point of recognizing the mood of the moment, and adapt their responses.

E-commerce is increasingly using recommendation systems to make targeted commercial proposals. Facebook uses an algorithm that chooses which messages and updates to show to users based on their historical behaviour. Similar mechanisms are used by Spotify to recommend music and by Netflix to suggest movies. Amazon's purchase suggestions are derived from the analysis of the vast database generated by the customer portfolio. German fragrance giant Symrise and IBM have jointly developed *Philyra*, an AI application that creates fragrances targeted at certain consumer segments by cross-analysing thousands of fragrance formulas and historical sales data organized by geography, age and gender.

Among the many applications in agriculture, there is an interesting one that helps beekeepers prevent the mite *Varroa destructor* from exterminating their bees. Cameras monitor the hives and send the images of the mites to an AI software that can determine in a few seconds whether they are harmless or destructive pests and prepare the appropriate defences. In the field of security, AI is used by some financial institutions to monitor clients' transactions and, by detecting inconsistencies in their behaviour, prevent fraud, abuse or money laundering. A well-known example is the bank's telephone message asking for confirmation of purchases considered abnormal. In the public administration, which produces, collects and stores a large amount of data, AI solutions can help to reduce costs, improve services and make better use of human resources. There are countless applications of AI in medicine and health care. Specifically, during the coronavirus pandemic, technology powered by AI has helped track the outbreak, clean hospitals, deliver supplies and develop vaccines.

AI algorithms can analyse data in different formats: verbal and written language but also images and videos. In August 2021, Sonantic—a U.K.-based software company that uses AI to copy voices for actors and film studios—digitally reconstructed the voice of actor Val Kilmer, who had lost it during his treatment for throat cancer effectively ending his career. Facial recognition applications can be used in various contexts, for example to increase security and prevent crime. Powerful software examines in real time large quantities of images collected by cameras in public places; the analysis then leads to the recognition of suspicious faces or behavioural patterns that can be an alarm signal. The same technology is used for commercial purposes to recognize people's emotions by reading their faces when they look at an advertisement or products on display. Facebook, Amazon, Microsoft and IBM are developing emotional recognition software.

Facial, voice and behavioural recognition can have applications that are controversial, in violation of privacy or even aimed at maintaining social and political control. It is believed that in China facial recognition applications record the faces of millions of people and the information collected is used to recognize, control and repress individuals belonging to minority groups, in particular the Uighurs.[12]

AI technology in general may have many problematic and arguable uses.[13] This raises a great ethical challenge. It seems important to find a way of inserting in the AI algorithms a decisional model that reconciles the utilitarian principles with the ethical-deontological ones.

Augmented and Virtual Reality

What Is It?

Augmented reality (AR) and virtual reality (VR) are two dimensions of mediated reality. Mediation usually occurs in real time and information about

---

[12] At the other end of the spectrum, the city of San Francisco has banned police from using this technology to avoid the risk of discrimination against minorities.

[13] A 2021 *New York Times* report revealed that Mossad—the national intelligence agency of Israel—assassinated in November 2020 Mohsen Fakhrizadeh, Iran top nuclear scientist, using an AI-powered remote-controlled machine gun.

the physical world surrounding the user can become interactive and digitally manipulable.

The first examples of mediated reality date back to 1957 when filmmaker Morton Heilig created Sensorama, a device designed to improve the cinematic experience of the viewer. Since then, the areas of application have multiplied. AR is the enrichment of human sensory perception by means of information—generally manipulated and conveyed electronically—that cannot be perceived with the five senses.

There are many applications that allow to get information about objects, products and places simply by framing them with the camera of a device. AR devices help with orientation in cities, act as tutors for tourists, provide details on products, suggest restaurants and shops, and facilitate the recognition of natural elements such as mountain peaks, stars and constellations. An example is Ikea Place, an application that allows to choose furniture from the catalogue, view it and position it at will within a floor plan. The same technique is used by other furniture retailers such as Wayfair and Anthropologie. Reality can also be "diminished" (DR), reducing the amount of information perceivable by human senses. Applications are mainly in the furniture sector but also in cinema, to remove wires and harnesses used to shoot action scenes.

If AR and DR modify perceived reality, VR is a realistic simulation of situations that do not exist. In VR, electronically added or subtracted information is predominant. This is to the point that people find themselves immersed in a situation in which the natural perceptions of many of the five senses no longer seem to be present and are replaced by others. The most widespread examples are video games. There are also many applications in architecture and interior design that place the client in environments that have been designed but do not yet exist.

All major hi-tech players are betting on these technologies, investing in research or making acquisitions. In recent years, Facebook acquired U.S.-based Oculus, which produces VR headsets, for about $2 billion; Apple has acquired German AR start-up Metaio; global action cam leader GoPro has bought French 360-degree video software start-up Kolor.

The Big Change: Threats and Opportunities

The use of AR and VR can create growth opportunities in many areas.

There are several applications in marketing, sales and tourism, which aim to bring the customer closer to the product. Among the precursors is the Danish Lego with its smart boxes: scanning a barcode on the box starts a video showing the characters of the game. Google's smart glasses are equipped with an AI system that increases the perception of the reality in which the individual moves. Similarly, Bose offers sunglasses with an audio system and AR that guide through streets, museums, shops and public offices.

The British retail chain Tesco uses AR in its promotional flyers: scanning the picture of the product gives the impression of holding it in your hands. Several car manufacturers use AR and VR for virtual test drives, to enhance the presentation of new models in showrooms, or even to create virtual showrooms. In tourism, the *Oculus Quest* headset with visor and high-resolution graphics makes it possible "visit" places and monuments, while special AR visors handed out in the Ara Pacis Museum in Rome allow visitors to perceive the three-dimensionality of bas-reliefs and sculptures.

Applications in the industrial field are growing, especially in the aeronautical, aerospace, automotive and mechanical sectors, where AR provides effective support for monitoring, maintenance, testing and simulation activities. Applications for maintenance are also used by service companies that own an infrastructure. The software *Acty* makes real time and remote maintenance operations possible, by having technicians visualize the problem through a smartphone. Italian utility company Enel's "smart helmet"—with microphone, headphones, adjustable cameras and wireless connectivity—lets operators in the field communicate with colleagues and show them the most complex cases.

As far as VR is concerned, the greatest growth opportunities are currently offered by the video game sector. The prospects in the medical field are also very interesting: in surgery, where VR can be used as a training tool, in motor and cognitive rehabilitation, and in the therapy of psychiatric disorders. A group of researchers in Virginia is using VR to study the learning process in mammals, useful for understanding the origin and evolution of pathologies such as Alzheimer's disease.

Various are the applications in architecture and design. Large studios manage projects from their offices all over the world thanks to mediated reality software that allows clients to interact and be involved. *Eyecadvr* allows designers and clients to "move" within projects and choose the desired combinations of materials, coverings and furnishings. In the judicial field, *Oculus Rift* is used in courtrooms to recreate crime scenes on a virtual platform. Many potential applications are in pedagogy and education, where mediated reality enhances student engagement and makes learning more enjoyable.

The greatest risk of VR is the possibility of influencing users' opinions and choices much more than television and the internet have done.

Blockchain

What Is It?

The blockchain is best known as the technology behind cryptocurrencies, particularly bitcoin.[14] The scope of the blockchain, however, is much broader. It is a trusted protocol on which transparent contracts, networks and exchange systems can be built, and it is potentially applicable in many areas.

The blockchain is a public, decentralized digital ledger that leverages technology to validate transactions between two parties in a secure, verifiable and permanent manner. The infrastructure that enables its use is a global network of devices, called nodes, interconnected through the internet. The term "blockchain" originates from its operation because each node in the network plays a role in verifying information, sending it to the next in a chain composed of blocks.

The blockchain is a *public* ledger because it is visible to everyone and it is *decentralized* because each participant has a copy of the same data, whereas in a centralized structure the data is stored in a central database. The data is *secure* because of the use of cryptography and it is *verifiable* because, being recorded in a ledger, it can be verified at any time. Finally, the data is *permanent* because once written in a block it cannot be retroactively altered without the consent of the other nodes in the network.

In a sense, the blockchain plays the role of notary to transfer, instantly and without intermediaries, the ownership of any asset: real estate, vehicles, financial securities, money, data and most recently artworks. Historically, the exchange of assets was direct and physical, through barter. Later, third parties emerged to secure the exchanges, such as the State being a guarantor for the circulation of currency and banks for the payment of checks or bills of exchange. With the blockchain, exchange can take place without the need for a guarantor and yet maintain a high level of security. From a technical point of view, this is possible because there is no single server controlled by someone, but all participants have a copy of the data and at any time they can check if data have been modified and by whom. To modify a piece of information, it is necessary to open a new block and declare it: this eliminates the possibility of fraud or theft.

The feature of reducing the level of uncertainty between parties is perhaps the most revolutionary aspect of the blockchain. Uncertainty has always been

---

[14] The idea of the blockchain came in 2008 to Satoshi Nakamoto, a pseudonym of one or more computer scientists who created bitcoin based on blockchain technology.

a constraint on the success of transactions and thus on economic growth. Throughout history, uncertainty has been contained, and transactions have been secured, in different ways. First through violence, then through a combination of laws and informal customs, including sometimes corruption. The modern institutions that guarantee transactions are the constitution, laws, governments, markets, banks and businesses.[15] The introduction of the internet has made transaction mechanisms more efficient—thanks to market platforms such as Amazon, eBay and Alibaba—but it has not eliminated the need for institutions and intermediaries that reduce uncertainty. With the blockchain, however, the revolution lies in the fact that—for the first time—the level of uncertainty can be reduced only by using technology and, moreover, in a decentralized way. This has the potential to replace the historic role of many centralized political and economic institutions.

The Big Change: Threats and Opportunities

One of the domains most affected by the blockchain is the financial sector, especially due to the possible applications in the settlement of both cash and securities transactions. The blockchain eliminates intermediaries by making money transfers and payments safer and faster, certified and less expensive.[16] Using this technology to transfer funds, clear and settle securities, assets and derivatives can increase the effectiveness of banks in capital markets. In lending, the blockchain allows banks to certify counterparty data— for example, creditworthiness—in a shared environment, reducing risk and containing costs across the system. In insurance, fraud can be prevented and the costs of management platforms reduced. Much of the investment in fin-tech is based on the blockchain. Recently, some 40 large international banks have decided to set a standard for using this technology in interbank operations.

The blockchain is also used as a general ledger tool for cryptocurrencies. Bitcoin is the best known but not the only one. Others are Monero, Zcash, Ethereum, Ripple, Litecoin, Waves, IOTA, Neo, Cardano, Stellar, the Petromoneda, backed by Venezuelan oil reserves, and Libra, launched by Facebook.

Due to the fact that it makes digital identity monitoring and management secure, efficient, irrefutable and fraud-proof, one area of potential application

---

[15] Nobel Laureate Douglass North (1971, 1989, 1990, 1991), an exponent of *New Institutional Economics*, studied the importance of institutions in reducing the level of uncertainty and increasing connections and exchanges of value in society.

[16] The cost of money transfers worldwide is estimated at around €30 billion per year.

for the blockchain is the administration of public records currently managed by centralized authorities, such as cadastre and registry, with the resulting responsibility for certificates and titles of ownership. The blockchain can manage the change of ownership of digital and physical objects through smart contracts, i.e. legally binding digital contracts between parties that do not require the presence of an intermediary. Fraud is impossible because blockchain data cannot be tampered with.

Bitnation, a blockchain-based government services platform, is designing an emergency virtual identity card for migrants and refugees—which could cryptographically prove a person's existence and family relationships—available on public record. This technology can also be useful in political elections, providing voting certainty and ballot transparency.

In health care, the blockchain allows doctors located in different parts of the world to securely share patients' records. In the pharmaceutical industry, medicines can be tracked and validated at each step of distribution, avoiding counterfeits and anticipating expirations. Similar applications can be extended to the agri-food sector. In retail, the blockchain can influence a wide range of processes, including payments, product traceability, certificates of authenticity, anti-counterfeiting mechanisms, supply chain management, sales and after-sales services.

This technology also has interesting applications to the logistics sector. The large Danish shipowner Maersk uses the blockchain to improve efficiency and security in transport: dozens of authorizations are sent simultaneously to all parties involved and the notification, being encrypted, constitutes endorsement. In the energy sector, the blockchain increases security of networks by defending them from hackers. In the future, the major applications will be in energy exchange platforms: automatic and decentralized distribution systems (*peer-to-peer*) that will replace centralized one. In the IoT field, the blockchain certifies the reliability of information transmitted by objects and sensors.

In the field of entertainment, the blockchain may become the core of a new system of interaction between those who produce it and those who use it. British singer Imogen Heap has used it to sell new songs directly to fans. The ability to eliminate middlemen prompted the United Nations (U.N.) to use the technology to collect donations in the World Food Programme (2017).

The blockchain, however, presents several critical issues. The main one is the difficulty of verifying the identity of participants. Anonymity increases the risk of cryptocurrency use in illegal transactions, money laundering and terrorist financing. It is estimated that bitcoins are used in almost half of the financial exchanges between criminal groups. Another problem with cryptocurrencies is their volatility, which can threaten the stability of financial markets.

Last but not least is the issue of the blockchain validation process, which requires thousands of computers to work incessantly to verify individual transactions. This results in very high computational costs, energy consumption and environmental impact. Each transaction is estimated to use about 800 kWh, which is equal to the daily consumption of twenty-six American households. The Dutch website "Digiconomist" (2018) calculates a "bitcoin energy consumption index" and estimates that the process of mining bitcoins requires more than three times the energy needed to mine gold of equivalent value!

Nanotechnologies and Nanomaterials

What Is It?

Nanotechnology deals with the creation, study and practical applications of nanostructures and nanomaterials. Working on the order of magnitude between 1 and 100 nanometres,[17] nanotechnology alters the traditional distinction between biology, chemistry and physics.

Nanotechnology makes it possible to modify the properties of matter by intervening directly on individual molecules, exploiting electromagnetic interactions (the van der Waals forces), and even atoms. This is possible due to the latest microscopy techniques such as the scanning probe: instruments such as the scanning tunnel microscope allow not only to visualize single atoms, but also to manipulate and move them.

The applications of nanotechnology therefore go far beyond the techniques for carrying out common chemical reactions, with which unknown molecules are synthesized. By manipulating individual molecules, it is possible to change their arrangement. In a sense, atoms and molecules become small bricks in a construction game that can be assembled at will. The result is advanced materials with special properties and innovative applications in many different fields.

---

[17] A nanometre is equal to one billionth of a meter or one millionth of a millimetre.

The Big Change: Threats and Opportunities

The applications of nanotechnology range from basic research to the development of new materials, from manufacturing to the improvement of production processes, from medicine to pharmacology, from electronics to information technology, from energy to the environment.

Industrial products based on nanotechnology include tyres that are particularly resistant to wear and tear, dyes and pigments that improve printing quality and stability, and drugs made up of nanoparticles for efficient and targeted delivery. Various batteries, auto parts, coatings, sporting goods, antibacterial clothing, cosmetics and food products also contain nanomaterials. In general, nanotechnology has made it possible to develop new materials with molecular structures which are much lighter than metals, but have similar or better mechanical strength or electrical conductivity. In manufacturing, they are used in automotive and sensor systems, aeronautics and aerospace, electronics and electromechanics, textiles, chemicals and cosmetics.

Many applications are in medicine, pharmacology and life sciences. Nanomedicine can provide an enormous contribution to the identification and treatment of many diseases. A real revolution may come from the development of molecules capable of selectively targeting the body's diseased cells while sparing healthy ones. Administration and dosing of drugs are also affected. Interesting applications are in the field of the environment, with industrial catalysts that reduce the dispersion of toxic substances to combat pollution, and security, with detectors of chemical and biological agents and miniaturized surveillance systems.

The main problems with nanotechnologies concern the production and release into the environment of microscopic particles, the consequences of which on ecosystems and health are not yet known. The concern is that, due to their small size, nanostructures released into the body for therapeutic or dietary purposes may exceed the chemical barrier that prevents the passage of harmful substances from the blood to the brain, causing damage to the nervous system. Several concerns exist about the use of nanotechnology in the production of dyes and additives used in the food industry. In order to deal with the environmental and health risks, the European Union (2021) has proposed adopting the same precautions for new nanocomposites as for the marketing of chemicals, i.e. carrying out *in vitro* and animal tests before marketing. Another major risk comes from the potential use of nanotechnology for military purposes.

Biotechnology

What Is It?

Biotechnology harnesses cellular and biomolecular processes in biological systems and living organisms to develop technologies and products that help improve human life and the health of the planet.

Biotechnology is an ancient discipline. In fact, one of the most traditional techniques for controlling and modifying living organisms is fermentation. Wine, beer, bread and yogurt are the result of biotechnology. So are penicillin and other antibiotics.

In recent decades, however, the range of action of biotechnology has widened. The great impetus came when progress in microbiology, biochemistry, molecular biology and genetic engineering made it possible to develop sophisticated methods to industrially obtain products—starting from plant or animal microorganisms—with multiple applications in medicine and pharmaceuticals, agriculture and animal husbandry, industry and energy, chemistry and cosmetics, food and the environment.

Biotechnology is central to the development of genetic engineering. It makes it possible to analyse the structure and function of genes, manipulate them and reintroduce them into the original cell or into a new one. Through manipulations, it is possible to construct new genes or even entire organisms.

The Big Change: Threats and Opportunities

Biotechnology affects multiple sectors.

In medicine, it is helping to diagnose, prevent and treat many diseases and is opening up interesting prospects in the study of hereditary and neurodegenerative illnesses. One important application is gene therapy, which can replace a gene mutated by a disease with a healthy copy, silence a mutated gene that is malfunctioning or introduce a new gene into a patient's body to help fight a disease. Biotechnology is also used to reconstruct parts of damaged tissues or organs and in the diagnosis of cancer, thanks to synthesized molecules that can selectively bind the diseased mass.

In the pharmaceutical industry, biotechnology makes it possible to design a new drug by predicting its absorption by the body. This is important because some drugs are efficient in *vitro* but not as much *in vivo*. In addition, biotechnology facilitates the large-scale production of antibiotics, vaccines, growth factors, hormones, anti-infective and anticancer drugs, blood products and products for both enzyme and gene therapy. In research, biotechnologies have reduced development times, with consequent economic savings, and have given excellent results in industrial transfer. Today, eight out of the ten best-selling drugs in the world come from biotech research.

A new frontier is the engineering of yeasts and plants for the synthesis of medicines. The twofold advantage is to make administration easier and to solve the problem—very common in many poor countries—of the lack of the cold chain, which is essential for preserving medicines. Freeze-dried yeasts and fruit resist longer than traditional vaccines.

In agriculture, biotechnology can be used for crop nutrition and protection, product diversification and quality improvement, including genetic manipulation. Gene therapy helps protect agrobiodiversity threatened by certain diseases and also improve certain characteristics required by the market, such as resistance to parasites, shelf life and product aesthetics. In animal husbandry, biotechnology can make reproduction, health control and animal nutrition more efficient and improve the health and productivity of animals by identifying traits to be passed on to the next generation, such as those that control the quality of the milk produced. Or, in the marine environment, the genetic manipulation of the biochemical characteristics of certain organisms allows for a more diversified use: for example, algae can become a combustible material or a source of active ingredients used in the cosmetic, pharmaceutical and food sectors.

Biotechnology can revolutionize the entire manufacturing sector, from the choice of raw materials to their bioprocessing, from the development of sustainable processes to the preservation of the final product. Biotechnology has many applications in the environmental field: it replaces chemical agents in some production processes of consumer goods, making them less polluting; it favours the biological treatment of waste water and gaseous emissions, the disposal of organic solid waste and sludge from water treatment plants and the development of biofuels with a lower environmental impact.

The potential risks are mainly related to the genetic alteration of plants, animals and even humans and the formulation of compounds that can be used in chemical weapons.

Other Innovations, Technologies and High-Potential Sectors

In addition to the twelve in-depth innovations illustrated in this chapter, several others can have a disruptive impact on the economy, society and labour.

The development of energy storage is very promising. Enhancing energy storage stimulates the production of renewable energy because it reduces waste and improves distribution. Increasing the capacity and reducing the price of batteries will be decisive for the spread of electric vehicles and will also make it possible to supply electricity to 1.2 billion people who do not have access to it today.

In science, advances in human genome engineering will make it possible to prevent and treat various diseases through DNA alterations. The cost of human genome sequencing has plummeted over the past decade from several million to a few thousand dollars, the time required has shrunk from a few years to a few hours. These trends, along with the development of microsensors, is paving the way for personalized medicine. There are already sensors in the form of finger rings or contact lenses—therefore easily wearable—that count heartbeats, detect body temperature and blood pressure, measure blood sugar levels and many other parameters. Their evolution will open up new possibilities for prediction and prevention in the near future. Nanosensors, today used mainly in medicine, could in the future form the basis of computers and robots working at the nanoscale.

Neurobionics, a cross between biology and electronics, is developing interfaces to connect computers with the central nervous system, which could advance the treatment of diseases such as sclerosis or dysfunctions such as paraplegia and quadriplegia. The space economy can be an important driver of development. Thanks to experiments conducted in space missions, many new technologies will be refined and find applications in the medical, scientific and industrial fields. The 5G infrastructure will greatly increase data transmission speed and capacity, accelerating the deployment of many technologies. This could lead to a new digital revolution and have very significant economic, social and geopolitical consequences.

* * *

Innovation is producing disruptive changes. New technologies almost always have two sides: on the one hand, they present threats, and on the other hand, they offer enormous opportunities. Having a good understanding of new technologies is a necessary condition to successfully manage the criticalities that will emerge and take advantage of the opportunities that will arise.

The challenge is to be able to use innovations to improve human life. This means satisfying the needs of present generations but not at the expense of future generations, expanding the economy without jeopardizing the health of the planet, increasing wealth but in such a way that as many as possible can benefit from it.

Bibliography

J. Allan et al., *Regulatory Landscape of Nanotechnology and Nanoplastics from a Global Perspective*, "Regulatory Toxology and Pharmacology", 122, June 2021.

W. B. Arthur, *The Nature of Technology: What It Is and How It Evolves*, Simon and Schuster, New York 2009.

K. Ashton, *Presentation to Procter & Gamble*, 1999.

J. Benyus, *Biomimicry: Innovation Inspired by Nature*, William Morrow & Company, New York 1997.

R. Bergman, F. Fassihi, *The Scientist and the A.I.-Assisted, Remote-Control Killing Machine*, "The New York Times", New York, 18 September 2021.

M. Cantamessa, F. Montagna, *Management of Innovation and Product Development: Integrating Business and Technological Perspectives*, Springer London Ltd, London 2015.

Digiconomist, "Bitcoin Mining Is More Polluting than Gold Mining", 16 January 2018.

R. Feynman, *Simulating Physics with Computers*, "International Journal of Theoretical Physics", 1982.

Pope Francis, *Address to the Participants in the Plenary Assembly of the Pontifical Academy for Life*, Rome, 28 February 2020.

R. Gen. Cone, Comment at the Army Aviation Symposium (as reported by "Defense News"), 15 January 2014.

M. Joerss et al., *How Customer Demands Are Reshaping Last-Mile Delivery*, McKinsey & Company, 19 October 2016.

J. McCarthy et al., *Automata Studies*, Princeton University Press, Princeton 1956.

McKinsey Global Institute, *The Internet of Things: Mapping the Value Beyond the Hype*, June 2015.

McKinsey Global Institute, *Notes from the AI Frontier: Applications and Value of Deep Learning*, September 2018.

S. Nakamoto, *Bitcoin: A Peer-to-Peer Electronic Cash System*, www.bitcoin.org, 2018.

D. C. North, L. Davis, *Institutional Change and American Economic Growth*, Cambridge University Press, 1971.

D. C. North, *Institutions and Economic Growth: An Historical Introduction*, "World Development", 1989.

D. C. North, *Institutions, Institutional Change and Economic Performance*, Cambridge University Press, 1990.

D. C. North, *Institutions*, "Journal of Economic Perspectives", 1991.

P. Z. Reizin, *Felicità per Umani*, Rizzoli, Milano 2019.

Robot Institute of America, 1979.

SAE International, www.sae.org

M. Scott, Cambridge Analytica Helped 'Cheat' Brexit Vote and US Election, Claims Whistleblower, "Politico", 27 March 2018.

S. Tibbits, *4D Printing: Multi-Material Shape Change*, "Architectural Design", pp. 116–121, 1 January 2014.

M. Tobias, *Comparing Facebook Data Use by Obama, Cambridge Analytica*, "Politifact", 22 March 2018.

A. M. Turing, *Computing Machinery and Intelligence*, "Mind", 59, pp. 433–460, 1950.

A. Vespignani, R. Rijitano, *L'algoritmo e l'oracolo. Come la scienza predice il futuro e ci aiuta a cambiarlo*, il Saggiatore, Milano 2019.

World Food Program, *Blockchain Against Hunger: Harnessing Technology in Support of Syrian Refugees*, 30 May 2017.

3

The Technological Revolution: Professions at Risk and New Jobs

The ongoing technological revolution will have an unprecedented impact on employment.

For Nouriel Roubini of New York University (2014), current technological innovations present three distortions. First, they are capital-intensive, so they favour those who invest over those who provide labour. Second, they are skill-intensive, so they benefit workers with strong technical skills. Third, they are labour-saving, so they tend to reduce the overall number of low-skilled workers. As a result, many occupations will inevitably disappear. Not only those heavy, dangerous and alienating, but also traditional roles; not only in manufacturing but also in services; not only those with simple and repetitive tasks but also those with complex and intellectual ones.

On the other hand, the same technologies are creating new economic activities and new jobs, so it is difficult to say what the final balance on employment will be. In many situations, machines replace humans in jobs that are heavy, dangerous alienating, or somehow impossible to perform.[1] Think of interventions in industrial accidents, natural disasters, terrorist attacks, or work in mines and nuclear power plants, submarine and space

---

[1] In announcing the Tesla Bot—a humanoid robot that is going to market in 2022—Elon Musk (2021) noted that it is intended to handle "tasks that are unsafe, repetitive or boring" because he thinks that "in the future physical work will be a choice".

© The Author(s), under exclusive license to Springer Nature Switzerland AG 2022
M. Magnani, *Making the Global Economy Work for Everyone*,
https://doi.org/10.1007/978-3-030-92084-5_3

missions.[2] Sometimes, as in Japan, automation is a necessary choice to compensate for the scarcity of workers due to the ageing population.

In other situations, technology does not replace humans but allows them to increase productivity and quality of work. Think of the factory worker aided by an exoskeleton, the surgeon assisted by robotic systems, the nurse who consults electronic medical records, the art historian who researches on digital databases. Traditional professions are evolving and humans are stimulated to acquire more skills. Workers' quality of life benefits too. Technology makes work more flexible and smart working helps reconcile professional and personal lives. In these cases, technology does not destroy work but transforms it, and it could even allow to spread opportunities more equally.[3] And this makes education and vocational training essential.

New technologies also encourage job creation. Some of the new jobs are directly linked to the development and implementation of emerging technologies. Other jobs are created either to respond to the new skills requirements in traditional sectors or to perform new economic activities that did not exist before.

In order to understand whether technology will have a positive or negative impact on employment, it is important to analyse the most exposed sectors and the most at-risk occupations and also to try to identify what might be the new jobs.

New Technologies: A Tsunami Affecting All Sectors and (Almost) All Professions

The current wave of technological innovation is affecting all sectors and many professions across the board.

The sectors at greatest risk of losing jobs are agriculture, manufacturing, transport, construction, commerce and large-scale distribution, banking and insurance, tourism and publishing.

---

[2] Several humanoid robots have been sent into space: from the American Robotnaut2 in 2011 to Japan's Kirobo in 2013, from Airbus and IBM's AI-equipped "flying brain" Cimon in 2018 to Russia's Fedor in 2019. In 2021, NASA's Perseverance rover and Chinese Zhurong rover landed on Mars.

[3] The COVID-19 outbreak has led to a surge of smart working. The trend may continue even post-pandemic, particularly in the Tech sector, for reasons beyond reducing office space and cutting costs. In an interview to The Verge (2020)—also reported by the New York Times (2020)—Facebook's co-founder, chairman and CEO Mark Zuckerberg pointed out some of the positive aspects of remote working: the advance of some of the future technology, the environmental benefit, the possibility for companies to access a larger and more diverse talent pool. Zuckerberg also pointed out that remote working may allow to spread opportunities more equally, because "rather than forcing people to come to cities for opportunity, you'll be able to spread that out more".

Professions with very different levels of skills and education are under threat. At risk are not only farmers, factory workers, assemblers, warehouse workers, cashiers, clerks, switchboard and call centre operators, doormen, mail carriers, porters, car and truck drivers, machinists, waiters, gardeners, inspectors, proof-readers and typists, claims and data entry clerks, but also notaries and tax experts, lawyers and paralegals, dieticians and dermatologists, financial and real estate brokers, insurance and financial consultants, credit and accounting analysts, journalists and press officers, technical writers and translators. In some areas, the speed of replacement of human labour will depend on the level of customer acceptance: as much as machines and robots are capable of performing certain functions, a strong and sustained demand for human contact may slow down their diffusion.

It is more difficult for machines to replace humans in roles where creativity, innovation, lateral thinking and flexibility are required. This applies to professions such as designers and architects, stylists and artists,[4] writers and authors, choreographers and composers, animation creators and sound engineers, researchers and mathematicians, software and algorithm developers, graphic designers and strategic consultants. Replacement is also difficult in professions that require empathy and in which personal contact is important. This is the case for specialist nurses, coaches, physiotherapists, athletic trainers, psychologists, teachers, sales consultants, purchasing office staff, supervisors and clergymen. The same is true for professions that, in addition to a certain degree of human interaction, require judgement and decision-making skills. This is the case of doctors and surgeons, dentists and veterinarians, police officers and firefighters, judges and top managers.

Although some of the tasks within these jobs can be automated, in many other duties humans are difficult to replace. Furthermore, in roles of entrepreneurship, leadership and people management, all of the characteristics mentioned are required.

In general, the risk of substitution of humans with machines decreases as certain characteristics increase.[5] First: the non-repetitiveness and complexity of the work. The simplest and most repetitive jobs—generally performed by workers with a low level of education—are more likely to be replaced by robots, algorithms or e-commerce sites. Second: the level of creativity

---

[4] Robot artists are still having a hard time. In October 2021, the Guardian reported that Ai-Da—a robot artist which creates paintings using algorithms, cameras and a robotic arm—was detained in jail by Egyptian security forces for 10 days because they feared it was part of an elaborate spy plot.

[5] David Autor and David Dorn (2013) have introduced the "routine task intensity index" to measure the substitutability of a job.

and innovation required to perform the work. Third: the presence of a relational component. A similar conclusion is reached by an Oxford University study (2013), according to which the three work tasks that are difficult to automate are perception and manipulation, creative intelligence and social intelligence.[6]

The new professions will require technical skills, but also creativity, flexibility, inventiveness, decision-making ability, judgement, organizational skills, empathy, inclination for interpersonal relations, aptitude for communication and multidisciplinary skills.

Agriculture and Animal Husbandry, Forestry and Mining

Agriculture is already highly automated in advanced economies, much less so in emerging economies where labour costs are lower. Robots, drones, self-driving vehicles and sensors are spreading very rapidly throughout the industry.

The *Spread and Vegetable Factory* in Japan is a farm run entirely by robots. In the United States, large farms are shifting from using individual machines to systems, or even systems of systems (i.e. sets of machines connected to each other and coordinated in their activities). Equipment manufacturer John Deere introduced a system that coordinates the operations of tractors, harvesting machines, and seeding vehicles, with humans acting only as supervisors.

A similar trend is visible in animal husbandry, with fully robotized and remotely managed stables. Robots and machines perform many tasks such as milking, shearing, feeding and cleaning. Digital technology helps monitor productivity and animal health. Human intervention is mostly a matter of supervision.

The level of automation is also very advanced in the forestry sector and in mining and oil extraction. The number of loggers and miners is steadily decreasing. Rio Tinto uses AI to monitor fleets of drills, excavators, transporters, self-driving trucks from a headquarter located thousands of miles away.

---

[6] Note that, in terms of their impact on employment, some new technologies—especially AI—do not necessarily align naturally with traditional classifications of occupations by social consideration and presumed status. Some jobs that are socially regarded as low status are difficult to automate, while others that are accorded high status are easy to perform and therefore replaceable.

The demand for agronomists, biotechnology experts, geneticist farmers and breeders, technicians with both mechanical and IT skills, logistics organizers, and sales and marketing personnel will grow and partially offset the many lost professions. A new, peculiar professional figure is the vertical farmer. Urban agriculture is growing and requires workers with scientific, engineering and commercial skills. In vertical farms, fruit and vegetables are grown inside buildings without using soil, therefore saving space, water and fertilizers. The outcome is the production of higher quality products at lower costs. And the environmental benefits as well, thanks to the elimination of pesticides and transport and the increase of urban greenery.

Manufacture

In manufacturing, robots are increasingly replacing not only labourers engaged in dangerous, wearisome and repetitive tasks, but also skilled workers. Of the roughly 5 million manufacturing jobs lost in the United States from 2000 to 2017, about half are due to automation. Emerging economies show a similar trend. Foxconn, the world's largest manufacturer of electronic components, is replacing tens of thousands of workers with robots. In China's Guangdong province, hundreds of factories are heavily investing in automation.

The process of automation is very advanced in factories and warehouses. However, a few things should be noted. First, instead of completely replacing human work, sometimes machines complement, support and improve it, as in the case of collaborative robots and exoskeletons. Furthermore, while inside factories the number of labourers is decreasing, that of workers controlling and supervising production is increasing. These are highly skilled technical personnel with a combination of mechanical, electronic and computer (mechatronics) skills. Finally, all professions involved in the development, design, production and maintenance of automation systems are on the rise.

The spread of advanced manufacturing technologies, such as additive manufacturing, could also put several jobs at risk. Manufacturers of industrial components risk losing 60% of the market within a decade because large companies will be able to print standard components in house. Less exposed is the employment of those who make complex parts requiring specialist skills. On the other hand, jobs associated with new technologies will arise, such as CAD technicians applied to 3D design, commercial and industrial designers.

The digitalization of the manufacturing sector is completely reshaping the set of professional skills required in many industries. Data analysts, application developers, systems engineers and cybersecurity specialists are some of the professional positions essential to the establishment and maintenance of the "Industry 4.0" infrastructure.

Finally, another consequence of automation in manufacturing—which benefits advanced economies—is the trend of reshoring.

When Automation Creates Jobs: Reshoring and Near-Shoring

The decision of offshoring economic activities is usually aimed at lowering labour costs. The expansion of automation makes this strategy less beneficial and sometimes irrelevant. Furthermore, in many emerging economies the quality of goods produced is not satisfactory and labour costs are continually rising. Sixty per cent of the jobs "returned" to the United States between 2010 and 2016 came from China, where average manufacturing wages more than tripled from 2005 to 2016.

In a global economy, these trends encourage the rise of reshoring, that is the return of certain manufacturing activities that had previously been relocated. The trend is clearly underway in the United States and Europe. Automated plants are opening close to the final outlet markets primarily in sectors such as electronics assembly, textiles, clothing and footwear. In recent years, many activities have been brought back to the United States by manufacturing groups such as General Electric, Emerson Electric, Johnson & Johnson, Lockheed Martin, General Motors, Ford, Caterpillar and Whirlpool. Adidas has opened automated shoe factories in Germany and the United States, and Boeing has repatriated some production to its factory in Saint Louis, Missouri. However, reshoring also involves important technology companies. Google is producing technology devices in Texas and Apple is returning to assemble computers in the United States. Microsoft, Oracle, Intel and Lenovo are also reshoring some of their activities.

Technological innovation has made reshoring possible but several other factors contribute explaining the trend. In addition to increasing labour costs in emerging countries, there is also the uncertainty about costs created by currency fluctuations, the greater efficiency of the supply chain when production is close to research and development centres and customers, the saving of customs duties, transport costs, packaging, insurance, storage and warehousing. In certain sectors, production was reshored to avoid the loss of intellectual property. In addition to these general factors, there are three more aspects that are specific to the United States: the *shale gas* boom that lowers domestic energy cost, the dynamism of many States and Counties that attract reshoring companies with incentives and infrastructures, and the shift of American consumers' preference towards products "made in the USA".

In terms of employment, the benefits of reshoring are not very significant from a quantitative stand point: the factories closed by the relocation were populated by workers, while those opened as part of the reshoring process are filled with robots. However, the overall economic impact is positive. First, because of the initial investment. Second, because automated production employs few workers but they are usually highly skilled. Finally, because the reopening of a production site generates an induced activity of local services that creates jobs.[7]

An indirect form of reshoring is near-shoring, that is the movement of manufacturing activities to countries adjacent to the final market. In the case of the United States, most of near-shoring is in Mexico for manufacturing and Canada for software and IT. Near-shoring allows to benefit from geographical and temporal proximity between production and the final market and, at the same time, to take advantage of lower labour costs in neighbour countries.

Reshoring as a Source of Quality Employment: The Italian Case

In Italy, the phenomenon of reshoring is less due to the growing degree of automation and more to product quality requirements—especially in manufacturing associated with *Made in Italy*—and to the necessity of having more control over complex productions.

Companies with sophisticated customers have realized that offshoring manufacturing lowers costs but can be detrimental to product quality and corporate brand. On the other hand, complex productions—such as industrial automation, plant systems and precision mechanics—require a mix of knowledge, technology and skilled labour that is difficult to replicate in emerging countries.

Several companies that had offshored production to China, Vietnam and Romania are reverting their decisions and returning to Italy. Reshoring is mainly in the textile and footwear industry (almost half of the total), typical

---

[7] In emerging economies, on the other hand, the trend of reshoring could undermine export-led growth models, causing dangerous local imbalances.

Made in Italy sectors, followed by electronics, electrical engineering, automotive, mechanics, furniture and furnishings. Ferragamo, Tod's and Prada have brought some productions back to Italy. The manufacture of bags and accessories by Furla, Piquadro and Nannini returned from Eastern Europe and Asia, Azimut Benetti yachts from Turkey, L'Oréal cosmetics from Poland. The choice of Maserati and Alfa Romeo to manufacture only in Italy confirms that for high-quality products the manufacturing location is more important than labour and transport costs. The trend is growing: the production of Fiamm car batteries goes back from the Czech Republic to Abruzzo, of Natuzzi sofas from Romania and China to Puglia, of Mediolanum Farmaceutici medicines from Paris to Lodi.

Complex and high-quality productions—those for which innovation, know-how, craft skills, tradition, control of the entire production cycle are important—are returning to Italy.

Transport (of People and Goods)

The development of AGVs, drones and unmanned cars threatens entire categories of traditional professions. In the passenger transport sector, taxi drivers, car chauffeurs, bus and metro conductors, train locomotive handlers and operators are at risk. So are truck drivers, construction machinery operators and delivery people in the goods transport sector.[8] AGVs and drones could shake up home deliveries, making the postman's job—already greatly undercut by electronic mail and online billing—disappear and threatening the jobs of many other similar roles.

The development of driverless cars will disrupt the labour market well beyond the disappearance of drivers. It will accentuate the trend, already underway, of shifting from vehicle ownership to renting "just for use", sometimes only for a few hours. The spread of car sharing will lead to a reduction in the number of vehicles, with repercussions on employment in manufacturing but also in services such as insurance and auto loans. This could also affect maintenance and repair jobs, which for car sharing vehicles would largely be carried out directly by manufacturers rather than by local workshops. This trend may be reinforced by the diffusion of electric cars that given their fewer number of components typically require a simplified maintenance compared to traditional vehicles.

---

[8] In the United States, the profession of truck driver is among the most widespread, with about 3.4 million employees, partly because it is immune to globalization and—at least until now—automation.

Fewer cars also mean less traffic, hence fewer traffic enforcement agents and urban police forces, whose jobs are already threatened by cameras and sensors. Unmanned driving should have the positive effect of reducing the number of accidents, but that also means less need for mechanics and car body repairers, and would make parking areas near airports, stations and city centres superfluous, with consequent loss of jobs.

As for new professions, the spread of drones and AGVs will create demand for new skills, for their design and development and for their efficient use. The professions of driverless car trainer and licenced drone operator will grow. There may also be higher demand for legal services to settle the rise in litigation related to accidents or privacy breaches caused by autonomous vehicles (both on the ground and in the air).

Trade and Sales

The introduction of new technologies is putting pressure on traditional trade, which has already been disrupted by the internet, with serious consequences for employment. The risks are particularly high in the large-scale retail trade where automatic cash registers and self-checkouts,[9] storage robots and mechanized home deliveries are spreading.

In general, all marketing, sales and after-sales functions of businesses will require strong digital skills and will displace many workers who, due to age or level of education, do not have them. Telemarketing and customer service will be revolutionized by big data and AI: automated chatbots and voice systems, currently answering only basic user queries, will soon provide satisfactory assistance and promote products and services over the phone and online. Many of the traditional jobs of market analysis, promotion and marketing will become redundant as increasingly sophisticated software makes predictions about people's consumption behaviour.

On the other hand, digitalization will create new professions. The results of data analysis performed by machines must be interpreted by professionals with expertise in the field. A key figure in e-commerce is the digital strategist, who designs the company's digital strategy coordinating it with the activities carried out in traditional manner. More technical is the search engine optimization (SEO) specialist, who attracts traffic to a site through search engines and then tries to turn visitors into customers. On the rise is the

---

[9] In the United States alone, it is estimated that automatic cash registers and self-checkouts could destroy 2.3 million jobs.

digital customer expert, a profile with sales, marketing and IT skills who helps companies in their digital transition.

New jobs will also emerge in the front office because interfacing with customers will remain crucial in selling products and services. Although machines will play an increasing role in customer service, their "personalities" will need to be programmed, updated and managed. Therefore, there will be a need for people to coach machines in conversation, empathy and even a sense of humour.

The spread of AR, VR and 3D printing could give new impetus to the retail of certain products leading to hiring salespeople with strong technical skills. Those involved in marketing, sales and logistics will also need to be familiar with blockchain applications.

Travel, Tourism, Hospitality, Catering

Over the past thirty years, the number of travel agencies in the United States has halved and large tour operators have had to significantly change their business model to survive. Both trends have had a negative impact on employment. Jobs in the traditional hospitality industry are also under pressure. This is caused by increasing competition on the supply side, mainly due to the success of the Airbnb model, and to the automation of many tourists' hospitality tasks. In 2015, the Henn-na chain opened a hotel in Nagasaki where robots welcome guests, the cloakroom is mechanized, access to rooms is managed by a facial recognition system, lighting and heating triggered by voice recognition software, security guaranteed by cameras, and room service and cleaning performed by humanoid robots.[10]

Robots equipped with hands, joints, sensors and AI are threatening traditional routine jobs in the restaurant industry, such as kitchen workers, waiters and bartenders. In Tokyo, there have been restaurants without waiters since 2013, in Berlin since 2017. San Francisco is the home of Cafe X, a chain of fully automated bars. In many fast-food restaurants across the world, orders are made only through a touchscreen without any human interaction.

Applications of AR and VR applications offer interactive tourist and cultural guides that replace human guides. Tourism back-office operations will be largely automated. Software capable of reading, sorting, filing and routing complaints is becoming increasingly popular. In some tasks, however, interpersonal and communication skills, expertise in crisis management and

---

[10] Three years after opening, the original 200 or so robots have been cut in half in response to customer complaints on slowness and inefficiency. Even robots can be fired!

fluent knowledge of foreign languages will continue to be essential. New professions in the field include web marketing experts, graphic designers, statisticians and behavioural analysts.

A professional figure on the rise is the revenue manager, an expert in real-time price customization. The task is to create mechanisms to modify the price of services in real time based on a number of variables—such as trends in demand and structure of customers personal preferences—with the goal of obtaining from each client the maximum amount they are willing to pay. The technique is used in many domains, such as the booking of hotel rooms, airplane or train seating, and theatre ticketing.

Banking, Insurance and Consulting

Technology has overturned the business model of traditional commercial banks. ATMs, home and mobile banking are leading to the closure of many branches with consequent staff reductions. The remaining employees are required to have at the same time technology skills, ability to interact with customers (both in person and remotely) and ability to provide advice and sell products and services (not only banking ones). The traditional branch clerk is being replaced by a sort of universal service advisor.

The development of AI and the enhancement of voice recognition capabilities will nearly empty the call centres. Only qualified operators, those capable to propose targeted promotions or solve complex problems, will survive. On the other hand, the need to develop new technological interfaces with clients requires new professional roles with creative, linguistic and anthropological skills, such as the conversational interface designer.

Financial and insurance advice is particularly exposed to the spread of AI. Robo-advisors are increasingly replacing consultants. For years now, *Warren*—a software named after legendary investor Warren Buffett—has been answering financial questions. Brokerage firm Charles Schwab has long had an automated advisory division. In 2015, BlackRock, the world's largest fund manager, acquired FutureAdvisor, a platform that manages portfolios with algorithms. Goldman Sachs, JPMorgan and Merrill Lynch use AI to identify investment opportunities by analysing millions of reports and news stories.

In the insurance sector, German start-up Clark introduced a few years ago the first digital broker that sells products from over 160 companies and helps customers identify the best solution. Japan's Fukoku Mutual Life replaced several consultants with AI software and announced productivity gains of 30% in two years.

Algorithmic trading is on the rise. Many investment banks have replaced financial analysts and traders with software that makes decisions by learning from experience. In 2021, between 70 and 80% of overall trading volume in the U.S. stock market and many other developed financial markets was generated through algorithmic trading. In emerging economies, such as India, algorithmic trading is estimated to be around 40%.

Technological innovation will also bring new jobs. Financial institutions will need more developers that combine the knowledge of software programming languages with that of industry regulations and clients' needs. In addition, changing financial regulations and changing products will require frequent updates and optimization of algorithms. Demand for skills in risk management, service design and financial literacy will also grow.

The growth of fin-tech—the use of technology to improve financial activities—will lead to the replacement of low-skilled professionals with highly skilled ones, boosting the number of jobs as data scientist, data analyst, controller, regulatory specialist and cybersecurity expert. Finally, the partnership gateway enabler will help manage relationships between financial institutions and their many digital partners.

Medicine, Health and Personal Care

Rather than destroying jobs, technology innovations in medicine will support doctors and improve their performance. New technology will, however, change the skills needed to carry out the profession. Sometimes in a profound way. In addition, the combination of AI and big data could jeopardize the work of several doctors due to the growing ability of machines to read test results, make diagnoses and predict diseases. British start-up Babylo has developed a chatbot that interacts with patients and suggests diagnoses. China's *Xiaoyi* AI system has passed the medical licensing exam: it collects and analyses test reports, considers patients' medical history and formulates diagnoses. For now, the robot joins the doctors for support and training; in the future, it could replace them.

The same kind of applications work in specialized medicine. In May 2018, "Annals of Oncology", the official journal of the European Society for Medical Oncology, has published the results of an experiment in which an AI system was more adept at diagnosing skin cancer than fifty-eight dermatologists (95% success rate vs. 86.6%). In the same days, "Radiology

Business" (2018) has disclosed an experiment in which *ByoMind* proved to be more accurate than fifteen Chinese doctors in diagnosing brain tumours: the AI system produced correct diagnoses in 87% of cases in only fifteen minutes, doctors in 66% of cases twice as long. In May 2019, "Nature Medicine" has documented that an AI system developed by Google and Northwestern University outperformed a team of experienced radiologists in both identifying and predicting lung cancers. Around the same time, "RadiologyToday" (2019) has published data from a model developed by MIT and Massachusetts General Hospital that accurately predicts the likelihood of developing breast cancer over five years. In 2019, Untromics—an Oxford University start-up, has launched *Echocardiography*, which predicts coronary artery disease with more than 90% accuracy.

In dietetics, AI and big data applications can recognize food, detect calories and suggest diets real time through the simple framing of a smartphone. A similar function is offered by Samsung's voice assistant, *Bixby*.

Robots are also successfully entering the operating room to support surgeons. Among the most common are those that correct sight defects or perform knee reconstruction operations. Some robot-surgeons programmed to stitch up soft tissue show greater precision than humans. Robot-anaesthesiologists, such as Johnson & Johnson's *Sedasys*, are also becoming popular.

In personal care services, the importance of relationships and the need for empathy could hold back the diffusion of machines. However, AI-equipped robotics is a threat to employment also in this field as social robots may replace nurses and caretakers for the elderly. In some hospitals in the United States, robots are in charge of distributing meals, linen and medicines. *Tug* is a "self-propelled bedside table" whose drawers containing medicines open only in the appropriate room and only with the fingerprints of the doctor or patient. The coronavirus crisis has accelerated the spread of robotic technologies and AI in health care, as they are seen as effective resources in combating the pandemic. Inside the hospitals, robots have been deployed for disinfection, medicine and food delivery, vital signs monitoring, thus helping to significantly reduce the infection risk of all personnel. Technology is also a spur to the growth of telemedicine and home care, two domains that are booming.

In general, in the medical field there will be an growing need for new professional figures with hybrid skills: medical and pharmaceutical but also computer science and data analysis. 3D printing—which is spreading for prosthesis, tissues, dental technology—will require engineers, computer scientists and designers, all with good medical knowledge. The development of biotechnology in the medical and pharmaceutical fields will be an opportunity for digitization experts, big data analysts and bioengineers. Advances in nanotechnology will create demand for experts in nanomedicine.

Office Work, Freelancing and Journalism

Technology is replacing and transforming many office and freelance jobs. The spread of virtual assistants puts many secretarial jobs at risk. Document sorting and archiving are increasingly being carried out by software—such as the *Kimonus* platform—interpreting e-mail texts and documents, matching them with a project and automatically archiving them.

More complex professions are also at risk. In the legal and paralegal fields, various AI applications are becoming popular. *Ross* is used to research law and jurisprudence, a task traditionally entrusted to practitioners, and can make logical connections and propose solutions that support lawyers in managing their cases. *Kira* analyses contracts in different languages, extracts parts of them, identifies clauses and suggests links.

In tax and accounting, there is software designed to fill out tax returns, make payroll and prepare financial statements. As applications become more and more sophisticated, the tasks of tax advisors and accountants will significantly change. The role of the notary, public official guarantor of transactions and agreements, could be seriously challenged by the rise of the blockchain.

Technology has radically changed the job of journalists. In some cases, it can replace them: *Wordsmith* is a software that generates reviews and articles on stock market trends, *StatsMonkey* specializes in sports reports, and *Quill* reads all the news and proposes to journalists the most interesting stories. Online news sites such as "AP", "Fox" and "Yahoo!" have long made extensive use of automated systems. Drones often replace humans for filming sporting events and movies, for photo shoots and topographical flights. Translators and interpreters are also at risk. Software that translates from one language to another—both written and audio texts—is improving very quickly.

In the corporate world, even roles that require critical sense and decision-making skills can be at risk. Project managers, especially in data-intensive projects, face growing competition from predictive AI models. Human resources departments use algorithms for important selection, evaluation and promotion decisions.

There will also be new professions. Recruitment firms and HR departments will need technical recruiters, who can assess the technological skills of candidates. There will be a growing demand for legal experts who can handle accidents caused by machines, intellectual property issues (because newer technologies make it easier to copy products), privacy protection cases, misuse of personal data and hacking. Reg-tech—the intersection of regulation and technology—will also be a source of employment.

Web Services

The enormous development of the internet and social networks has strongly contributed to the rise of communication agencies that manage the web presence of individuals and companies. Firms seek to improve corporate image and reputation, enhance products positioning and increase sales. This creates many new professions. The digital PR establishes a relationship with the main players of the web—influencers, community managers, bloggers, journalists—in order to give natural visibility to products or promote corporate events. The e-reputation manager monitors online conversations and performs keyword analysis in order to catch trends, identify network influencers and monitor critical online discussions of the product or brand. Some consultants are in charge of removing negative news about companies, products and people from the web. The web content editor produces content and generates active online discussions to generate traffic. The personal brander helps build a brand through social media and other mass media by defining the positioning of a new product.

School and Training

Technology penetration in most schools is slow. This is because of the huge investments required and also for organizational and cultural reasons. At the university level, telecommunications technology has led to the growth of telematic universities and MOOCs, through which a course is followed by tens of thousands of students all over the world. Rather than taking work away from teachers, these phenomena have broadened the student base and helped teaching. In the future, virtual teachers will be introduced in schools and universities to help, and in some cases replace, the real ones. However, the role of the teacher is a difficult one to replace as it requires strong relational and interpersonal skills.

Education and training seem to be domains that will benefit the most in terms of job creation from the introduction of new technologies. The need to train appropriate professional figures to manage the new systems, at both technical and managerial levels, will be a source of employment. There will also be an growing demand for people with classical training who can deal with the many ethical issues raised by technology. Finally, it is possible that the continuous progress of science in areas such as AI, self-driving cars, cloning and nanotechnologies will make it necessary to create a new generation of philosophers specializing in ethics.

Start-Ups and New Entrepreneurial Activities

Entrepreneurial activity is an important source of new employment. Technological innovation contributes to it in two ways. First, the need to develop and improve on the latest technologies stimulates the emergence of start-ups. Second, technology is often a growth accelerator for small businesses in traditional industries. Let's see some examples.

While shedding jobs among traditional IT and software service providers, cloud computing allows start-ups and businesses with limited financial resources to grow rapidly. 3D printing allows a small firm to offer customized products without incurring heavy investments in machinery and distribution network. Similarly, with IoT firms of any size can easily and accurately track consumer needs without the expense of market research and strategic consultants.

Similarly, VR applications put even small companies in a position to do very effective marketing without excessive investment. In a virtual showroom, it is possible to show customers all the models of clothes or types of furniture that can be made, without keeping them in stock. This way even a craftsman can offer his products worldwide.

Digital platforms have contributed to the closure of many small traditional businesses, but they can also represent growth opportunities for local micro-activities. This is how social commerce—which gives consumers the chance to discover artisanal products through social platforms such as Instagram or Facebook—has started and flourished.

New Jobs and Skills

The rise of machines will create new jobs. Humans will be employed in designing, developing and building machines but also in tasks that allow to use them effectively. In particular, there will be a need for professionals who know how to manage and integrate the latest technologies into business strategy; for trainers who educate machines by teaching algorithms to mimic human behaviour and make fewer mistakes; more in general, for roles capable of bridging the gap in knowledge and communication between technology experts and traditional managers. There will also be demand for ethical compliance officers who act as mediators; for sentinels who prevent machines from going out of control; for security experts who know how to manage increasingly sophisticated cyber threats.

The strong development of AI and big data requires workers with a strong multidisciplinary vocation, who combine technical skills and business knowledge, logic and creativity, empathy and ethics. Some new professional figures are becoming strategic across many sectors. The data scientist— defined by "Harvard Business Review" (2012) as "the sexiest job of the twenty-first century"—is the person who develops and tests predictive models that can help define company objectives and create new products. The role requires statistical knowledge and programming skills. The data engineer creates automated processes to generate, collect and catalogue large amounts of data in an efficient and usable manner. This requires mastery of data mining techniques and management of cloud computing platforms. The data analyst is responsible for interpreting data—by looking for trends and patterns—and extrapolating decision-making information to support senior management. The chief data officer is responsible for defining strategies for data exploitation.

The growth of IoT makes certain new professions strategic for many traditional companies. It is the case of the chief IoT officer, who directs the strategic choices proposing the introduction of new technologies, the business IoT designer, a creative thought leader able to design an IoT project, the full stack developer, an "all-round" developer able to adopt different languages and exploit the potential of various platforms. The boom of the cloud and the growth of mediated reality are creating the need, within traditional companies, for new professions with specific technical skills such as the cloud architect, responsible for managing and optimizing the use of the cloud. Similar professions could sprout from the development of the blockchain and quantum computing.

* * *

The impact of innovation on employment will be huge. In many cases, humans will be replaced by machines and entire professions will be eliminated. Replacing humans with machines will be more difficult for those jobs with a strong emotional, creative and relational component and requiring decision-making and judgement ability.[11] In a number of cases, technology will not substitute human labour but will support it by increasing its efficiency. Even at these junctures, however, job transformation will profoundly change the skills required of workers, making the transition complex. Moreover, new jobs will be created, but their quantity, quality and geographical location are very uncertain.

Bibliography

U. Amaldi, Conversation with the Author on 20 September 2021.

D. Ardila et al., *End-to-End Lung Cancer Screening with Three-Dimensional Deep Learning on Low-Dose Chest Computed Tomography*, "Nature Medicine", 20 May 2019.

D. Autor, D. Dorn, *The Growth of Low Skill Service Jobs and the Polarization of the U.S. Labor Market*, "American Economic Review", 103, no. 5, 2013.

C. Conger, *Facebook Starts Planning for Permanent Remote Workers*, The New York Times, 21 May 2020.

R. Cormack, *Elon Musk's New AI 'Tesla Bots' Can Be Overpowered by the Average Human*, RRI-RobbReport, 20 August 2021.

N. Correll, *How Investing in Robotics Actually Helps Human Jobs*, "Time", 2 April 2017.

T.H. Davenport, D.J. Patil, *Data Scientist: The Sexiest Job of the 21st Century*, "Harvard Business Review", October 2012.

C.B. Frey, M. Osborne, *The Future of Employment: How Susceptible are Jobs to Computerization?*, Oxford Martin University, Oxford 2013.

H.A. Haenssle et al., *Man Against Machine: Diagnostic Performance of a Deep Learning Convolutional Neural Network for Dermoscopic Melanoma Recognition in Comparison to 58 Dermatologists*, "Annals Oncology" 29: 1 August 2018.

N. Khomami, *Egypt Detains Artist Robot Ai-Da Before Historic Pyramid Show*, "The Guardian", 20 October 2021.

McKinsey Global Institute, *Skill Shift: Automation and the Future of the Workforce*, May 2018.

M. Magnani, *Reshoring manifattura, una questione di qualità*, "IlSole24Ore", 20 October 2015.

M. Magnani, *Reshoring all'italiana per evitare il declino*, "IlSole24Ore", 17 December 2015.

C. Newton, *Mark Zuckerberg on Taking His Massive Workforce Remote*, "The Verge", 21 May 2020.

---

[11] Italian physicist Ugo Amaldi (2021) notes that a fundamental and permanent difference between human beings and robots is the fact that the latter have never been loved by anyone as children.

B.W. Orenstein, *Mammographer's Helper - AI Shows Much Promise in Cancer Detection, Treatment,* "Radiology Today", 21, no. 2, 2019.

M. Purdy, P. Daugherty, *Why Artificial Intelligence Is the Future of Growth,* Accenture, December 2016.

N. Roubini, *Where Will All the Workers Go?,* "Project Syndicate", 31 December 2014.

M. Walter, *AI System Beats Team of 15 Doctors in Competition,* "Radiology Business", 2 July 2018.

4

Constraints to Economic Growth: Sustainability, Happiness and Other Issues

Innovation has always generated economic growth. In two ways: first, by producing continuous increase in productivity that has led to expanded supply, lower prices for products and services, and higher average wages; second, by favouring a progressive enlargement of the economy, through the development of new products and services, the start of new activities, and the opening of new markets.

Both drivers have always had a positive impact on employment. Lower product prices and higher wages stimulated consumption. The expansion of the economy led to investment. The resulting greater aggregate demand boosted employment. (And in turn, more jobs further reinforced the positive impact on demand and growth.) Thus, innovation has always been able to trigger a virtuous circle involving growth, employment and welfare.

Will this virtuous circle work in the same way in the future? Is the current growth model sustainable in the long term? Will the wave of innovation that characterizes our time be able to generate an increase in the economy and employment?

There is no consensus on the answers to these questions. This chapter focuses on the relationship between innovation and economic growth and the constraints on its sustainability. Chapter 5 analyses the impact of innovation on the labour market.

© The Author(s), under exclusive license to Springer Nature Switzerland AG 2022
M. Magnani, *Making the Global Economy Work for Everyone*, https://doi.org/10.1007/978-3-030-92084-5_4

Economic Growth and Sustainability

As recalled, Malthusian fears about the sustainability of economic growth have been disproved by history. This is largely due to innovation that has always made it possible to overcome constraints of population growth and scarcity of natural resources. John Maynard Keynes also raised the problem of growth sustainability. In *Economic Possibilities for Our Grandchildren* (1930), he predicted that "the standard of life in progressive countries in a hundred years will be between four and eight times as high as it is today". However, he was optimistic that "the economic problem [of producing sufficient goods] may be solved, or be at least within sight of solution, within a hundred years".

The last two very harsh recessions[1] have brought back to the forefront the debate on the limits of growth, the concern on sustainability and the different views on how well-being should be measured. The consequence has been a growing criticism of the traditional growth model. Some are calling for its "scrapping". For others, an "adjustment" is sufficient to direct it towards growth capable of recreating the conditions for its future. Sustainability means "holding on" (from Latin *sustinere*), that is maintaining a certain condition over time, preventing it from losing its characteristics.

Sustainability goes far beyond the strictly environmental aspect with which it is often associated. In fact, the term has several dimensions and they are often interconnected. Already in the first official use of the word "sustainability" at the international level—the U.N. Conference on the Human Environment that took place in Stockholm in 1972—reference was made to the much broader concept of "human environment". Economic growth is sustainable if it is attentive to pollution and ecological balance, but also to demographic stability, which is threatened by a growing and ageing population and by increasing intergenerational tensions. Moreover, economic growth should be compatible with the availability of natural resources— especially food and energy—and be able to preserve in the long term a socio-institutional equilibrium. Key elements of this balance are the provision of adequate levels of education and training, the existence of job opportunities, and a fair and inclusive redistribution of the produced wealth. Last but not least, as the recent pandemic has clearly shown, there can be no economic growth without health sustainability.

---

[1] The recession triggered by the subprime mortgage crisis in 2007–2008 and the economic downturn caused by the spread of the COVID-19 pandemic in 2020.

Sustainable Growth and the Environment

An important part of sustainability is associated with the ecological constraints of carrying out economic activities. This includes, *inter alia*, phenomena like climate change and global warming, combating air, water, sea and soil pollution, preserving animal and plant biodiversity, hampering food and energy waste, enhancing waste management and recycling, and land protection activities such as hydrogeological care, earthquake prevention and fire management.

In *Reflections on the Economics of Climate Change* (1993), Nobel Prize-winning economist William Nordhaus raises the alarm noting that "mankind is playing dice with the natural environment [...] injecting into the atmosphere toxins like greenhouse gases or ozone-depleting chemicals, engineering massive land-use changes such as deforestation, depleting multitudes of species in their natural habitats even while creating transgenic ones in the laboratory, and accumulating sufficient nuclear weapons to destroy human civilizations".[2]

The focus on sustainability constraints has an impact on the economy but also on people's lifestyles, it affects growth models but also social organizations. Phenomena such as car sharing and smart working, whose success depends in part on the desire to reduce pollution, have economic relevance but are also disrupting the concept of mobility and way of working.

Pollution is one of the most important variables of environmental sustainability as it has negative consequences across the board. It contributes to climate change and global warming,[3] it disrupts ecosystems and threatens biodiversity, and it worsens the quality of food resources and affects people's health. According to "New Scientist" (2010), one species—either plant or animal—becomes extinct in the world every twenty minutes. There is also the risk of a vicious circle between climate change and pollution. Indeed, to cope with greater changes in temperature, people tend to consume more

---

[2] Nordhaus' studies focus on the influence of the economy on climate change and the consequences of climate change on social dynamics such as living standards and the well-being of future generations.

[3] Much of the scientific community agrees that human activities are the dominant cause of current global warming. However, a minority of climatologists—including atmospheric physicist Franco Prodi (2019)—believes that at the moment no scientific research establishes a certain relationship in this sense. The main argument is that throughout history Earth has undergone climatic changes even before humans developed industrial activities. This is the case in the *Mediaeval warm period* between 800 and 1200 and the *Little Ice Age* between 1300 and 1850. Raphael Neukom of the University of Bern disputes this thesis and—in a study published by "Nature" (2019)—shows that previous climate changes were local (not global) phenomena while the current warming affects 98% of Earth's surface.

energy—for heating and air conditioning—and this amplifies the greenhouse effect, pollution and global warming.[4]

Pollution negatively affects the health of people through air, water and food. This diminishes the quality of life and results in higher health care costs. The World Health Organization (WHO) (2018) estimates that exposure to air pollution causes 7 million deaths a year worldwide and costs 5.1 trillion dollars in lost welfare. In the fifteen largest greenhouse gas emitting countries, the negative impact on health costs more than 4% of GDP.

Pollution also negatively affects the quantity and quality of available food resources, starting with water which is increasingly scarce and polluted. Agriculture and animal husbandry are particularly sensitive to climate change and pollution. A real emergency is the pollution of the seas, which kills fish and—indirectly—poisons people who eat them. Apart from lost fishing gear abandoned at sea, 80% of the waste in the oceans consists of plastic, especially single-use items such as bottles, glasses and cutlery. World production of virgin plastic has increased from 15 million tons per year in 1964 to almost 400 million today. According to the World Wide Fund for Nature (WWF) (2019), plastic waste is now 300 million tons per year and about one-third of this is dispersed in nature, mainly in the sea.[5]

There are currently five large plastic "islands" in the oceans. The largest—the Great Pacific Garbage Patch, located in the east side of the Pacific Ocean—covers more than eight million square kilometres and consists of around 79,000 tonnes of debris.[6] Even more dangerous than visible plastic is the invisible microplastic that enters the food chain of both fish and humans. An estimated 250 billion microplastic particles floating in the Mediterranean Sea are ingested by 134 animal species. The problem is worsening rapidly. A 2016 study by the Ellen MacArthur Foundation (2016) predicts that by 2025 there will be one tonne of plastic for every three tonnes of fish in the seas, and by 2050, there will be more plastic than fish.

Technological innovation can help increase sustainability. In turn, greater attention to the environment can be an important driver of innovation. Many

---

[4] With annual sales of about 135 million units, the current 1.6 billion air conditioners worldwide could grow to 5–6 billion by 2050 resulting in an energy consumption second only to that of industrial use.

[5] More than 90% of the plastic dumped in the oceans comes from ten rivers, eight of which are in Asia (including the Blue River—or Yangtze—and Yellow River in China and the Indus River in India).

[6] The other four islands are in the west side of the Pacific Ocean (0.7 million square kilometres), in the Indian Ocean (2.2 million square kilometres) and in the north and south Atlantic Ocean (3.6 and 1.3 million square kilometres). Italian artist Maria Cristina Finucci (2013), whose work has denounced the pollution of the oceans for many years, has provocatively proclaimed herself president of the *Garbage Patch State*, an ideal "waste nation" made up of plastic islands!

are the examples. *LifeStraw*, the three-dollar portable straw-filter designed by Swiss company Vestergaard Frandsen, makes non-potable water drinkable: this helps to combat water scarcity, to avoid the spread of disease in poor countries and to reduce the use of plastic bottles in rich ones. Robot scavengers contribute to clean up the seas, like those involved in the *Blue Resolution* project launched by the Sant'Anna School of Advanced Studies in Pisa to eliminate invisible microplastics. ENI's "digital diviner", thanks to AI and fast calculation capabilities, diminishes the number of drilling errors and hydrocarbon leaks, thus cutting exploration and extraction downtime by 30%. This significantly reduces both costs and environmental impact. Finally, the progress in battery technology encourages the spread of non-polluting electric vehicles.

Innovation helps but it is not enough. A widespread culture of respect for the environment and a strong political will are also necessary. Unfortunately, it is not uncommon for politicians to show a worrying combination of incompetence and poor foresight regarding these issues. In addition, the downturns of the economy sometimes push those who govern to put environmental sustainability in second place to growth. One example is the green light given by Trump in January 2017—primarily for economic and employment reasons—to the completion of Keystone XL, the long pipeline to connect Canada to the refineries in Texas and Louisiana that had been blocked by Obama for environmental reasons.[7]

Global Warming Changes the Economy, Finance and Geopolitics

Although the front of those who deny the existence of climate change—or downplay its consequences—remains strong, in recent years there has been a marked increase in awareness and a growing sense of urgency on environmental issues, at least in advanced economies. Public opinion, governments, companies and financial institutions are understanding that the phenomenon could upset not only the environment, but also have serious economic, financial and geopolitical consequences.

Climate change is a growing concern also for central banks. In a speech delivered in September 2015 at a dinner at Lloyd's in London, the then governor of the Bank of England spoke in detail about the risks of global warming. One could argue that his speech "froze" the many insurers and

---

[7] In June 2021, the Keystone XL pipeline's developer has halted all construction on the project months after its permit was revoked by the incoming Biden administration.

bankers in the room. Since then, Mark Carney has returned to this topic several times during public speeches. The data are alarming. Since 1980, climatic events causing heavy damage have tripled and insurance losses, net of inflation, have increased fivefold, reaching 50 billion dollars a year.

The consequences go well beyond the insurance sector and are a threat to global financial stability. There are three main risks. The "physical" risk, relating to insurance reimbursements for damage caused by floods and storms, in particular to agriculture and commerce. The "liability" risk, linked to possible future claims for compensation filed by the damaged parties against the presumed responsible parties, first and foremost the mining and oil sector. Finally, the "transition" risk, that is the costs of adjusting the economy towards a more sustainable model.

In the absence of international agreements and shared choices of sustainable growth, the risk is an increase in instability of the macroeconomic framework.[8] A study by the University of Cambridge (2019) estimates that in the face of an increase in global temperatures of 4 °C, the per capita GDP of the United States could fall by over 10% by 2100. If the Paris 2015 constraints were respected, the reduction would stop at 2%.[9] Clearly, growth rate volatility and uncertainty make economic policy by governments and central banks more complex and less effective. However, if the necessary adjustment were planned with a certain degree of international cooperation, the transition could be more gradual and predictable, thus creating opportunities for growth and employment through the development of new technologies and renewable energy sources. In any event, even in this scenario, the profound changes in production structures would generate some degree of instability.

Other variables that should be taken into account are the likely greater volatility of agricultural prices due to more frequent and sudden droughts, floods and frosts, and the possible higher fossil fuel prices due to increasing taxes and disincentives. Rising agricultural prices have a major impact on the cost of living in developing countries, where a large share of income is devoted to the purchase of food. Energy prices can have a significant impact—as they have in the past—on overall price trends and growth rates. Greater volatility

---

[8] This has clearly emerged also during the COP26 meeting that took place in Glasgow, Scotland in November 2021.

[9] The central objective of the Paris Agreement (2015) is its long-term temperature goal to hold global average temperature increase to "*well below 2 °C above preindustrial levels and pursuing efforts to limit the temperature increase to 1.5 °C above pre-industrial levels*". In November 2021, in the COP26 in Glasgow nearly 200 countries agreed to keep the target of 1.5 °C alive and finalized the outstanding elements of the Paris Agreement. The U.N. (2021) predicts a global temperature increase of about 3 °C by 2100.

of food and energy prices increases the difficulty for central banks to adopt an appropriate monetary policy and predict its impact on the economy.

Important economic and geopolitical consequences of global warming also derive from the progressive melting of Arctic ice, which facilitates the discovery and exploitation of natural resources and the opening of new navigation routes, usable for commercial and military purposes.[10] For this reason, all countries bordering the Arctic Sea—and sometimes even those not bordering it—are investing in explorations, observation stations and the opening of new routes.[11]

Other possible geopolitical consequences of global warming are the spread of diseases, such as malaria and dengue fever, the rising of the seas, which would submerge inhabited centres and cultivable lands and affect fresh water supplies,[12] the drastic worsening of agricultural harvests in the sub-Saharan zone, which would lead to very serious famines in Africa, and the uninhabitability of some areas of the world, which would cause mass migrations.[13]

Climate change also has some positive effects. These include a reduced consumption for heating, the ability to cultivate previously non-agricultural areas, faster growth of some crops and reduced cold-related mortality. However, there is broad consensus that with temperature increases above 2 °C compared to pre-industrial times, negative effects outweigh positive ones.

Excessive climate change represents a serious limit to the sustainability of the current growth model. It may affect the activities of companies and financial institutions, but also the economic, social and political balance of cities,

---

[10] It should be noted that in the last forty years the Arctic has lost about 3 million square kilometres of ice while the Antarctic ice area—perhaps due to the different impact of winds and currents—is stable and sometimes increasing. This contrast offers arguments to those who deny the existence of a climate crisis.

[11] The case of China is emblematic: although it is very distant from the Artic, Beijing has described itself as a "quasi-arctic power" and, in addition to the terrestrial Silk Road, is investing in a polar Silk Road. On this route, navigation from Shanghai to Rotterdam takes thirty-three days compared to forty-eight to fifty days required when going through the Suez Canal. The passage between the Atlantic and the Pacific—skirting Greenland, Canada and Alaska—takes a week less than the Panama Canal route.

[12] A study published by "Nature" (2019) notes that by 2050 areas currently populated by about 300 million people could be at risk of flooding. The Indonesian government has announced plans to move the capital Jakarta, which is subject to constant flooding, by about 100 kms.

[13] Desertification, floods and droughts are already causing migrations. For example, the 90% decrease in surface area of Lake Chad over the last fifty years has damaged fisheries and agriculture, causing a food emergency for 7.5 million people and the displacement of at least 2.5 million to neighbouring countries. Various sources estimate that 30% of the inhabitants of the Sahel area of Burkina Faso have had to migrate over the last 20 years. According to the British scholar Norman Myers (2005), environmental migrants could reach 200 million by 2050.

territories and countries, with significant geopolitical implications. It is essential that the level of international cooperation on such a "hot", transversal and global issue increases. Internationally shared choices would make it possible to better manage the timing of adjustment, minimize the degree of uncertainty and volatility, and open up new avenues for growth.

Sustainable Growth and Food Resources

A key element of sustainability is the availability of natural resources, such as agricultural and livestock products, minerals and energy sources. This matter is closely linked to demography. It is basically Malthus' fear extended to the entire world and to all natural resources.

With regard to food, there are both grounds for concern and optimism. The latter outweigh the former.

Among the critical issues are the scarcity of water and the decreasing fish population of the seas. Water is increasingly a scarce resource. According to the U.N. (2019), in one century, the global demand for water has increased sixfold and continues to grow by 1% a year. Today, we consume about 4600 cubic kilometres of water a year: about 70% in agriculture, 20% in industry and the rest in households. According to a study by the University of Twente (2020), the shortage of water resources is not only one of the most dangerous challenges the world is facing but it is probably far worse than expected. The main causes of water scarcity are global warming, that increases areas of drought, population growth, that causes water consumption to average twice as much as rain that replenishing aquifers, and a sharp increase in the consumption of foods whose production has a high water footprint, such as meat.[14] The consequences range from quotas and price increases, as in California in recent years, to full-blown "water wars", as in South Sudan in early 2017.[15]

---

[14] According to the Food and Agriculture Organization (FAO) (2018), the production of one kilo of beef requires 15,000 L of water, 6000 L are necessary for pork and 4000 L for chicken, compared to only 50 L for the equivalent quantity of protein-rich legumes. Moreover, 98% of the water used for zootechnics goes to fodder cultivation and only 2% to watering, cleaning, waste disposal and slaughtering.

[15] The South Sudanese civil war (December 2013–February 2020) left some 5 million people with no access to safe water, basic sanitation and hygiene. This led to a fight for water within the conflict. Conflicts for water take place in different regions of the world. Sometimes water is not the main factor affecting the conflict, but it is one of the outstanding issues. The 2019 U.N. World Water Development Report lists 94 "water wars" in the period 2000–2009, growing to 263 in the period 2010–2018. Some examples are the civil war in Syria, the dispute between Bolivia and Chile over the waters of the Silala, the Tigris and Euphrates conflict involving Turkey, Syria and Iraq, the

As for the fish population of the seas, it is at an all-time low. According to FAO (2018), today more than 90% of the world's fish stocks are fully exploited and the risk of collapse is very high. Among the main causes of this situation are the exponential increase in consumption due to the growth of the world population, the spread of industrial fishing and the use of harmful techniques.[16]

Once again, climate change is making things worse. According to a study of the University of California Irvine published in "Science" (2018), at the current rate of increase in temperature, fish stocks will decrease by an average of 20% over the next 300 years, with peaks of 60% in the western Pacific. The quality of fish—but also of meat and other foods—is increasingly compromised by pollution. Moreover, in the long term, variations in rainfall and average temperatures influence the productivity and geographical distribution of crops. And the increase in temperature and CO_2 encourages the development and spread of new pests and pathogens, responsible for about 30% of the loss of agricultural production.

In spite of all this, there are some reasons to be optimistic. First of all, greater attention to pollution and a more conscious exploitation of resources can contribute to limiting many of the current problems. The growing sensitivity to these issues on the part of young people gives hope for the future in a greater commitment on the part of business and politics, at least for reasons of profitability and consensus respectively.

Secondly, technology can help. In the case of water, improvements in desalination techniques are continuous. Today, less than 1% of the world's population depends on desalinated seawater, thanks to more than 20,000 plants in operation mainly located in the Middle East. The use of *graphene*—a nanomaterial obtained from graphite—could allow the construction of plants with better yields, lower energy costs and limited environmental impact. Innovations such as Sharp's *Skywell*, which transforms air into water, could also be useful in areas with severe drought.

For agriculture and livestock, the main challenge is to increase the productivity per plant, per head and per unit area, by selecting more productive crops and animals. In agriculture, it is important to seek—where it is possible—a second harvest per year, given that the availability of uncultivated land is modest and deforestation undermines the environmental

---

Zambezi River basin fight between Mozambique and Zimbabwe, the Nile Basin conflict between Egypt, Ethiopia and Sudan, and the Cochabamba Water War.

[16] Among the most damaging fishing techniques are *bottom trawling*, which destroys marine habitats, *drift longlines*, which catch dolphins and turtles together with tuna and swordfish, *flying traps*, which are not very selective in what they catch, *dredgers*, which damage the seabed and do not distinguish between catches, and the use of *fish aggregating devices* (FAD), floating objects that attract small fish.

balance.[17] Urban agriculture is growing in its various forms—such as rooftop and vertical farming, hydroponic cultivation—which helps sustainability and combats food shortages and poverty in cities.

However, there is still considerable scope for increasing food productivity. Only by extending the use of existing techniques, agricultural and livestock production could increase significantly. In addition to mechanization, benefits can come from spreading techniques to hinder desertification, combat erosion, protect vulnerable soils, safeguard soil fertility, and prevent and treat plant and livestock diseases and pests. Moreover, positive impact will come from the spread of precision agriculture, the creation of digital twins[18] and the laboratory development of alternative proteins, such as vegetable meat and "clean meat".

Great opportunities come from the techniques of genetic improvement of plants and animals, which can be carried out using traditional methods—such as hybridization, backcrossing, selection and mutagenesis—or genetic engineering. Genetically modified or transgenic organisms—GMOs—are a field with great potential, but one that raises many fears, especially with regard to food safety.[19] On the other hand, the history of agriculture is characterized by continuous human intervention in nature, and agriculture itself is not a discovery but rather a human invention.[20]

A note of optimism comes for nature's unexplored reserves. At the World Exposition hosted in Milan in 2015 with the theme "Feeding the planet, energy for life", it emerged that compared to a world reserve of about 300 thousand plants, only 4% are toxic, currently only 50 thousand are considered edible and only 200 are commonly used as food for humans. These

---

[17] According to FAO (2010), deforestation destroyed about 16 million hectares per year in the 1990s and about 13 million per year in the following decade (about the same size of Greece). The main reason for deforestation is conversion into agricultural land, the second cause is fires.

[18] Digital twin is the perfect digital copy of something real—a product or a process—through which it is easier to interact. An example is the seed, whose digital twin makes it possible to save on the creation of a physical prototype and test its performance only on a digital level. The digital twin of a farm is a virtual copy of it that reproduces its operation, facilitating management activities and improving decisions. Every component of the farm—such as seeds, plants, animals and farm equipment—can have its virtual twin.

[19] According to agricultural genetics expert Salvatore Ceccarelli (2019), the real weakness of GMOs is that although they are effective in the short term—because they make crops more resistant to insects, fungi and weeds—their introduction stimulates the evolution of certain parasites—similar to the reaction of bacteria to antibiotics—which become more resistant and require different solutions (such as a new GMO!).

[20] The field of comparative and evolutionary genomics is developing fast, driven by the availability of genome sequence data. Evolutionary genomics improves the characteristics of plants and animals without abruptly changing their genetics—as it is the case with GMOs—but rather by regularly replicating the mutations that nature occasionally produces.

numbers may increase significantly. The same applies to animal species, especially insects.

The spread of a proper diet can contribute to sustainability as it reduces the consumption of water and the use of agricultural land, as well as the impact on the production of greenhouse gases and biodiversity. Not to mention the savings in health spending, given that diet is one of the main risk factors for chronic diseases. Finally, the potential for efficiency gains, distribution optimization and waste reduction is enormous. Between pest attacks in the fields and losses both post-harvest and during processing, FAO (2017) estimates that approximately 1.3 billion tonnes of edible food are wasted every year.[21] That is the equivalent of one-third of the world production for human consumption.

Technological, logistical and organizational innovations—as well as greater international cooperation—can significantly increase productivity, reduce inefficiencies and combat world hunger.

Sustainable Growth and Energy Sources

Global energy needs are constantly growing. The International Energy Agency (2019) estimates an increase in demand between 1 and 1.3% per year to 2040.[22] Long term there is a risk of depletion of energy resources; shorter term the risk is inability to meet increasing requirements with negative consequence of energy price level. Technological progress can be of great help in facing these challenges.

Firstly, technology allows a more efficient use of current energy resources: it improves storage and distribution and it reduces waste. Secondly, technological progress enables the discovery of new deposits, for example through the use of satellites, and makes it possible to exploit others that are known but inaccessible, for example through improved extraction techniques that permit to reach greater depths on land and at sea. The combination of technology with the gradual melting of the Arctic Sea ice is making oil and gas fields accessible that were previously untapped due to technical difficulties and excessive drilling costs. According to a U.S. Geological Survey (2008),

---

[21] F.A.O. (International Day of Awareness of Food Loss and Waste, 2021) estimates that globally, about 14% of food produced is lost between harvest and retail, while an estimated 17% of total global food production is wasted (11% in households, 5% in the food service and 2% in retail).

[22] In the "Current Policies Scenario"—that is if the world continues along its present path, without any additional changes in policy—the estimated increase in energy demand is 1.3% each year; in the "Stated Policies Scenario"—which incorporates today's policy intentions and targets—the estimate is 1%.

approximately 30% of natural gas reserves and nearly 15% of undiscovered global oil reserves are to be found in the Arctic region.

Technological development has led to the exploitation of shale gas and shale oil—methane gas and oil trapped in the microporosity of clay rocks—the extraction of which is radically changing the sector with significant economic and geopolitical consequences. The surge in production of shale oil has caused the price of methane gas to fall worldwide and has influenced the price of oil. The United States, a net importer of energy since 1953, has recently become a net exporter of oil and could soon show a positive trade balance in energy.[23] China has huge reserves of shale gas but its extraction is technically difficult due to the complex geology. Other countries rich in shale gas are Argentina, Algeria, Poland, UK, Germany, Lithuania, Romania, Russia, Iran and Qatar, while Venezuela, Saudi Arabia and Canada have mostly shale oil. Shale resources are estimated at about 10% of the world's crude oil and about a third of the technically recoverable gas. The exploitation of shale is not due to a discovery but to innovation. The introduction and development of new technologies made it possible to first reach vertical drilling depths of between 2 and 4 thousand metres, then carry out horizontal drilling and finally—albeit with a certain environmental risk—carry out hydraulic fracturing to extract gas or oil from the rocks.

Technological innovation is fundamental to discover and improve the use and diffusion of new energy sources. Some compelling examples are the progress made in nuclear and solar energy, the improvements in the production of wind, water and geothermal energy, the experiments on the exploitation of wave motion. Various waste-to-energy processes are also being developed for the production of energy starting from organic and non-organic waste. Among these, the production of energy from biomass is the only one that is "carbon negative", thanks to the anaerobic digestion process that decomposes organic waste without combustion but with the sole intervention of microorganisms.

Technology will help the deployment of renewable energies, which are by nature intermittent and non-programmable, by ensuring continuity of supply through improvements in production, storage and distribution. In particular, the development of batteries and the rediscovery of hydroelectric pumped storage plants will increase energy storage capacity. And the spread of smart grids—electricity networks equipped with smart sensors to collect information in real time—will optimize distribution. This will allow

---

[23] Thanks to shale energy, the United States has become the world's leading producer of hydrocarbons: of natural gas since 2009, surpassing Russia, and of oil since 2013, overtaking Saudi Arabia.

constant coordination between supply and demand. On this subject, American sociologist Jeremy Rifkin (2014) has a strong view, as he thinks that "the bulk of the energy we use to heat our homes and run our appliances, power our businesses, drive our vehicles and operate every part of the global economy will be generated at near zero marginal cost and be nearly free in the coming decades". This is already happening in countries like Germany and Denmark, where thousands of homes have become small power plants thanks to photovoltaics and wind power. Moreover, the growth of renewable sources—potentially ubiquitous and less influenced by geographical elements than traditional ones—will lead to less concentration of political power related to energy.[24]

In the energy field, as in food, innovation is essential to overcome the constraints imposed by the scarcity of available resources.

Sustainable Growth, Demographic and Generational Balance

Demographics can be a limitation to the sustainability of economic growth.

First of all, the rapid growth of the global population raises concerns that there will not be enough resources to meet its needs in the future. Considering the extraordinary growth in consumption in countries with a strong demographic weight such as China and India, the worry extends to the environmental impact. In addition, there is an issue of progressive ageing of the population worldwide, which creates problems of generational balance. Finally, one should consider the tensions caused by migration flows, especially between countries with very different economic growth rates and average ages.

On a global level, demographic growth is impressive: from about one billion people in Malthus' time to 7.7 billion today. In the twentieth century, the trend accelerated: from two billion in 1927 to three in 1960, four in 1974, five in 1987 and six in 1999. The U.N. (2019) estimates that by 2050

---

[24] Rifkin's conclusions on energy should be read in the context of the zero marginal cost society he envisions. According to Rifkin, the increasing level of productivity will reduce the quantity of resources, energy and labour needed to produce anything, converging in a system where fewer goods will be produced and shared by more people. In this scenario, "access" is more important than "ownership" and the new key figure is the *prosumer*, someone who is at the same time producer and consumer of goods, services and energy. Current examples of prosumers are those who share their cars and homes using sharing economy platforms. In the future, people will be able to produce and share information, energy and 3D printed goods. And this will occur at almost zero marginal cost.

the world population will reach about nine billion, and in 2100, it will exceed eleven.[25]

The progressive ageing of population is a very strong trend worldwide. The OECD (2015) estimates that the world population over sixty years old will rise from 12% today to 21% in 2050. According to the U.N. (2019), the average world age—that in 1990 was twenty-six—will reach thirty-eight in 2050: a 46% increase in just sixty years. The order of magnitude of the phenomenon is unprecedented in the history of mankind, in both relative and absolute terms.

Of course, there are countries—such as India and most of Africa—with a very low average age and a population heavily skewed towards young people. In other areas of the world, the average age is very high—or the future projections show a strong upward trend—due to the combined effect of increased longevity and a sharp drop in the birth rate. In all cases, there is a generational imbalance.

Among the most significant cases of demographic ageing are Japan, Russia and several European countries, including Germany and Italy.[26] In the EU, France has the highest birth rate. In the United States, ageing is less pronounced than in other advanced economies thanks to strong migration inflows—largely made up of young people with a high birth rate—which have kept the demography, as well as the labour market, in balance. China shows population imbalances both by age, with rapid ageing, and by gender, with a clear preponderance of men over women in the generation of the one-child policy.[27]

The issue of demographic sustainability has different relevance in the South and the North of the world. In emerging countries, the problems are mainly related to population growth. The challenges are eradication of extreme poverty and hunger, reduction of child mortality, improvement of maternal health, fight against diseases (in particular HIV-AIDS and malaria) and environmental sustainability. In advanced economies, the ageing trend

---

[25] Austrian demographer Wolfgang Lutz (2015) and others have a different view. They believe that the world population will stabilize at 8 billion around 2040 and then begin to decline. This is because of the rapid fall in fertility rates in developing countries due to the urbanization of rural populations and to higher education of girls.

[26] Italy has an average age of about forty-five, higher than the EU average of 42.6 and lower only than Germany.

[27] *One-child* policy is a birth control programme introduced in China in 1979 by Deng Xiaoping, which prohibited couples from having more than one child. In the mid-1980s, it was amended to counter selective abortions and female infanticide, allowing rural families to have a second child only if the first was a girl. Despite this, it is estimated that there are currently about 30 million fewer women than men in China. The law was only removed in late 2015 allowing couples to have up to two children. The limit was increased to three children in May 2021, after a census data showed a steep decline in birth rates.

reduces the labour force and puts the sustainability of the welfare state at risk. In these countries, the allocation of resources is a source of inter-generational tensions: the youngest ask for family policies, childcare and employment support, while the oldest demand more spending on health care and pensions. Resources are not sufficient and an already high gap between demand and supply of welfare is increasing. In the world of work, longer life expectancy and public budget constraints are pushing for a higher retirement age. However, in many countries, youth unemployment is very high and this could trigger a serious social problem.

In this context, the theme of migration becomes. In developing countries, migration consists of outflows of young people that threaten to deplete local economies of manpower and brains. In advanced economies, migration is made up of inflows: on the one hand, they are a source of social tensions, and on the other hand, they are an important factor in demographic and labour market rebalancing.

Growth and Socio-Institutional Sustainability

For economic growth to be sustainable over time, it is important that societies and institutions are stable. Socio-institutional balance is based on the provision of security, health, culture, employment and the ability to guarantee conditions of stability, democracy, participation and fairness. This requires efficient infrastructures and reliable and trustworthy institutions.

There are some alarming trends in this respect. First of all, the spread of social networks is contributing to increasingly question the credibility of many institutions, highlighting their slowness and bureaucracy. Also, technology has favoured a strong tendency towards disintermediation, and this affects politics and democratic processes, the economy and the labour market. Intermediate bodies—such as political parties, business associations and trade unions, ecclesiastical and non-profit organizations—have historically been the transmission channel between ideologies and citizens. However, today intermediate bodies seem to have lost much of their purpose and authority.

From an economic point of view, a reason of concern in many countries is unemployment, especially in certain demographic groups. Particularly alarming is the growing number in many countries of NEETs (Not in Education, Employment or Training), young people between the ages of twenty and thirty-four who are not studying, not working and not following training courses.[28] Another critical issue is the excessive size of public debt, both in advanced and in emerging economies, which reduces the margins for investing in welfare, health care, infrastructure, education and culture. Finally, one of the greatest threats to social sustainability is the growing inequality.

Social sustainability also depends on a fair—and not only efficient—allocation of the produced wealth. As to the best method for achieving this goal, there are those who believe it is necessary to introduce redistribution policies and those who think this task should be left to the free market.

Redistribution mechanisms are generally considered necessary to protect vulnerable categories of a society and are associated with solidarity and welfarism. It is with great modernity, however, that in the encyclical *Evangelii Gaudium* (2013) Pope Francis considers redistribution mechanisms as an evolution of growth and speaks of "growth in justice", or growth in equity. The pope writes: "Growth in justice requires more than economic growth, while presupposing such growth: it requires decisions, programmes, mechanisms and processes specifically geared to a better distribution of income, the creation of sources of employment and an integral promotion of the poor which goes beyond a simple welfare mentality".

Redistribution is not in contradiction with economic growth nor it denies its importance. Indeed, without growth, redistribution is more complex and becomes a source of social tensions. Hence, growth allows and facilitates redistribution. On the other hand, a fair redistribution is necessary for growth to be sustainable in the long term. According to the sociologist Mauro Magatti (2017) "in the long run, if there is no social development - with a fair and inclusive redistribution of wealth, a strong investment in education, cultural, technical, scientific and infrastructural flourishing - there can be no economic growth".

There are also those who believe that redistribution mechanisms can create distortions and eliminate the incentive for growth that could derive from the existence of economic inequalities. In this view, public intervention is not necessary as the best allocation of the produced wealth can be achieved by the free market. According to Milton Friedman, technological development is an important redistributive tool, because it primarily benefits social classes that are less well-off. In *Free to Choose* (2016), the Nobel Prize-winning economist from the University of Chicago argues that "industrial progress, mechanical improvement, all of the great wonders of the modern era have meant

---

[28] According to Eurostat (2021), in 2020 the NEETs in Italy were 29.4% of the relevant age group: the highest percentage in the EU, whose average was 17.6%.

relatively little to the wealthy. The rich in Ancient Greece would have bene-fited hardly at all from modern plumbing: running servants replaced running water. Television and radio? The patricians of Rome could enjoy the leading musicians and actors in their home, could have the leading actors as domestic retainers. Ready-to-wear clothing, supermarkets—all these and many other modern developments would have added little to their life". According to Friedman, the consequence is that "the great achievements of Western capitalism have redounded primarily to the benefit of the ordinary person. These achievements have made available to the masses conveniences and amenities that were previously the exclusive prerogative of the rich and powerful".

Friedman captures a very important point that is also applicable to today's innovations. The benefits produced by the introduction of many technologies—especially in terms of increased access to information, education, opportunities, markets, cheaper products and services—are available to all. And people with fewer opportunities benefit proportionally more. However, it should be noted that today in many cases technological innovations are replacing human labour, which is the traditional mechanism for redistributing the produced wealth. Moreover, technology and globalization are polarizing the labour market and increasing wage inequality. On the one hand, lower product prices benefit consumers, and on the other hand, they put pressure on wages, therefore reducing the disposable income of the less well-off. These elements make less compelling the argument that, in the current context, no redistributive mechanism—other than the free market—is needed.

Finally, it should be noted that growth and entrenchment of poverty are problems distinct from inequality, although in many cases they are linked to that of unemployment.[29] Despite the worldwide declining trend, poverty is a major source of concern.[30]

A socio-institutional balance is fundamental to sustainable growth. Rising inequality, unemployment and poverty are undermining it.

---

[29] For Pope Francis (2013), "there is no worse poverty than that which does not allow us to earn our bread, which deprives us of the dignity of work" (Lecture to Fondazione "Centesimus Annus Pro Pontefice", 25 May 2013).

[30] The formal decline in world poverty over the last fifty years—from over 2.2 billion people in 1970 to just over 700 million today—is also due to the very low threshold used by statistics. Despite the fact that the World Bank has raised it from 1.25 to 1.90 dollars of income per day, this threshold does not seem realistic and is perhaps kept low on purpose in order to be able to meet—at least formally—the objectives of the international institutions for fighting poverty.

Growth and Sustainable Demand: The Risk of Secular Stagnation

Sustainability also needs to be considered from the demand side. The risk is that aggregate demand, a key growth driver, may suffer a structural contraction. In other words, there may be prolonged periods of zero growth due to a downsizing—not temporary one due to the economic cycle, but a prolonged and structural one— of consumption, investment and public spending.

The issue of secular stagnation was introduced in the 1930s by Keynesian economist Alvin Hansen (1939) and recently revived by Larry Summers (2014). For the former Secretary of the Treasury of the Clinton administration, "a prolonged period in which satisfactory growth can only be achieved by unsustainable financial conditions, may be the defining macro-economic challenge of our times".

These fears are considered excessive by many, particularly after the expansionary fiscal and monetary policies of the post-COVID-19 pandemic. However, some profound changes currently underway are causing structural declines in several components of the aggregate demand. A first trend is a decline in consumption. Companies in the digital economy have fewer employees than their traditional competitors: Amazon sells online and employees 550 thousand people while Walmart has stores on the ground and 2.3 million workers. In general, a smaller workforce translates into a structural decline in consumption. Similar consequences derive from the growth of precarious work, because uncertainty about the future forces people to postpone many purchasing decisions, especially of intermediate goods. The rise of inequality and the crisis of the middle class in advanced economies also have a negative impact on demand. In addition, there is a greater propensity to save—aimed at recovering from the high levels of debt reached—and a more prudent attitude of banks in granting credit.

A second major trend is the decline in investment. Companies in the digital economy invest a lot less in tangible assets than traditional firms: Google or Facebook do not need factories, plants and warehouses like General Motors or Dow Chemical. The world's number one retailer—Amazon— owned no stores prior to the acquisition of Whole Foods supermarkets. Just as a telecommunications leader like Skype owns no infrastructure, an urban transport leader like Uber owns no cars, a hospitality leader like Airbnb owns no hotels, and a film distribution leader like Netflix owns no movie theatres.

Finally, the ability to expand aggregate demand through public spending is largely limited by high public debt in both advanced and emerging economies.

As the governor of the Bank of Italy, Ignazio Visco (2014), points out, "in these conditions, the balance between savings and investments, necessary for full employment, could require a negative level of real interest rates (net of inflation) that monetary policy is unable to determine and that could give rise to phenomena of financial instability" which "could negatively affect the economy's capacity for growth in the medium to long term".

Some economists, including Robert Gordon (2012), argue that the risk of secular stagnation stems not so much from the demand side as it does from the supply side. The cause is a slowdown in productivity growth. The underlying assumption is that most of the major innovations leading to significant productivity gains have already been introduced and that a return to lower growth rates is therefore inevitable.[31]

Fears of secular stagnation are perhaps overblown. The alarm that emerged in the 1930s was dispelled by the long period of expansion that followed World War II. More recently, the very aggressive expansionary fiscal and monetary policies implemented by most countries following the 2008 financial crisis and the 2020 coronavirus pandemic have boosted aggregate demand and fostered growth, putting aside most concerns of stagnation. However, it is a fact that advanced economies are in the midst of facing radical changes that are affecting both the composition and the size of aggregate demand. The long-term consequences of these changes are difficult to predict. Traditional economic policies may not be sufficient to successfully deal with the situation.

Alternatives to the Traditional Growth Model

The severe economic crisis of recent years and the increased attention to sustainability issues have led some people to consider the liberal-capitalist growth model a failure. However, among the various proposals to replace it, none seems to be a fully convincing alternative. Nonetheless, from some of these proposals arise ideas that could make the traditional system more sustainable.

---

[31] In a supply-side view of secular stagnation, slower growth in potential output is a consequence not only of lower productivity growth but also of reduced population growth and declining labour-force participation.

The *blue economy*, proposed by Belgian entrepreneur Gunter Pauli (2010), is inspired by sustainable ecosystems and considers nature as a source of inspiration.[32] The idea is that nature can teach us to do much more with less. In nature, there is no unemployment because everyone contributes to the best of their ability, there is no waste because what is waste for some is raw material for others. Some small but emblematic examples in the food sector are the use of coffee waste to cultivate *shiitake* mushrooms, or orange peels to produce natural detergent, or slaughterhouse waste to feed flies whose larvae become animal feed and produce disinfectant.

The *civil economy* places human beings at the centre, exalting values such as reciprocity and fraternity. Both the capitalist and the civil economy are market driven. The difference is that the former pursues the so-called total good, while the latter targets the "common good". Luigino Bruni and Stefano Zamagni (2015)—for whom the civil economy has its close roots in Humanism and its more remote ties in Aristotle, Cicero, Thomas Aquinas and the Franciscan school—explain that civil economy "seeks answers not outside the market economy but under the banner of a different market, a civil market, where the words happiness, honour, virtue, common good can be rediscovered precisely in an economic key, leaving room for an ethical perspective and not a purely individualistic one". Because "private interest is not naturally resolved in public happiness, this being the fruit of civil virtues".

Particular attention should be paid to the *circular economy*, the aim of which is to eliminate waste. The key is to view what some consider waste as a resource for others. For the precursors of the circular economy Nicholas Georgescu-Roegen (1971, 1975) and Kenneth Boulding (1941), the economic cycle—which currently depletes nature with resource extraction and the accumulation of environmentally harmful waste—should be inspired by the ecological cycle, in which almost all waste is put back into circulation and becomes useful for other forms of life. The key is to move from the current linear "take-make-dispose" model to a circular one that has the capability of limiting the input of materials and energy and of minimizing the output of waste. The circular economy is therefore an economic system planned to be self-regenerating, reusing materials in subsequent production

---

[32] Similarly, biomimicry (or biomimetics) studies the biological and biomechanical processes of nature as a source of inspiration for solving human problems. Leonardo da Vinci studied birds to design flying machines. The structure of the Eiffel Tower is inspired by human anatomy, in particular the joint between the femur and the kneecap. Insects, plants and animals are mines of ideas. The sociability of ants has inspired mathematical models to optimize traffic. The lotus leaf has been a model for the development of water-repellent materials. The burdock for that of Velcro. Geckos, which walk on walls, have inspired new adhesive materials, the properties of shark skin the design of the suit of swimming champion Michael Phelps!

cycles and reducing waste to a minimum. Interestingly, in the encyclical *Laudato si'* (2015) Pope Francis condemns the "throwaway culture" because the disposal of physical things is linked in many ways to the "discardability" of human life.

The *sharing economy* is widespread. The basic assumption is that there are many unused resources[33] and therefore it is more efficient to share ownership of certain goods. There are countless examples. In the transport sector, Zipcar, Uber, Lyft, BlaBlaCar and DriveMyCar operate with different business models but they all provide vehicle sharing. Airbnb allows to rent houses for short periods, Couchsurfing to offer a bed, VoulezVousDiner a home-cooked meal, Parkatmyhouse the parking next to home, Poshmark used clothes, Withlocals services for tourists, Busuu foreign language lessons. With Spinlister people can share sports equipment, with Marinanow berths, with Parcel delivery and shipping services, with Waze real-time traffic information. With Streetbank, people can share everything—from work tools to skills—with their neighbours.

The size of the sharing economy is certainly growing thanks to technology but also because it meets different needs and values. This includes the respect for the environment,[34] money saving,[35] flexibility, the search for sociability, the desire to be fashionable and part of a community. Many of these values are now widely shared among generations such as millennials and post-millennials. Clearly, such a philosophy has a significant economic impact, on both the demand side and the supply side. However, the growth of the sharing economy poses a problem of rules. The sharing of goods and means has always existed in history but the introduction of technology has a disruptive effect, making it necessary to rewrite old rules. Think of the economic and legal tensions caused by the success of Uber or the difficulty of regulating Airbnb from a fiscal point of view.

In recent years, there have been many interesting ideas about alternative growth models. Jean-Paul Fitoussi (2009) has called for a new political ecology and has pointed out that a new development can be sustainable only if it is democratic, in the sense that it is able to ensure everyone the right of

---

[33] Fortune (2016) reports that on average cars are parked 95% of the time. A Royal Automobile Club Foundation report (2021) shows that personal vehicles in the U.K. are parked 96% of the time and driven only 4%.

[34] Martin, Shaheen and Lidicker (2010) estimate that in the United States on average a carpool "replaces" 9 to 13 owned vehicles; Myers and Cairns (2009) show that in the United Kingdom the cars "replaced" are 9 to 14. In both countries, the reduction in terms of mileage and greenhouse gas emissions is significant (up to 40%).

[35] In the short term, the sharing economy increases supply and lowers prices, creating value for consumers. However, in the long term, it can sometimes have negative effects, such as the case of Airbnb which in some cities is taking homes away from the residential market thus driving rents up.

subsistence. Alain Caillé and other intellectuals have launched the *Convivialist Manifesto* (2014, 2020) envisioning an ethic of the future that allows to manage rivalry between human beings. Convivialism values the art of living together and aims to teach people they can and should cooperate by "opposing without slaughtering each other". There has also been a resurgence of *Commons* movements, due to the rediscovery of the importance of the commons.

Economic Growth, Well-Being and Happiness

Some of the criticism to the traditional growth model has prompted to question the methods of measuring well-being that are based only—or primarily—on Gross Domestic Product (GDP). Several new methodologies, while still taking into account GDP size and growth, put a lot more emphasis on sustainability goals.

The human development index used by the U.N. since 1993 to assess the quality of life in member countries—and to the construction of which Nobel Prize winner for economics Amartya Sen has contributed—goes in this direction. In addition to traditional measures of wealth, such as GDP per capita, the index takes into account life expectancy at birth and level of education. The idea is to reconcile economic growth, measured by the increase in GDP, with economic development, which is a function of many other variables. Sen himself acknowledges that the index should be further expanded. For example, including indicators of environmental sustainability, technological development and culture, and taking into account factors such as the existence of free elections, an independent press, a multi-party political system and freedom of expression.

An important step in this direction has been taken in Italy with the measurement of fair and sustainable well-being. The BES index[36] evaluates the progress of a society from an economic point of view but also from a social and environmental one, and it also takes into account inequality and sustainability. The BES index includes twelve indicators: health, education and training, work-life balance, economic well-being, social relations, politics and institutions, security, subjective well-being, landscape and cultural heritage, environment, research and innovation, and quality of services.[37]

---

[36] Benessere Equo e Sostenibile (BES)—Equitable and Sustainable Well-being—is an index introduced by ISTAT (Italian National Institute of Statistics) and Cnel (National Council for Economics and Labour).

[37] For example, the BES index is more accurate than GDP fluctuations at assessing the negative impact that the COVID-19 pandemic has on the economy and society. This is because, in addition

Broadening the definition of well-being does not mean giving up on growth. The end goal is a model that measures not just people's economic prosperity but also their overall well-being and happiness. In other words, their happiness. In this scenario, income is no longer the only variable that matters, although it continues to be an important one.

More extreme is the view of Richard Easterlin (1974), for whom there is no significant correlation between income and happiness. In a survey on economic growth in the 1970s, the American economist concludes that over the course of a lifetime people's happiness depends very little on variations in income and wealth. Easterlin's well-known paradox shows that human happiness grows in parallel with increasing income only up to a certain point, after which it decreases following a parabolic trajectory.

Easterlin uses the metaphor of the treadmill (*treadmill effect*). Higher income brings with it also more ambitions and greater expectations of happiness. This leaves the sense of dissatisfaction unchanged, and sometimes even worsening. Just like the individual running on a treadmill thinks he is progressing while he actually remains in the same spot. The explanation of Easterlin's paradox is that a correct measure of happiness must also include relational goods. Wealth (or utility) and happiness (or social well-being) are not the same thing. In order to be happier, it is not sufficient to try to increase utility: it is necessary to enter the sphere of relationships between people.

Serge Latouche (2003, 2004, 2006, 2011) is well known for his thoughts on the subject. According to the French economist and philosopher, growth does not necessarily make people happy. In fact, it may have the opposite effect. Studying the population of Laos, Latouche observes that people are happy despite not pursuing economic growth. This is the starting point for his harsh criticism of the capitalist model, which is his view is "condemned to growth" and in which human beings are at war among themselves and with the planet to pursue accumulation.

Latouche's proposal is to pursue a "happy degrowth". He points out that "enacting *décroissance* means [...] abandon the economic imaginary, that is the belief that more equals better". Degrowth is a conscious choice to produce and consume fewer goods and services. This is different from a recession, which is an unwanted and uncontrolled drop in GDP that inevitably damages aspects of the quality of life such as education, health and employment. Happy degrowth is a selective reduction, a choice not to produce what is not necessary. In this scenario, it is not demand that stimulates production but vice versa: only what is considered necessary is produced. Latouche is

---

to showing the decline of economic wealth produced, it also takes into account the damage in terms of health, education, social relations, and other dimensions.

inspired by some of the ideas introduced by Georgescu-Roegen (1971), such as the sense of limits, sobriety, durability and reparability of products.[38]

Grazia Francescato, a convinced environmentalist for more than fifty years and patroness of the Italian green movements, also thinks that an adjustment of the current system is not sufficient to guarantee the salvation of the planet and its inhabitants. For Francescato, it is necessary to pursue "a radical ecological conversion of economy and society", because "without a qualitative leap in collective conscience and an authentic recovery of the limit, we will devour Earth's resources, triggering increasingly devastating social inequalities and many conflicts (including armed conflicts)".

An actual policy pursuing degrowth is difficult to implement, in both advanced and emerging economies. It is hard for those who live in the former to change their habits after decades of growth. It is just as complicated for those who live in the latter—who have just started to benefit from growth—to give up the opportunity to improve their well-being.

* * *

Sustainability constraints, both on the demand and on the supply side, must be taken very seriously. It is difficult to say whether economic policy and international cooperation will be sufficient to deal with the risks of a structural contraction of consumption and investment. Or whether innovation will allow to overcome once again sustainability constraints. Perhaps even more difficult is to understand whether mankind will be able to make in time the necessary mind changes to bring growth back onto the tracks of sustainability. What is certain is that the current situation leaves no room for errors, indecisions or deferrals. Now more than ever, it is necessary to make the right choices. With urgency.

Bibliography

Artistic Agenda: The State of Eco-Art, "New Scientist", 24 June 2010.

J. Attali, *For a Positive Economy*, Egea Università Bocconi, Milan 2014.

K. Boulding, *Economic Analysis*, Harper and Brothers, New York 1941.

Brundtland Report, *Our Common Future*, World Commission on Environment and Development, 1987.

L. Bruni, S. Zamagni, *L'economia civile*, il Mulino, Bologna 2015.

---

[38] The Romanian mathematician argues that "goods must be made more durable through design that then allows them to be repaired". A very topical position given the current controversy over planned obsolescence.

Alain Caillé, *Convivialist Manifesto: A Declaration of Interdependence,* "Global Dialogues" n. 3, Duisburg 2014.

Alain Caillé, *Second Convivialist Manifesto: Towards a Post-Neoliberal World*, "Civic Sociology" n. 1, 2020.

M. Carney, Br*eaking the Tragedy of the Horizon—Climate Change and Financial Stability,* Speech at Lloyd's, London 29 September 2015.

S. Ceccarelli, *I dubbi sugli OGM in agricoltura,* "Corriere della Sera", Milano 21 September 2019.

R.A. Easterlin, *Does Economic Growth Improve the Human Lot?* Academic Press, Inc., New York 1974.

Eurostat Statistics Explained, June 2021.

FAO, *Global Forest Resource Assessment,* 2010.

FAO, *Water for Sustainable Food and Agriculture,* Rome 2017.

FAO, *The State of World Fisheries and Aquaculture,* Rome 2018.

FAO, *International Day of Awareness of Food Loss and Waste,* 29 September 2021 http://www.fao.org/international-day-awareness-food-loss-waste/en/.

M.C. Finucci, *The Garbage Patch State – Wasteland,* Presentation and First Installation at UNESCO, Paris 11 April 2013.

J.-P. Fitoussi, É. Laurent, *The New Political Ecology. Economics and Human Development,* Feltrinelli, Milan 2009.

Pope Francis, *Lecture to Fondazione "Centesimus Annus Pro Pontefice",* 25 May 2013.

Pope Francis, *Apostolic Exhortation Evangeli Gaudium,* 24 November 2013.

Pope Francis, *Laudato si',* Encyclical Letter, 24 May 2015.

M. Friedman, R. Friedman, *Free to Choose. A Personal Perspective,* IBL Books, Turin-Milan 2016.

L. Gallino, *Finanzcapitalismo,* Einaudi, Turin 2011.

R.J. Gordon, *Is US Economic Growth Over?* "NBER Working Paper", 18315, 2012.

N. Georgescu-Roegen, *The Entropy Law and Economic Process,* Harvard University Press, Cambridge, MA, 1971.

N. Georgescu-Roegen, *Energy and Economic Myths,* "Southern Economic Journal", 41, 1975.

S. Gianpio, *Water Scarcity, A Problem to be Addressed,* "Ecoland.it" Reference to Study of University of Twente, 9 March 2020.

A.H. Hansen, *Economic Progress and Declining Population Growth,* "American Economic Review", n. 29, 1939.

G. Hardin, *The Tragedy of the Commons,* "Science", 162, no. 3859, pp. 1243–1248, 1968.

International Energy Agency, *World Energy Outlook,* 2019.

ISTAT, The BES Report, https://www.istat.it/en/well-being-and-sustainability/the-measurement-of-well-being/bes-report.

M.E. Kahn et al., *Long-Term Macroeconomic Effects of Climate Change,* University of Cambridge, Cambridge 2019.

J.M. Keynes, *Economic Possibilities for Our Grandchildren,* lecture in Madrid, 1930.

J.M. Keynes, *Economic Possibilities for Our Grandchildren*, in *"Essays in Persuasion"*, Norton & Co., New York 1930.

S. Latouche, *Would the West Actually be Happier with Less? The World Downscaled*, "Le Monde Diplomatique", December 2003.

S. Latouche, *Why Less Should be So Much More: Degrowth Economics*, "Le Monde Diplomatique", December 2004.

S. Latouche, *Conference on Degrowth*, Greenrport, Lastra a Signa September 2006.

S. Latouche, *Come si esce dalla società dei consumi. Corsi e percorsi della decrescita*, Bollati Boringhieri, Torino 2011.

W. Lutz et al., *The Uncertain Timing of Reaching 8 Billion, Peak World Population, and Other Demographic Milestones*, "Population and Development Review", 37, September 2011.

M. Magatti, *Cambio di paradigma*, Feltrinelli, Milano 2017.

M. Magnani e G. Giordani, *Why Central Bankers Should Worry About Climate Change*, "World Economic Forum", Geneva 17 December 2015.

M. Magnani, *Con la Sharing Economy Rivoluzione a 360 Gradi*, "IlSole 24Ore", 20 March 2016.

M. Magnani, *Se i social premiano l'eticamente corretto*, "IlSole 24Ore", 28 August 2016.

E. Martin, S. Shaheen, J. Lidicker, *Carsharing's Impact on Household Vehicle Holdings: Results from a North American Shared-Use Vehicle Survey*, "Journal of the Transportation Research Board", 2143, pp. 150–158, 2010.

N. Mirenzi, *Con Greta siamo di fronte a un abbaglio mondiale* (interview to Franco Prodi), Huffington Post, 6 October 2019.

N. Myers, *Environmental Refugees: An Emergent Security Issue*, 13th Economic Forum, Prague May 2005.

D. Myers, S. Cairns, *Carplus Annual Survey of Car Clubs 2008/09, Transport Research Laboratory*, Published Project Report PPR 399, Wokingham 2009.

J. K. Moore et al., *Sustained Climate Warming Drives Declining Marine Biological Productivity*, "Science", 9 March 2018.

D.Z. Morris, Today's Cars Are Parket 95% of the Time, Fortune, 13 March 2016.

R. Neukom et al., *No Evidence for Globally Coherent Warm and Cold Periods Over the Preindustrial Common Era*, "Nature", 24 July 2019.

W.D. Nordhaus, *Reflections on the Economics of Climate Change*, "The Journal of Economic Perspectives", 7, no. 4, pp. 11–25, 1993.

OECD, *Ageing: Debate the Issue*, edited by P. Love, 2015.

E. Ostrom, *Governing the Commons. The Evolution of Institutions for Collective Action*, Cambridge University Press, Cambridge 1990.

G. Pauli, *The Blue Economy*, Paradigm Publication, Taos (New Mexico) 2010.

J. Rifkin, *La società a costo marginale zero*, Mondadori, Milano 2014.

Royal Automobile Club Foundation, *Standing Still*, July 2021.

A.K. Scott, B.H. Strauss, *New Elevation Data Triple Estimates of Global Vulnerability to Sea-Level Rise and Coastal Flooding*, "Nature Communications", 2019.

L.H. Summers, *IMF Economic Forum: Policy Responses to Crises*, Speech to the 14th Annual IMF Conference, Washington DC, 8 November 2013.

L.H. Summers, *U.S. Economic Prospects: Secular Stagnation, Hysteresis and the Zero Lower Bound*, "Business Economics", 49, no. 2, 2014.

United Nations, *World Water Development Report*, 2019.

United Nations, *The World Population Prospects*, 2019.

United Nations, *Climate Change 2021: The Physical Science Basis*, IPCC Report, 2021.

United Nations, Paris Agreement, United Nations Treaty Collection, www.treaties.un.org, Paris 12 December 2015.

U.S. Geological Survey, *Circum-Arctic Resource Appraisal: Estimates of Undiscovered Oil and Gas North of the Arctic Circle*, May 2008.

I. Visco, "Perché i tempi stanno cambiando…", XXX Lettura del Mulino, Bologna 18 October 2014.

World Economic Forum, Ellen Mac Arthur Foundation, McKinsey Company, *The New Plastic Economy: Rethinking the Future of Plastic*, 2016.

World Health Organization, *Health & Climate Change*, Special Report, 3 December 2018.

WWF, *Responsabilità e rendicontazione, le chiavi per risolvere l'inquinamento da plastica*, 2019.

5

New Jobs or Technological Unemployment?

In the course of history, innovation has always fostered employment. And economic growth has been the main conduit between innovation and employment.

In the short term, innovation has often led to the sacrifice of certain sectors and related jobs. However, in the longer term it has brought productivity gains, growth in average wages, enlargement of the size of the economy and creation of new jobs. The transition has never been easy. The positive impact on employment emerged only after a certain period of time—due to the necessary adaptations to new technologies and working methods—and the beneficiaries were not necessarily the same people who had lost their traditional occupations. Nevertheless, once the transition was complete, the impact on employment—in terms of both quantity and quality—was positive.

Things may be different in the future. First of all, it is no longer a foregone conclusion that innovation will continue to produce economic growth. And in a scenario of either degrowth or secular stagnation, employment suffers. Second, even if innovation leads to an expansion of the economy, it could pave the way for a jobless growth. When economic growth is conditioned by sustainability constraints the effect on employment is uncertain. In this scenario, the newly created jobs may be fewer than those lost, the relative value of work may decline, and transitioning to new professions may be challenging. The overall wealth would grow but significant redistribution problems would emerge.

© The Author(s), under exclusive license to Springer Nature Switzerland AG 2022
M. Magnani, *Making the Global Economy Work for Everyone*,
https://doi.org/10.1007/978-3-030-92084-5_5

In the future, what will be the impact of innovation on employment? Will economic growth continue to act as the transmission belt between innovation and employment?

Economic Growth, the Transmission Belt Between Innovation and Work

Technological innovation has a twofold impact on the economy. First, it creates economic value by increasing productivity and customizing supply. Second, it expands the size of the economy by opening new development cycles.

On the first front, strong productivity gains reduce production costs and increase supply, transforming an economy of scarcity into an economy of abundance. In addition, technology—especially digital—increasingly allows products and services to be personalized. Abundance and customization of supply create economic value for consumers but do not necessarily lead to an increase in employment.

In the past, productivity gains due to innovation were shared with workers, thus increasing their compensation. This stimulated consumption and increased aggregate demand, with a positive impact on employment. However, in the digital economy, this is no longer a given. In fact, the economic value created by innovations is largely shared between the consumers purchasing the end product, who benefit in terms of price reductions, and the investors providing the capital. A smaller portion of the created value goes into improving the remuneration of labour. The consequence is that greater productive efficiency may not have positive effects on employment.

The second transmission channel between innovation, growth and employment is stronger and more reliable than the first one. The introduction of technology makes it possible to produce new products and services, create new activities and access new markets. In short, it broadens the economy by opening up new cycles of development. It happened in the past with the introduction of revolutionary technologies such as the steam engine and electricity. It is happening today with digital technology. It will happen again in the future with other innovations.

Often the enlargement of economic activity has taken some time, and in the short term, innovations have even slowed down growth. However, after a period of transition, the economy expanded and employment grew with it. There are several good examples of these dynamics. The spread of the automobile in the 1920s caused the horse population to plummet and related businesses and services to fail. Nonetheless, new businesses and professions related to the new mode of transportation have subsequently emerged. More recently, the introduction of personal computers and software—which initially caused the loss of many jobs—in the longer run has dramatically reduced the fixed costs of launching new businesses, expanding the economy and creating jobs. Similarly, for e-commerce: while severely penalizing traditional distribution activities and employment, it has allowed artisans and micro-businesses to access new markets, creating new jobs. Finally, the sharing economy has undermined traditional sectors and firms with established positions, but it has also stimulated the emergence of new market segments and new professions.[1]

This transmission channel works even when economic growth is subject to sustainability constraints. Indeed, while adapting the growth model to sustainability criteria may slow down growth and employment in some sectors, it is also likely to favour the rise of completely new sectors and professions. The examples are many. Greater attention to the environment stimulates the development of new materials and production processes, economic activities and professions. An ageing population supports employment by increasing the demand of health and personal services. Increased awareness of the scarcity of natural resources drives the energy sector to innovate and find alternative sources, thus creating jobs.

The long-term prospects inspire some optimism in Lawrence Katz (2008), who has studied the historical relationship between technological progress and labour. The Harvard University economist notes that, although it has sometimes taken decades to acquire the skills needed to perform new jobs, "in the long run, employment rates remain relatively stable and there has always been success in creating new work, new things to do". David Autor (2003, 2013) of MIT comes to similar conclusions, arguing that jobs can go through transformations without necessarily bringing about significant negative changes in employment rates.

This Time May Be Different

Some simple figures show that something has changed with respect to the past in the innovation-growth-employment relationship. A few years ago, the "Economist" (2016) noted that while in 1990 the combination of the *Big*

---

[1] In many cases, however, e-commerce and sharing economy jobs are—in terms of pay, social security and insurance contributions, job protection and stability—of lower quality than those lost.

Three of the automobile industry—General Motors, Ford and Chrysler—capitalized about 36 billion dollars, had a turnover of 250 billion and employed 1.2 million people, in 2014 the three giants of technology—Apple, Google and Microsoft—had a similar aggregate turnover (about 247 billion) but capitalized together over a thousand billion and had only a little more than 227 thousand workers. Today, each of the three *Big-Tech* has alone a market capitalization of between two and three trillion and the aggregate number of employees is around 360 thousand. The data confirms that in the digital economy much more value can be created with far fewer employees than in the traditional economy.

Many of the challenges posed by current technological innovations are unprecedented. Some of them concern labour. First of all, it cannot be taken for granted that productivity growth will translate—as it has in the past—into employment. Empirical data show that since the year 2000 in the United States the two variables are no longer closely correlated. Hence, jobless growth and technological unemployment are real risks. Secondly, the frequency with which disruptive innovations are introduced is much higher than in the past. This significantly reduces the time available for workers to adapt to the changes in the labour market triggered by innovations.

Another challenge comes from the penetration rate and pervasiveness of new technologies. The main consequence is that the number of new jobs created by innovations may not compensate for job cuts in sectors that have become obsolete. Moreover, the average wage of the new jobs will not necessarily be higher than that of the old ones, because automation is increasingly threatening even medium- to high-paid jobs and because productivity gains are likely to reward capital investment more than labour. In particular, the knowledge economy—which is growing exponentially in the digital age—is characterized by decreasing marginal costs. This leads to lower prices for products and services and, consequently, lower wage levels.

The combination of technological innovation and globalization determines other disruptive effects, such as a big increase in international labour mobility. The new digital professions, those with a high level of creativity and high added value, will concentrate in the most attractive territories, transforming them into innovation hubs that can service the whole world. Of course, this is a favourable juncture for skilled workers and for those territories that are able to attract talent. However, not all of them will be able to seize the opportunity. There will be winners and losers.

A scenario with high unemployment and low value placed on work requires a shift of focus towards wealth distribution. Without an effective distribution of produced wealth, in the long run, the foundations of the democratic system itself are at risk. In a speech to the U.S. Congress on 29 April 1939, the father of the New Deal Franklin Delano Roosevelt warned that "true individual freedom cannot exist without economic security and independence" because "people who are hungry and out of a job are the stuff of which dictatorships are made".

This time things may be different than in the past. Even if innovation continues to be an engine of economic growth, the positive impact on jobs should not be taken for granted. And, in any event, the transition will be very complex. There are several reasons for this, many of which have never been contemplated. Until now.

The Risk of Jobless Growth

A first aspect is that technological innovations could replace human labour at a faster rate than that of new job creation. This is a challenge of Okun's law, an empirically observed inverse relationship between GDP growth and unemployment rate.

According to Erik Brynjolfsson and Andrew McAfee, the trend has been going on for some time. In *Race Against the Machine* (2011), the two MIT economists analyse productivity and employment in the United States since 1947. The study shows that until 2000 the two variables have grown proportionally, but after that there is a *decoupling* effect: productivity grows while employment (and wages) decline. The main cause of decoupling is technology, which destroys jobs faster than it creates them.[2]

According to Brynjolfsson, technological progress and our inability to keep up with it are "the great paradox of our time". While productivity and innovation are at record levels, we are witnessing a decrease in employment. Moreover, the difficulty of schools and training institutions to keep up with the changes that innovation brings to the labour market is one of the causes of the growing mismatch between the skills required by companies and those offered by workers.[3]

The relationship between technological change and employment is a much-discussed point in economic analysis. David Ricardo (1821) feared

---

[2] While increasing offshoring of manufacturing activities and the entry of China in the World Trade Organization (WTO) also contributed to decoupling, the role of technology seems to be preponderant. Indeed, decoupling started in 2000: too late to be only the effect of offshoring and too early to be caused only by China's entry in the WTO (which took place in December 2001).

[3] A Unioncamere report (2020) indicates that in Italy companies have difficulty finding the required professional profiles in 29.7% of cases.

that the use of new machines could be harmful to workers and employment. The risk of technological unemployment was also discussed in the 1930s by Keynes, who believed that within a century the available wealth would at least quadruple and the working week would be reduced to fifteen hours. Keynes (1930) wrote: "We are suffering from a new disease [...] of which [we] will hear a great deal in the years to come – namely, technological unemployment". This is "due to our discovery of means of economizing the use of labour outrunning the pace at which we can find new uses for labour". Keynes, however, was more optimistic than Ricardo and saw this as a temporary adjustment phase. He considered progress as an opportunity for mankind to engage in other activities. Wassily Leontief (1952) pessimistically drew an analogy with the technologies of the early twentieth century that made horses redundant. The Russian economist and Nobel prize laureate speculated that "labour will become less and less important [...] More and more workers will be replaced by machines" and he did "not see that new industries can employ everybody who wants a job".

British Nobel Prize winner for economics, James Meade (1964) wondered "what shall we all do when output per man-hour of work is extremely high but practically the whole of the output goes to a few property owners, while the mass of the workers are relatively (or even absolutely) worse off than before". American economic historian Robert Heilbroner (1965) asserted that "as machines continue to invade society, duplicating greater and greater numbers of social tasks, it is human labour itself—at least, as we now think of 'labour'—that is gradually rendered redundant". Technology has very often modified the organization of work throughout history (think of the transition from horse-drawn carriages to cars) but, as American economists Jeffrey Sachs and Laurence Kotlikoff (2012) point out, the latest wave of innovations risks making the worker disappear (as in the case of the driverless car)!

For William Brian Arthur (2011), digital technology is creating a "second economy" alongside the traditional physical one. The "second economy" is "vast, silent, connected, unseen [...] it is remotely executing and global, always on, and endlessly configurable". And it is "autonomous", meaning that "human beings may design it but are not directly involved in running it". Since the mid-1990s, this parallel economy has enabled productivity gains but it has also destroyed many jobs. The trend has involved all sectors and it is still rapidly growing. Think of the proliferation of devices that replace housework and secretarial work, such as Google Home and Amazon Alexa. Or look at the rise of driverless taxi services, such as Delphi and nuTonomy (in Singapore). Or consider the DoorDash initiative that delivers food and packages to the client's doorstep with miniature self-driving vehicles.[4]

The growing decoupling of productivity (which is increasing thanks to innovation) from employment (which is decreasing as technology replaces workers) is a reason of great concern because it challenges the traditional virtuous transmission channel between innovation and labour.

High Frequency of Disruptive Innovations

Another unprecedented aspect affecting the labour market is the frequency with which disruptive innovations occur today.

Think of the great technical innovations at the origin of the industrial revolutions. The distance in time between the invention of the steam engine and that of the dynamo—respectively the catalysts of the first and second industrial revolutions—is almost a century. The third industrial revolution, marked by the introduction of electronics and information technology, also arrived just under a century after the previous one. The internet paved the way to the digital revolution only a few decades later, marking a sharp acceleration. Today, important innovations follow one another much more rapidly than in past. Robots, drones, unmanned cars, 3D printing, IoT, cloud, big data, AI, quantum computing, blockchain, mediated reality, biotechnology and nanotechnology are all emerging at a rapid pace. And each can disrupt established equilibria. In the past, the new equilibrium that followed the introduction of a radical innovation lasted a few generations; today, each generation witnesses several disruptive innovations in the course of its professional life.

The high frequency of disruptive innovations has a twofold effect on the labour market. First, it is more complex for workers to reposition themselves in the new professional environment. The time needed to acquire the necessary skills to transition to a new job—or to learn how to use new technologies in the current job—can be longer than the time between one innovation and the next. Hence, by the time a worker adapts to the new labour environment and learns a new job, there has already been significant change. The transition that took place in several European countries in the first part of the twentieth century from agricultural to industrial economy—and later the one from manufacturing to services—occurred over a couple of generations;

---

[4] The image of high productivity of new technologies is sometimes tarnished by embarrassing setbacks. At the end of 2018, the Wall Street Journal revealed that Alexa is unable to make a simple call to 911, the single emergency number in North America.

today, the same generation is dealing with several professional transitions. This is a cause of great tensions, especially where the labour market is rigid and professional training is inadequate.

A second effect of the high frequency of innovations is that it is difficult to imagine today what work skills will be required in the future. According to the World Economic Forum (WEF) (2016), 65% of the children currently attending primary schools will be performing jobs that do not yet exist. The degree of uncertainty about new professions is unprecedented. In the 20 years of Italy's post-war economic miracle, the jobs lost in agriculture were replaced by others concentrated in well-identified sectors and locations (such as manufacturing in Northern Italy or abroad) and requiring similar skills (manual labour). In other words, it was clear where the new jobs were and what skills they required. Today, the professions at risk of disappearing are easy to identify but it is very difficult to imagine what the jobs of the future will be and where they will be located.

In recent years, the frequency in the introduction of disruptive innovations into the economy and society has been exceptional. There is not enough time to digest them, sometimes not even to fully understand them. This makes it very difficult to adequately prepare those entering the labour market and to continuously update the skills of those who are already in it.

Penetration Rate and Pervasiveness of Innovations

The impact of new technologies on the economy and employment is unprecedented also due to the speed with which they are introduced into production mechanisms and to their pervasiveness, i.e. their ability to spread everywhere in a deep and transversal way so as to prevail over other technologies and dominate.

Penetration rate and pervasiveness of innovations have never been greater in history. The invention of the wheel by the Sumerians in about 3500 BC did not have immediate repercussions in the rest of the ancient world because technical knowledge was transmitted slowly. It is believed that the initial application was as a lathe for handicrafts and only three centuries later it was extended to means of transport. Moreover, even in this use, the wheel was adopted by the Chinese and Greeks only at a later time. The compass—which was revolutionary because it allowed safe navigation far from the coasts and stimulated maritime traffic and geographical exploration—was invented by the Chinese between the ninth and the eleventh centuries. However, it took some time for the technology to be transferred to Europeans and Arabs through naval contact.

Today, the penetration rate of new technologies is impressive. The number of robots introduced into production processes globally has increased exponentially in only two decades. More in general, innovations are reaching large numbers of people much faster than in the past. It took radio thirty-eight years to reach the first 50 million users, TV needed thirteen years and the internet only four. Facebook reached 100 million people in approximately nine months![5]

There are several reasons why the innovation process has become faster and more pervasive in recent years. One is technological development itself, especially in the telecommunications field. Another reason is the unprecedented degree of interdependence of world economies. A third factor is the rapid succession of incremental innovations: the continuous upgrade of technologies that are already widespread has made Moore's law obsolete. Think of the electric car, whose autonomy has gone from eighty to almost six hundred kilometres in just a few years. Or the sequencing of the human genome, the cost of which has fallen in a decade from several million to a few thousand dollars while the time required to perform it has collapsed from several years to a few hours.

Another phenomenon, not new but much more relevant than in the past, is the *"combinatorial effect"*. The various technological innovations intersect, combine, integrate and feed off each other, each contributing to the development and improvement of the others. This further accelerates the development and diffusion of the technologies themselves and it also enables new and unexpected applications.

High penetration rate and pervasiveness are typically the features of the so-called general-purpose technologies. These are innovations that can change the entire way of producing, overturning business models, competitive scenarios and consolidated leadership positions. In the past, this happened with steam power and electricity. More recently, the rise of digital photography has swept away Kodak, the smartphone has hurt Nokia and Motorola, e-commerce has revolutionized distribution and logistics. We may see similar impacts in blockchain-based payment systems on financial institutions, 3D printing on certain manufacturing activities, big data, IoT and AI on many businesses across sectors.

---

[5] It is important to remember that when dealing with social networks numbers of accounts may include fakes and duplicates. For example, Facebook estimates them to be about 16% of the total (Statista 2021).

The impact on employment will be extraordinary. More and more studies list occupations that will disappear or profoundly change in the coming years. For Carl Benedikt Frey and Michael Osborne (2013) of Oxford University, 47% of jobs in the US are at high risk of automation over the next two decades, 19% are at medium risk, and only a third is relatively safe. The think tank Bruegel (2014) estimates that more than 50% of workers in major European countries are at risk. According to Nomura Research Institute (2015), by 2035 half of the jobs in Japan could be carried out by robots. In Italy, consulting firm Ambrosetti (2017) estimates that about 15% of employees will be at risk of replacement in the next fifteen years.

Rather than looking at the professions at risk of being replaced by machines, the OECD (2019) focuses on how the tasks of the individual worker change when introducing a new technology. This approach is based on the fact that automation more often replaces tasks rather than entire jobs. Therefore, more than job *destruction* the real challenge is job *transformation*. Machines will make certain skills obsolete, de-qualifying them, and will require workers to be retrained in order to perform other tasks more productively. In this scenario, the share of jobs at high risk of automation (those in which more than 70% of tasks can be replaced) is only 14%. However, another 31.6%—although not disappearing—is at high risk because it will undergo profound changes (having between 50 and 70% of the replaceable tasks).[6] Incidentally, it should be noted that the fact that it is technically possible to replace people with machines to perform certain jobs does not necessarily mean it is economically advantageous to do so. At least not immediately.

The Challenge to Intellectual Work

In recent decades, technological innovations have generally led to the loss of low-to-medium wage jobs that required limited levels of education. Today, technology is undermining occupations with medium to high wages and high skill levels.

In the past, the arrival of automation in factories prompted advanced economies to reposition themselves, focusing on more complex manufacturing and services, creating new higher value-added employment. Similarly, the spread of personal computers and software made many low-skilled jobs obsolete and prompted the development of new higher competences.

---

[6] For Italy, jobs at high risk of automation and at risk of substantial change are 15.2% and 35.5%, respectively.

Today, the situation is different. The challenge of automation is no longer limited to manual work and repetitive activities and instead threatens intellectual work and specialized functions. Many professions with medium–high skill level are under threat and in danger of being replaced or greatly reduced in size. It should be noted that replacing humans in performing clerical tasks with new technologies—such as AI—presents fewer difficulties than automating blue-collar jobs. This is because handling information and data is easier than dealing with the physical world and, in addition, clerical work is usually not as "real-time" as blue-collar work.

New technologies are increasingly used in sectors that are human capital intensive. In medicine, AI is used to carry out complex tasks of diagnosis and prevention. In business, machines with ever-increasing cognitive capabilities are undermining some managerial positions. In the financial sector, many professions are being replaced by software that provides advice to clients and makes decisions based on algorithms. Translators and interpreters are experiencing increasing competition from ad hoc software. The same happens in the legal field, for drafting contracts, analysing documents, searching for precedents and referring to judgements. AI is changing the job of journalists and e-learning that of teachers. Wireless applications and AR are replacing traditional tourist guides, both printed and in person.

The recursive nature of some of the new technologies poses a further threat to professions with a high intellectual content. There are already robots capable of reprogramming or updating themselves, machines that improve their performance over time based on experience and self-learning. According Swedish philosopher Nick Bostrom of Oxford University (2018), this recursive nature may allow machines to reach a level of superintelligence that would pose "a greater threat to human existence than climate change".

Technological innovations will shake up the labour market as never before. Machines with increasing mobility, sensory perception, cognitive skills and language processing will threaten not only jobs in manufacturing and repetitive services, but also some highly intellectual professions. In addition to blue-collar and white-collar workers, also doctors, lawyers, journalists, traders and managers are at risk of being seriously affected.

Technological Revolution and Globalization: An Unprecedented Combination

Another important new element to consider is the combined effect of globalization and technological innovation.

In the 1980s and 1990s, the offshoring of much industrial production made many jobs redundant in advanced economies, which shifted their focus to more complex manufacturing and services. The new jobs were often more value-added than those lost. Today, the combination of technology and globalization is affecting the jobs of the knowledge economy: creating extraordinary opportunities but also putting them at risk. If in the past entire factories and industrial operations were relocated, today it's even easier to offshore activities such as design of software, production of content and supply of services.

Some of the largest software companies, such as Microsoft, Oracle, SAP and Alcatel, have long since transferred much of their product development to countries offering high levels of technical and scientific education and low labour costs. Bangalore, the Indian Silicon Valley located in the state of Karnataka, is home to giants such as Infosys, Wipro and Mindtree and is one of the world's largest IT districts. This trend is the result of globalization, which allows activities to be moved to countries that offer lower labour costs and greater flexibility. But it is also the consequence of technological innovations that make it possible to work remotely, communicate and transmit data easily and at limited costs.

A similar trend is underway for some services. Telemedicine makes it possible to treat patients remotely, even from one country to another. A patient in the United States who has to undergo an X-ray, CT scan, ultrasound or other tests may go to a clinic where a nurse administers the examination. The results are transmitted to India or Pakistan and analysed by a local doctor—less expensive than his American colleagues—who produces the report in excellent English. The prescription is forwarded in real time to the pharmacy in the United States and the drug delivered directly to the patient's home. As a result, the patient benefits because he receives a good service at a lower cost and the US lab reduces costs and makes a higher margin. However, from the point of view of employment, there is a reallocation between countries. In the United States, a highly skilled job, the doctor's, is eliminated and only those with less added value, such as the nurse and the medicine courier, remain. In India or Pakistan, there is a new doctor's job, which in turn stimulates the creation of new lower-paid jobs related to services needed by the doctor (e.g. food delivery, dry cleaning, house cleaning, grass mowing services).

Another interesting example is the increasing use by companies of software platforms for the management of product life cycles. These are systems that integrate data, processes, business systems and people located in different places, with the aim of making a new product. An interesting example is that of sports shoe manufacturers, such as Adidas, Nike and Lotto. The physical production of the shoe takes place in a factory. However, other phases of the product creation—such as idea development, design, choice of materials and colours, marketing tests—are managed using a common software platform to which hundreds of people physically located in different parts of the world are connected and contribute. A product lifecycle management (PLM) platform allows many distant people to work together: it records all inputs, regulates work times, sets deadlines and shares the work in progress as appropriate.

The use of PLM software is also widespread in the automotive and aerospace sectors, in shipbuilding, transport and electronics. Companies have obvious advantages in terms of work coordination and efficiency, project tracking, control and continuity (in case of staff turnover). Most importantly, they can attract and hire highly skilled workers, regardless of their geographical location. The use of PLM software is more than an IT solution: it is a business strategy.

At a more macrolevel, an important consequence of the combination of globalization and technological innovations is that attractive territories become hubs hosting qualified workers, who offer their services remotely, while less competitive areas lose traditional jobs and are not able to create new employment.

Telemedicine and software platforms are just two examples of the impact technological progress may have in a global environment. The higher mobility of intellectual labour will put local territories in fierce competition with each other to attract economic activities and employment. There will be winners and losers. The result can be disruptive for less attractive economies as they risk to lose jobs even in the service sector (which, being very local, has traditionally been protected by globalization, or at least less penalized than manufacturing).

Detachment Between Presence and Location

The detachment between presence and location is one of the main consequences of the success of digital technologies. This phenomenon is unprecedented and is profoundly changing human work and life.[7]

Until recently, the location of an economic activity and the physical presence of the people involved (workers and customers) have gone hand in hand. In order to perform their job, farmers had to go to the fields, workers to

---

[7] For Floridi (2014, 2019), one of the main characteristics of the digital era is precisely the "ability to attach and detach a large part of the elements we have inherited from modern culture".

a factory and clerks to an office. Similarly, a customer would physically go to a bookstore to buy a book and to a bank to deposit a check. In the digital economy, automated tractors and drones, personal computers and smartphones, e-commerce platforms and online banking, make it possible to operate remotely, thus splitting physical presence and location.

The trend is increasingly evident and it has been accelerated by the recent pandemic. Many physical locations of bank branches, travel agencies and commercial businesses are closing. Uber has "detached" the car service from the vehicles, Airbnb the hospitality service from the hotel, smart working and homeworking the worker from the office, telemedicine the patient from the doctor and both of them from the clinic. There are also some interesting countertrend attempts to reunite presence and location, for example the opening of coffee shops inside bookstores.

As Floridi (2014, 2019) noted, a revolutionary consequence of this possibility of splitting presence and location is that humans, after a very long period in which space was used to manage time (think of the importance of the clock), can now use time to manage space. This is possible because with digital transformation and the access to broadband networks, latency—which in computer science and telecommunications is the time interval between the moment when an input is sent and the moment when its output is available—tends to zero. Thus, it is possible to interact in real time with places and people that are physically located on the other side of the world.

This phenomenon upsets established dynamics of social and economic interaction. And it also disrupts the labour market.

New Geography of Work: "Open" Countries Win

In many countries, there is a growing sentiment that introducing tariffs on goods and strong restrictions on immigration are useful (and necessary) actions to protect employment. Restricted markets and closed borders may protect traditional jobs, at least in the short term. However, this is certainly not the case for professions with high added value, which in the new geography of work are concentrated in "open" countries and territories: those that offer good infrastructure and a high quality of life, but also flexibility, diversity, creativity and circulation of ideas. It is not by chance that all of the above are fundamental ingredients of innovation.

In the short run, a tightening of trade and immigration policies can benefit employment and GDP. In the longer term, policies of rising tariffs, customs barriers and restricted markets are likely to lead to a general decline in trade, and thus also in wealth creation. Similarly, restrictive immigration policies diminish a country's appeal to people and investment.

In addition to generating backlash and having negative side effects, these policies are short-sighted because they take no account whatsoever of the technological revolution. Most of the workers they are trying to protect today will soon be replaced by robots, software and AI. Neither customs duties nor quotas on immigration can stop the rise of technology. And they cannot avoid the combined effect of technology and globalization nor the growing disconnect between presence and location, both of which increase international mobility of intellectual labour. This particularly concerns professions with a high level of creativity and high added value, which are concentrated in the most attractive and innovative areas. And in those areas they also generate lower-paid jobs in the local services market.

The geographical distribution of new jobs is therefore a key factor for employment. In a global economy, cities, territories and countries compete with each other to attract both financial and human capital. Only those who are successful can benefit from the enlargement of markets resulting from globalization and have a positive impact on employment. Moreover, the gap between winning and losing territories is widening over time. Areas with talented people are innovative and grow rapidly, attracting further human capital and triggering a virtuous circle. Conversely, those that are unattractive risk decline.

The growing economic gap between territories clearly emerges in a 2018 Brookings Institution paper, which illustrates why innovative companies and talented people tend to concentrate in urban centres. Companies have access to greater and better infrastructure and resources; people have the opportunity to have their skills better valued. The study compares an urban and a rural area in the United States. The first, made up of fifty-three cities with more than a million people, has produced more than three-quarters of the job growth since the 2008 crisis. The second, made up of small and medium-sized towns, shows a much slower growth. In fact, since 2010 more than 200 thousand rural towns and micro-communities have had negative growth rates.

The shift from a production economy to a knowledge economy—which is based on know-how and innovation—is profoundly changing the labour market. It generates enormous disparities between territories, in terms of employment and income but also in terms of schooling, family stability and life expectancy.

More tariffs and fewer entry visas may protect non-innovative industries and traditional jobs in the short term. But they cannot stop the repercussions of technological innovation.

In order for territories to play a leading role in the new geography of work, it is crucial that they attract talents whose activities create wealth and employment. And to do so they need to be "open". That means being open-minded, but also having open borders (for talent, trade and investment) and free markets (for goods, services, labour and capital).[8]

Polarization of the Labour Market and Increasing Wage Inequality

The spread of technological innovation is creating a dichotomy in the labour market—widening the gap between those who know how to use the new technology and those who do not—with consequent polarization of incomes. A study conducted by Matthew Slaughter and Phillip Swagel for the International Monetary Fund (1997) confirms that the introduction of technology is leading to a scenario where workers with higher skills are rewarded with better pay while less skilled ones are penalized.

The jobs surviving to the rise of technology and automation are on opposite sides of a metaphorical pyramid. At the top, new high value-added positions are emerging: they require technical knowledge, creativity, judgement and decision-making skills. At the bottom, there is an increasing number of people doing simple jobs: they do not require special skills nor education, but rather physical proximity and personal contact (and for this reason cannot be automated). These are mainly personal services, such as care for the elderly, children, the sick and the disabled,[9] but also include job such as barbers, manicurists, personal trainers and shoe shiners. In addition, there are jobs for which automation would be difficult or economically unviable. These include carpenters, electricians, plumbers, dog walkers and people who supervise automated activities (such as supermarkets' cash registers and check-outs, airport baggage claim desks, and ATMs). The end result is a growth in

---

[8] Dani Rodrik has studied in depth the consequences of globalization. In *The Globalization Paradox* (2011), the Harvard University economist argues that it is not possible to simultaneously pursue democracy, national self-determination and economic globalization. Rodrik argues that a globalized economy (globalization), the ability of governments to make decisions (national sovereignty) and the correspondence between those decisions and majority preferences (democracy) are compatible only two by two, but not all three together.

[9] ILO (International Labour Organization) (2018) estimates for the period 2015–2030 a global growth of 269 million people employed in this type of personal services.

demand of two opposite types of professions: on the one hand the creative and managerial jobs, that tend to be enhanced by technology, and on the other hand the "simple" jobs, that are not threatened by technology. The "middle" jobs are increasingly performed by machines.

Bank of Italy Governor Ignazio Visco (2015) underlines how "the rapid advancement of digital technologies is profoundly segmenting the workforce: on the one hand a highly qualified elite, estimated at around one tenth of the American population, which works alongside the new technologies and receives high incomes; on the other hand, the remaining population, less educated, which faces increased employment difficulties and stagnant or decreasing salaries".[10]

The segmentation of the labour market is reflected in a strong increase in wage inequalities. OECD data (2019) shows that in the last twenty years the average wage growth has been higher than that of the median wage. This confirms the crisis of the middle class. At the top, there is what American economist Tyler Cowen calls—in his essay aptly titled *Average Is Over* (2013)—the *technological oligarchy*. At the bottom, there are those that former Secretary of Labour in the Clinton administration Robert Reich defines—in his book *The Work of Nations* (1992)—as the *in-person servers*. Reich thinks that they "are, yes, protected from the effects of technological innovation and from those of planetary competition due to the particular nature of the service they offer, but they suffer and are destined to suffer more and more from the competition of unqualified workers expelled from the system of companies".

For Stefano Scarpetta (2017) of the OECD "the real point is not which jobs will emerge and which ones will disappear, but how much inequality will be produced by innovation. The gap will be between those who are able to access new hi-tech job opportunities with high pay and career prospects and those - the majority - who are forced to fall back on low-skill jobs".

In this regard, Larry Summers (2014) criticizes Thomas Piketty for not giving sufficient relevance—in his *Capital in the 21st Century* (2014)—to the role of technology among the causes of growing inequality. Summers believes that in the future the central aspect of the "connecting capital accumulation and inequality will not be Piketty's tale of amassing fortunes [but rather] the

---

[10] According to Visco (2015), segmentation of the workforce occurs in two stages. First there is a *skill-biased technical change* that involves the replacement of workers with others who more qualified in order to adapt to changes in production techniques. Then—in the face of increasing automation and the "unbundling" of production phases—a *task-biased technical change* emerges, causing the displacement of workers based on the degree of repetitiveness of their tasks rather than their skills and competences.

devastating consequences of robots, 3D printing, AI, and the like for those who perform routine tasks".

Autor (2014) is less pessimistic: while he acknowledges the growing polarization of the labour market, he considers it a transition shock because "when employees update their training and skills and employers are able to create job opportunities from these new technologies, technological unemployment could become employment". In addition, Autor believes the loss of middle-class jobs could be at least partly compensated by the need for professionals who perform routine tasks but with a certain degree of flexibility and personal interaction. There will be room for coaching experts, therapists, trainers, medical staff, teachers, as long as they learn to use technology to improve the quality and efficiency of performance.

On the same page is Katz (2008), who believes that some of the simple occupations—those that by their nature make the presence of a human being indispensable—could become a lifeline for the middle class. According to Katz, people who lose their jobs due to major changes tend to rediscover—and reinvent—old professions, thus creating new jobs. The opportunity for these "new artisans" is to transform— leveraging culture, education and interpersonal skills—traditionally low-paid trades into well-paid economic activities. While technological progress transforms almost everything into commodities (products and services offered in large quantities at low prices), the offer of the "new artisans" is unique and non-standardizable, capable of earning a price premium. So, for example, whoever was making sandwiches can make them gourmet, whoever was making ice cream can make it organic, pastry chefs can offer products for celiacs. Similarly, carpenters, electricians and plumbers can use innovative and eco-sustainable materials and tools. Crafts such as shoemaking, baking and tailoring are reappearing. There is an increase in the number of artisans who make handmade and made-to-measure objects, especially clothing, footwear, accessories and jewellery. The entire maintenance and repair chain is growing.[11]

In disagreement with the employment potential of local craftsmanship is Enrico Moretti (2012), of the University of Berkeley. Moretti believes that this craftsmanship "is something very nice but it can't act as an engine for employment growth".[12] Handicrafts will not be able to make a difference for lack of critical mass and because "these activities are rather the result of wealth produced in some other sector". It is true that the demand for goods and

---

[11] Some of the growing "new artisan" jobs are exterminator, urban farmer, object repairer, natural cosmetics manufacturer, caregiver for people with dementia, food waste collector.

[12] Moretti refers to traditional craftsmanship but his considerations are extendable to many of Katz's "new artisan" trades.

services from the economic oligarchy will stimulate the rise of new activities and support employment and wages of less educated workers.[13] However, while helping overall employment this will not prevent an exacerbation of polarization in incomes.

Autor's considerations on transitions shocks, Katz's studies on the *New Artisan Economy* (2008) and Moretti's analysis on the employment indirectly generated by hi-tech jobs, are all very insightful. However, how strong will the shock be? How long will the transition be? And will either the new artisan economy or the employment indirectly generated by the new rich be robust enough to sustain the middle class?

Decrease in the Value Placed on Work

An important difference from the past is the growing tendency to place less value on work.

In addition to the decoupling of employment from productivity—which explains the jobless growth—there is also a trend of decoupling of wages from the train of economic progress. OECD data shows that in the last twenty years average wages have not kept pace with labour productivity. That means that an increasing share of productivity gains has gone to profits and rents and a decreasing portion to labour.

The fall in wages can in part be attributed to globalization, which has increased offshoring, and to the recent economic crisis, which has led labour supply to exceed demand. Another factor is the change over time in the political-contractual balance between workers and companies: negotiating capacity of the former has decreased while market power of the latter has increased. However, an important role in this trend is played by technology: both because by replacing workers it puts downward pressure on their wages and because it is the main cause of polarization in the labour market.

Technology stimulates productivity growth, and therefore value creation, but this does not necessarily translate into higher wages. Most of the greater wealth produced is transferred to consumers, through the reduction of prices, and is destined to the remuneration of the capital invested in machines. An exception is innovative products and services, not easily replicable because they are the result of creative work. Moretti uses the example of the iPhone to explain that in these cases "the competitive advantage that comes from

---

[13] In *The New Geography of Jobs* (2012), Moretti shows that in certain U.S. metropolitan areas for every new hi-tech job, there are five new low-education jobs—such as yoga classes, home meal delivery and laundry services—that are generated to meet new needs.

them allows us to extract more value from global consumer markets: a sort of dividend that for about one-third goes to (creative) labour and the remaining two-thirds remunerates invested capital".

Wage compression is also partially explained by an entirely new phenomenon, closely related to the nature of digital technologies. In contrast to Ricardo's basic idea of diminishing returns, which applies to the industrial world, in the digital economy returns tend to be increasing: an additional investment generates a more than proportional benefit. In the knowledge economy, productivity can grow faster than output, and therefore, marginal costs are decreasing and tend to zero.

A few examples may be helpful to better understand this point. There are no additional costs in selling a software application to an extra customer, just as it costs nothing to extend an online newspaper subscription to new subscribers, to increase the number of users of an online course or to allow more people to download films or music on demand. The dynamics of the information economy are very different from those of physical goods. In the physical world, producing, reproducing, archiving and transferring are all activities that generate costs in terms of both time and money. In the immaterial world on the other hand, although the production of contents requires an initial investment of time and money, the marginal costs of reproduction, archive and transfer are close to zero.

Decreasing marginal costs tend to drive down the prices at which digital products and services are offered, fuelling the growth of an economy that can be considered almost entirely "free" (the trend is only partly slowed by intellectual property laws). This produces two main consequences: first, value creation can be very quick, as evidenced by the enormous and rapid growth of several multinationals in the digital economy; second, if prices tend to zero, so will profits and wages. This is the basis for Jeremy Rifkin's interesting thesis (2014) that technological progress will generate a free economy and, consequently, will lead to the end of work.

The sharing economy also contributes to the declining value placed on labour. Most of the value produced by the sharing economy goes to the consumer, through lower prices, and to the entrepreneur who owns the platform, as a return on the investment. The value placed on work tends to decrease mainly because the sharing economy puts those who perform a certain service professionally in competition with those who are willing to offer the same service—in person or online (e.g. using crowd working platforms)—in an amateur and occasional way. This creates a race to the bottom that inevitably squeezes wages.

Crisis of the Man-Work Relationship

Another important change that is altering the dynamics of labour market concerns the relationship between man and his work, which seems to have broken down.

In many ancient civilizations, work was left to slaves and was not one of the requirements of citizenship. On the contrary, in modern culture work is central: it is a source of sustenance, dignity and personal fulfilment. Work also gives people an identity and is closely linked to the social dimension of an individual.

The nature and the role of work are profoundly changing. First of all, there is more and more talk of "jobs", in the plural form. This is because individuals tend to have several jobs throughout their professional lives, even several jobs at the same time. Work is no longer a lifelong activity. Part-time work is growing while full-time jobs are declining as a percentage of the labour market. Working relationships are often precarious and discontinuous.

In addition, there is a growing number of people who are dissatisfied with their work, do not identify with it or even have the perception that it is useless. In this regard, two quotes seem to be more relevant than ever. Italian entrepreneur and intellectual Adriano Olivetti (2013) notes that "work should be a great joy and yet for many it is still a torment: the torment of not having it, the torment of doing work that is not useful, that does not serve a noble purpose". The Polish philosopher Zygmunt Bauman in *Work, Consumerism and New Poverty* (2007), regrets that work "rich in gratifying experiences, which develops one's personality and gives meaning to one's life, a supreme value, a source of pride and self-esteem, of respect or notoriety, work understood, in short, as a vocation, has become the privilege of the few".

The consequence is that less and less of a person's identity is represented by their work. This is a difficult change to manage, and it can be a source of anxiety and bewilderment. Because man comes from centuries of a clear identity in society, identity that is often closely linked to his work. Today, technological innovations are radically changing production processes and revolutionizing employment: many jobs will be abolished and new ones will be created. Regardless of the final employment balance, this process has a profound effect on identity. Some professions with a strong and defined identity will disappear. It is the case of factory workers, truck drivers and bankers. Of course, other occupations are emerging—such as data scientists, algorithm trainers, revenue managers and technical recruiters, but also urban farmers, dog walkers and personal trainers—but their identities are still undefined, they are "under construction".

The traditional man-work relationship is going through a crisis. In some cases, work is still a means of ensuring sustenance (but not much more than that); in others even this function has been weakened. It almost seems as if work were no longer necessary to men. Technological development is not the only cause of this change but it certainly is contributing to it. Companies seem to want to replace human capital with physical capital as much as possible by investing in technology. The need for human work seems to be limited only to creative or top management roles.

The deterioration of the man-work relationship is dangerous because it could prevent humans to react to the rise of machines and rather push them to choose to retreat. Either out of fear or laziness. The risk is real. If man no longer recognizes himself in his own work nor does he need it for sustenance, then the "surrender" of mankind to robots risks to be total.[14]

Sense of Uncertainty, Social Anxiety and Political Distrust

The challenge triggered by technological change is complex also due to a widespread and growing sense of uncertainty. There is economic uncertainty, but there is also social anxiety, political distrust and ethical confusion.

As Magatti (2017) well illustrates, "the great historical frames of reference have progressively been exhausted. Religion [...] oscillates between fundamentalist impulses and aspirations of relaunching [...]. Politics is going through a very difficult moment in an interconnected world, in which the effects of an action in any part of the planet can be directly reflected on what happens in another".

Technology contributes to these trends: it fosters individualism and increases the risk of authority erosion. Decision-making mechanisms are changing radically. Social networks favour a process of disintermediation that significantly undermines the authority of intermediate bodies, which are often decisive in decision-making processes and fundamental to the well-functioning of democratic systems. The spread of information in real time at

---

[14] The temptation to delegate thinking skills to machines is big. The risk is that man may become slow, lazy, incomplete, inadequate and de-qualified. In his *L'uomo col cervello in tasca* (2019) (*The Man with the Brain in His Pocket*), the psychiatrist Vittorino Andreoli observes that the digital era is shaping a hybrid individual and he emphasizes the danger that the "second brain"—the digital one—takes over from the human one.

a global level and the strong interconnection between countries make decisions more complex and their consequences more unpredictable. The focus is increasingly on short-term objectives, while the political challenges to be faced require a long-term vision. Sometimes, the democratic model itself is questioned because it is not always considered capable of guaranteeing long-term political stability and vision.

For Bauman (2007), the uncertainty that characterizes the postmodern society (which the Polish philosopher famously defines as *liquid*) and the consequent discomfort of man are closely linked to technological progress that has "made mass work increasingly useless in relation to the volume of production" and has essentially transformed postmodern man from producer to consumer, from "supplier of goods to seeker of pleasures and sensations".

The high speed of technological progress further adds to the existing confusion and anxiety. The first industrial revolution had opened a process that lasted several centuries. During the course of that very long period, factories were built and urbanization increased, transport and mobility were organized, the way of thinking and relating to other people changed, a society was shaped, a role of work was defined, and a certain identity of man was developed. Today, an equally radical transformation is compressed into a very short time.

Other sources of the current social and economic insecurity are the strong demographic trends, the increasing diversity and multiculturalism, the crisis of the role of the family.

To make matters worse, the two recent economic crises—the one triggered by the subprime mortgage crisis in 2007–2008 and the one started by the spread of COVID-19 in 2020—have highlighted some critical aspects of the market economy and the capitalist system.

Globalization has led to some excesses. Emerging countries entered a formidable growth race, which on the one hand has improved people's quality of life and workers' average income but on the other hand has created social tensions and sometimes encouraged authoritarian political turns. In Europe and the United States, inequality has increased and the middle class has weakened. This has facilitated the rise of a sovereignist vision with repercussions on international trade, economic and monetary policies. Finally, the rapid and deadly spread of coronavirus around the world has revealed the fragility of global supply chains.

There are two other aspects—specific to technological innovations—that characterize what English poet Wystan Hugh Auden (1994) calls the "age of anxiety". The first is the uncertainty about the ethical consequences of the technological revolution. Innovations have often raised ethical issues throughout the course of history, but the development of robots, drones and unmanned cars, AI and ML, biotechnology and genetic engineering, poses some unprecedented questions and challenges. The second aspect is the great difficulty—perhaps greater than in the past—of predicting the limit of the technological development that is currently underway.

Uncertainty and a general sense of bewilderment make it more difficult to navigate the impact of innovations on the labour market.

Inadequate Leadership and Poor Vision

Innovation, globalization and more recently the pandemic are bringing about major changes to the labour market. The economic, social and political consequences could be disruptive. However, in most countries, the leadership does not seem to be too concerned about it. Many trade associations are not considering this a priority issue. Many entrepreneurs are focused on short-term goals and lack the foresight—and sometimes the financial resources—to set up long-term strategies. Labour unions, with a few minor exceptions, do not seem to be able to act with the necessary speed and flexibility. Politicians often lack both the intention of facing the challenge and the skills to do so.

The current scenario is certainly very complex and there is no easy way to deal with it. However, as it is often the case, successful strategies are also a matter of people. In the past, for example, periods of great transition, such as industrial revolutions and major economic downturns, have been managed by statesmen of the calibre of Bismarck in Germany, Gladstone and Disraeli in the United Kingdom, Wilson and the two Roosevelts in the United States. All leaders with a long-term vision who were able to make bold decisions. The general feeling today is that these characteristics are rare in the leadership of many countries.

* * *

This is not the first time that innovations disrupt the labour market. Just as in 1831 silk weavers destroyed looms because they feared losing their jobs, in 2015 taxi drivers set fire to Uber's cars in Paris, and in 2019 dockworkers went on strike against increasing automation of logistics giant Maersk in Los Angeles.

History has shown that innovation—even though it replaces humans in various occupations—gives rise to new needs, activities and professions with greater added value. In the past, the new professional figures have compensated for job cuts and the growth in productivity has facilitated the increase in average wages. Today, as in the past, new jobs are emerging. Nonetheless, it cannot be taken for granted that they will be sufficient to compensate—in terms quantity and quality—for those lost.

The only certainty is that the transition period will be long and the competition between territories fierce. And that there will be winners and losers. For the most part, those taking on new jobs will not be the same workers who have lost the old occupations, and the territories where the new employment emerges will not necessarily be the same ones that have lost the traditional jobs. Moreover, the high speed of change will give losers (people and territories) little time to adapt. This is likely to lead to further increases in inequality, with consequent social tensions and political repercussions, and to a weaker aggregate demand, with negative effects on growth.

In such a scenario, it is crucial to identify possible solutions to face the challenge, managing the transition and trying to seize the opportunities.

Bibliography

D. Acemoğlu, P. Restrepo, *Robots and Jobs: Evidence from US Labor Markets*, "NBER Working Papers", No. 23285, March 2017.

D. Acemoğlu, P. Restrepo, *The Race Between Machine and Man: Implications of Technology for Growth, Factor Shares and Employment*, "NBER Working Paper", No. 22252, 2016.

D. Acemoğlu, G. Gancia, F. Zilibotti, *Competing Engines of Growth: Innovation and Standardization*, "Journal of Economic Theory", 147, no. 2, pp. 570–601, 2010.

L. Addati et al., *Care Work and Care Jobs for the Future of Decent Work*, ILO-International Labour Organization, 28 June 2018.

Ambrosetti Club, *Tecnologia e Lavoro: Governare il Cambiamento*, 2017.

V. Andreoli, *L'uomo col cervello in tasca*, Solferino, Milano 2019.

W. B. Arthur, *The Nature of Technology: What It Is and How It Evolves*, Simon and Schuster, New York 2009.

W. B. Arthur, *The Second Economy*, McKinsey Quarterly, 1 October 2011.

W. H. Auden, *The Age of Anxiety*, edited by V. Magrelli, Il Nuovo Melangolo, Genoa 1994.

D. Autor, *Skills, Education and the Rise of Earnings Inequality Among the "Other 99 Percent"*, "Science", 344, no. 6186, pp. 843–850, 2014.

D. Autor, D. Dorn, *The Growth of Low Skill Service Jobs and the Polarization of the U.S. Labor Market*, "American Economic Review", 103, no. 5, pp. 1553–1597, 2013.

D. Autor, F. Levy, R. J. Murnane, *The Skill Content of Recent Technological Change: An Empirical Exploration*, "The Quarterly Journal of Economics", 118, no. 4, pp. 1279–1333, 2003.

Z. Bauman, *Lavoro, consumismo e nuove povertà*, Città Aperta, Enna 2007.

N. Bostrom, *Superintelligenza*, Bollati Boringhieri, Turin 2018.

J. Bowles, *The Computerisation of European Jobs*, "Bruegel", July 2014.

E. Brynjolfsson, A. McAfee, *Race Against the Machine*, Digital Frontier Press, Lexington 2011.

E. Brynjolfsson, A. McAfee, *The Second Machine Age: Work, Progress, and Prosperity in a Time of Brilliant Technologies*, W. W. Norton, 2014

J. Bughin et al., *"Tech for Good": Using Technology to Smooth Disruption and Improve Well-Being*, McKinsey Global Institute, 2019.

T. Cowen, *Average Is Over: Powering America Beyond the Age of the Great Stagnation*, Penguin, London 2013.

The Rise of the Superstars, "The Economist", 17 September 2016.

Excelsior Report, Unioncamere and Anpal, Rome 2020.

L. Floridi, *The Fourth Revolution*, Oxford University Press, Oxford 2014.

L. Floridi, *Convegno AGI—Avvocati Giuslavoristi Italiani "Diritto al lavoro"*, Verona, 4 October 2019.

C. B. Frey, M. Osborne, *The Future of Employment: How Susceptible Are Jobs to Computerization?*, Oxford Martin University, Oxford 2013.

C. Goldin, L. Katz, *The Race Between Education and Technology*, Harvard University Press, Cambridge, MA 2008.

R. Heilbroner quoted in D. Akst, *What Can We Learn From Past Anxiety Over Automation?*, "Wilson Quarterly", 2013.

C. Hendrickson, M. Muro, W. A. Galston, *Countering the Geography of Discontent: Strategies for Left-Behind Places*, Brookings Institution, November 2018.

L. Karabarbounis, B. Neiman, *The Global Decline of the Labor Share*, "The Quarterly Journal of Economics", 129, 2014.

J. M. Keynes, *Economic Possibilities for Our Grandchildren*, Lecture in Madrid, 1930.

J. M. Keynes, "Economic Possibilities for Our Grandchildren", in *Essays in Persuasion*, Norton & Co., New York 1930.

S. Krause, *Alexa Can Do Many Things But Won't Call 911*, "The Wall Street Journal", 6 November 2018.

W. Leontief, *Machines and Man*, "Scientific American", 1952.

M. Magatti, *Cambio di paradigma*, Feltrinelli, Milano 2017.

M. Magnani, *I robot minacciano i paesi emergenti*, "IlSole24Ore", 1 October 2017.

M. Magnani, *Globalizzazione e tecnologia: ora i robot insidiano anche le professioni*, "IlSole24Ore", 3 December 2017.

M. Magnani, *Mestieri di qualità richiedono mercati aperti*, "IlSole24Ore", 10 January 2019.

J. E. Meade, *Efficiency, Equality and the Ownership of Property*, George Allen & Unwin, London 1964.

E. Moretti, *The New Geography of Jobs*, Mariner Books, Boston 2012.

Nomura Research Institute report, 2015.

OECD, *The Future of the Work*, Employment Outlook, Paris 2019.

A. Olivetti, *Il mondo che nasce. Dieci scritti per la cultura, la politica, la società*, edited by A. Saibene, Edizioni di Comunità, Ivrea 2013.

T. Piketty, *Capital in the Twenty-First Century*, Harvard University Press, Cambridge 2014.

R. Reich, *The Work of Nations Preparing Ourselves for 21st Century Capitalism*, Alfred A. Knopf, New York 1992.

D. Ricardo, "On Machinery", in *On the Principles of Political Economy and Taxation*, John Murray, London 1821.

J. Rifkin, *La società a costo marginale zero*, Mondadori, Milano 2014.

D. Rodrik, *The Globalization Paradox: Democracy and the Future of the World Economy*, W. W. Norton, New York 2011.

J. D. Sachs, L. J. Kotlikoff, *Smart Machines and Long-Term Misery*, "NBER Working Papers", No. 18629, 2012.

S. Scarpetta, *OECD Lecture at the Jobless Society Forum*, Fondazione Feltrinelli, Milan 2017.

M. J. Slaugher, P. Swagel, *Effect of Globalization on Wages in the Advanced Economies*, IMF, April 1997.

Statista Research Department, *Facebook—Statistics & Facts*, Statista, 5 February 2021, https://www.statista.com/topics/751/facebook/

L. Summers, *The Inequality Puzzle: Piketty Book Review*, "DEMOCRACY: A Journal of Ideas", no. 32, Spring 2014.

I. Visco, *Come affrontare il cambiamento: sfide per il lavoro*, Note del Governatore in Giornate del Lavoro della CGIL, Firenze, 13 giugno 2015.

World Economic Forum, *The Future of Jobs*, Geneva 2016.

6

Many Proposals, Few Resources: Difficult Choices for the Future of Labour

An unprecedented wave of innovation is sweeping through the world of work. There are different views on how to deal with it. According to the most optimistic one, technological innovation will open new cycles of development with positive consequences on employment. This has happened on other similar occasions in history. In the more pessimistic view, human labour will be largely replaced by machines and the impact on employment will be negative.

In the first case, the transition will be long and complex and the main challenge is to manage it in the best possible way across all sectors and professions. The difficulty is to integrate new technologies into the economy and society quickly while at the same time causing as little trauma as possible, seizing the new opportunities for economic and employment growth, and ensuring that the benefits are available to as many people as possible. In this case, the education system, training programmes and redistribution mechanisms play a crucial role. The second scenario is more complex and several alternative paths emerge. Some recommend hindering and slowing down technology. However, Ricardo (1821) had already warned that the outcome of Luddite approach is that progress—and growth and employment with it—is transferred abroad.[1]

Setting aside the possibility of stopping the rise of machines, what are the alternatives? There are those who believe it is inevitable (or even desirable)

---

[1] In some cases, such as AI or driverless cars, the diffusion of technology could be slowed down by the complexity of ethical choices.

© The Author(s), under exclusive license to Springer Nature
Switzerland AG 2022
M. Magnani, *Making the Global Economy Work for Everyone*,
https://doi.org/10.1007/978-3-030-92084-5_6

to delegate work to machines—in whole or in part—and to increase free time for humans. This means rethinking the function of work and people's lifestyle. In this case, humans have three possible alternatives: devoting themselves completely to idleness, reducing their working hours or offering their work for free. Such a radical change in the traditional relationship between humans and labour makes it necessary to identify alternative sources of income and it raises questions regarding the sustainability of the welfare system. Some of the possible answers are the introduction of universal basic income, guaranteed minimum income, negative tax and social dividend. The focus is on redistribution mechanisms and on identifying the necessary sources of financing.

At the other extreme, others argue that eliminating—or drastically reducing—human labour is a mistake, both socially and economically. This is because high level of unemployment may have consequences far wider than the mere loss of income. Therefore, the state should pursue full employment and guarantee everyone an occupation, regardless of the level of automation (and of the actual necessity of certain jobs). The implementation of the "job guarantee" requires very significant financial resources. However, in this scenario income from labour maintains a redistributive role and supports demand.

There is also a third path: accepting the challenge of an intelligent coexistence between human beings and machines. This can be pursued on two levels, which are not alternative to one another. At a macroeconomic level, coexistence may result in the division of labour between humans and machines: the rise of machines becomes an opportunity to invest massively in labour-intensive activities—such as education, cultural heritage, health and personal services—leaving those that require high capital intensity, such as most manufacturing, to technology. At the level of the individual profession, coexistence can be achieved through a close collaboration between humans and machines, harnessing technological innovations to improve human performance. In this scenario, technology provides human beings with the opportunity to focus on those tasks within each profession that generate added value. These are tasks based on skills that are difficult to mechanize, such as empathy, creativity, decision-making and interaction. Such a strategy requires re-evaluating the role of work and investing heavily in knowledge to make the best use of technology.

Many are the proposals and few are the resources to implement them. Hence, it is important to understand all the alternatives and their implications in order to make the right choices.

Work for Machines, Idleness (and Universal Basic Income) for Humans

In a nutshell, the idea is that production is entrusted to machines and human beings devote themselves to recreational, cultural or even idle activities.[2] By choice or by necessity. This raises the issue of finding sources of income alternative to labour, to give humans a means of sustenance and to support aggregate demand. A solution often put forward is the introduction of universal basic income.[3]

Universal basic income is a monetary payment distributed—starting at birth or at some other time—to all people with citizenship or residence regardless of their employment status and it can be combined with other income. It is therefore received by the unemployed but also by those who are employed. Historically, universal basic income was not conceived as an instrument strictly linked to employment, but rather it was designed to address situations of poverty by guaranteeing a minimum level of income and to enhance the status of citizenship or residency within a community.[4]

There are two main reasons for its introduction: justice and efficiency. Universal basic income helps to pursue a fair distribution of economic resources. It also allows for a more transparent and efficient redistribution compared to traditional welfare, which is often fragmented and sometimes discretionary. A part of economic theory supports the introduction of a universal basic income mainly to achieve efficiency and waste reduction (rather than fairness). Indeed, the guarantee of a minimum income allows individuals to make more efficient choices regarding their family, education, housing and employment. On the contrary, excessive inequalities in the distribution of wealth often lead to the search for benefits and clientelist privileges which result in a waste of resources. In short: limitation of inequalities tends

---

[2] The Greeks were the first to celebrate idleness (*scholé*), which was considered a gift of the gods and was associated to freedom because idleness is possible only if one does not depend on others. Work, on the other hand, was despised and linked to servile conditions. In Plato (*Republic*) the primacy of contemplation over work—which is considered a forced and unworthy activity for a free man—is evident. For Aristotle (*Politics*) "we need idleness"—and not work—"to develop virtues and political activities". Similarly, for the Romans *otium* was the time free from *negotia* (public affairs), and it was dedicated to domestic care or studies (school).

[3] Universal basic income (UBI) is sometimes also referred to as unconditional basic income or citizen's basic income. Experiments have been made at the local level in various countries, including Finland, The Netherlands, South Korea, Namibia, Kenya, Ukraine and India.

[4] One of the first ideas of universal basic income emerged in *Agrarian Justice* (1795) by Thomas Paine, one of the founding fathers of the United States of America. Faced with rampant poverty in France, Paine proposed a land tax to establish a fund that would provide all citizens with a substantial sum upon reaching the age of majority, followed by an annual payment from age fifty.

to reduce waste, therefore redistribution is not only a matter of justice but also of efficiency.

In recent years the debate on universal basic income has become topical again based on the belief that rising unemployment is a structural issue and not a cyclical one. This is due to the dual effect of globalization and automation. In this context, the main objective of universal basic income is to facilitate reintegration of unemployed workers into the labour market. To this end, it is generally regarded as a more effective means than unemployment benefits. In fact, benefits often are a disincentive for the recipients to look for a job because their payment stops when an occupation is found. This is not the case—at least in theory[5]—with universal basic income, which can be combined with other income and is not taxable.

In a machine-dominated economy—in which innovation is an engine of growth and a driver of prosperity but not a source of employment—universal basic income can be a tool to redistribute the wealth produced, provide an alternative means of human sustenance and stimulate aggregate demand.

The replacement of humans by machines and the concurrent introduction of universal basic income require a radical change in the current economic and social model. And it raises several critical points. First, the introduction of a source of income that is disconnected from labour transforms workers into simple citizen-consumers and goes against an anthropology of labour for which it is hard work that procures sustenance. In the Bible (Genesis 3,19) it is recalled that "by the sweat of thy face shalt thou eat bread". Moreover, for most people work is not only a means of generating income but it provides an identity and it carries a significant social value. As the sociologist Luciano Gallino (2015) well explains, "professionally qualified work, which is engaging, motivating and allows us to express ourselves, is a fundamental component of human identity".

A big challenge is how to finance universal basic income. Note that if universal income is conceived primarily as an instrument of justice and equity, then the decision is purely a political one. On the other hand, if limiting inequality is seen as a way to reduce waste and increase efficiency, then the decision has some economic implications. In this case, the costs of the introduction of basic income—although high—should be compared with benefits similar to those of other universalistic reforms, such as the public pension system, education and universal basic health care. Finally, in a scenario where most workers are replaced by machines, a criticality is also the sustainability of the welfare system.

---

[5] In practice, a universal basic income experiment conducted by the Finnish government in 2017–2018 did not show a significant increase in incentives among beneficiaries to seek new employment.

Work Less, Work for All

In the face of the unstoppable rise of machines, another possible reaction of humans is to try to distribute the remaining work. The idea is immediate and simple: reducing work hours to allow a larger number of people to be employed.

The risk of technological unemployment was also discussed in the 1930s by Keynes, who believed that within a century the available wealth would at least quadruple and the working week would be reduced to fifteen hours. In 1933, the U.S. Senate passed a bill reducing the working week to thirty hours with the objective of cutting unemployment and boosting consumption after the Great Depression of 1929.[6]

In the 1930s the issue emerged in Italy in a debate between the economist and future President of the Republic, Luigi Einaudi and the chairman of Fiat Giovanni Agnelli. Einaudi made a detailed reconstruction of this exchange of opinions in a book (1933). Agnelli argued for the necessity of reducing working hours to fight unemployment, "a frightening chain" that endangered demand.[7] In the highly standardized factory of the time workers were easily replaceable, therefore the reduction of working hours would probably have led to an increase in employment. Einaudi agreed that "in the long run unemployment must be eliminated" but he also argued that "technical unemployment is not a serious illness. It is a factor of growth, a fruit of vigour and health. It is a disease which doctors need not worry much about, because it cures itself". Einaudi referred to the fact that a certain rate of temporary unemployment can be determined by an increase in the productivity of companies, which is a positive factor for the competitiveness of an industry and the growth of the country. And, precisely to preserve competitiveness he was sceptical about reducing working hours.[8]

---

[6] In 1932, Senator Hugo Black (a Democrat representing Alabama) introduced the Thirty-Hour Work Week Bill—drafted by the American Federation of Labor with the expectation of creating 6 million jobs—to "prohibit, in interstate or foreign commerce, all goods produced by establishments where workers were employed more than five days a week or six hours a day". On 6 April 1933 the Senate passed the bill by a vote of 53–30. However, the bill remained in the House of Representatives committees for five years and when the Fair Labor Standard Act became law in 1938, the thirty-hour work week provision was not included.

[7] In the 1970s Giovanni Agnelli's grandson—often referred to as "Avvocato Gianni Agnelli"—was the Chairman of Fiat and as president of Confindustria (the main association representing manufacturing and service companies in Italy) defended similar arguments to those of his grandfather.

[8] As a young journalist at the end of the nineteenth century, Einaudi had followed the struggles of the Biella wool workers for the reduction of the working time (from sixteen to ten hours a day!) and in his reports he pointed out the risk that diminishing the working time could make companies of the Italian district less competitive than their foreign competitors, causing a capital flight.

The analytical weakness of the proposal stems from some underlying assumptions that are far from obvious. A first assumption is that the number of hours worked in the market is fixed and therefore a reduction of working hours of employed workers should be automatically compensated by new hires. In reality, the labour market is more complex and dynamic.

Secondly, the unemployed are not necessarily perfect substitutes for workers whose hours are reduced. This may be because they don't have the same skill set or because, even if they have the necessary skills for the job, they may not be willing to relocate for it, or may not be aware of all available work opportunities due to lack of information in the labour market.[9] In addition to these problems on the labour supply side, there are some other issues on the demand side. For example, labour costs do not necessarily decrease as the number of hours worked is reduced. On the contrary, hourly wages may increase slightly. There are several reasons for this. One is the higher incidence of fixed costs, which are independent of the number of hours worked. Another reason is that the employer may decide to use more expensive—but also more flexible—overtime to make up for the reduced availability of labour. In these cases, the rise in labour costs does not leave sufficient resources to compensate for the reduction in hours worked with new hires. Another possible consequence is that the reduction in working time encourages organizational improvements and new investment in technology rather than new recruitment.

"Work less, work for all" is a recipe that historically has not yielded satisfactory results in terms of employment. The only positive effect is that employees who reduce the number of working hours have more free time. Hence, rather than for fighting unemployment this proposal may be useful for increasing flexibility. This is relevant because a greater work-life balance helps productivity. While "working less" at the individual level is unlikely to translate into "work for all", it may lead to "better work".

---

[9] As labour economist Pietro Ichino (1996) well summarizes in his *Il lavoro e il mercato* (*Work and the Market*), "in the vast majority of cases the unemployed suffer from a position of disadvantage in the labour market, compared to those already employed, which the reduction in maximum working hours is certainly not enough to eliminate". At the opposite extreme, workers with greater abilities, faced with the cut in working hours, generally do not accept the reduction in income and pursue more overtime, second jobs, or the start of self-employment activities.

Work for Free, Work for All

Domenico De Masi supports the idea that employment may benefit from a reduction in working hours but he also recognizes the difficulty of implementation. In his *Lavorare gratis, lavorare tutti*[10] (2017) he concludes that this "will not happen, so the only thing the unemployed can do is to disrupt the situation by offering their work for free". The premise is that "technological progress will provide us with more and more goods and services without using human labour" and therefore it is necessary to find "new paths to follow".

The path indicated by the Neapolitan sociologist is a sort of "revolt of the free". A "white strike" instead of a traditional one. "Because staying at home means rotting [...]. Instead, leaving home and giving someone who needs it a shred of one's professionalism means self-fulfilment". Therefore, it is "a thousand times better to work for free than not to work at all". According to De Masi, if pursued by the unemployed in an organized manner, this strategy can "profoundly modify the labour market making the whole of humanity more just and peaceful". The objective is "not only full employment but also the realization of happiness" and therefore implies the adoption of a new model of society and lifestyle.

The idea of offering labour for free may be an original form of protest but it raises several doubts about its practical applicability and effectiveness. Generally, those who are left without work are often in a condition of frustration and sense of impotence that makes it difficult to formulate strategies, to think long-term and to coordinate with others. De Masi himself acknowledges this, stressing that "the docile non-rebellion is ensured by poverty itself, which weakens the body and dulls the mind, pinning the whole person to the search for minimal and unreliable resources, so that no residual energy remains, no further intelligence to apply to a long-term project, since even the medium term is a luxury that the poor cannot afford". To facilitate the transition the sociologist suggests the introduction of a minimum income.

The main objection to the proposal, however, is to its effectiveness. Leaving the intellectual provocation aside, is it realistic to assume that millions of unemployed young people offering their work for free can disrupt the labour market and determine an increase of (paid) employment? As it has been demonstrated by the current trend in several sectors—such as publishing, journalism, video-photo services, various sharing economy activities and crowdworking—once the idea of placing little or no value on work is widespread and accepted, it is very difficult to turn back.

---

[10] The title of the book—that can be literally translated in "work for free, work for all"—well summarizes the author's proposal.

Job Guarantee

According to some, the answer to technological innovation is the *job guarantee*. Guaranteeing a job to all is considered not only a political duty but also a better strategy compared to those of working less, working for free or not working at all, which all need to be accompanied by significant redistribution to replace the income from work.

The idea of a job guarantee stems from Hyman Minsky (2013), who argues that public intervention must go beyond traditional redistribution measures—such as progressive taxation and unemployment benefits—in order to protect workers during recessions. Governments need to guarantee full employment and they can do so by introducing regulations that limit layoffs and by offering jobs to anyone who is unemployed.

The post-Keynesian economist proposes guaranteed work plans similar to those instituted by Franklin Delano Roosevelt to deal with the Great Depression of the 1930s. Programmes such as the *Works Progress Administration* (public works, infrastructure, arts), the *National Youth Administration* (work in public services for young people) and the *Civilian Conservative Corps* (environmental care) were aimed at putting people immediately to work, without any period of training. Instead, according to Minsky, programmes that focus mainly on training—such as *War on Poverty* launched by Lyndon Johnson in 1964—are less incisive.

According to Italian economist Federico Caffè (2013), full employment must be the central objective of economic policy. Because "employment is not only a means to increase production [...], it is an end in itself, since it puts an end to the servile attitude of those who find it difficult to obtain a job opportunity or have the continuous fear of being deprived of it. In other words, the advantages of a situation of full employment must be considered also and above all from the point of view of human dignity".

Amartya Sen (1973, 1975, 1997b) demonstrates that unemployment has negative consequences of an exceptionally wider scope than just the loss of income. Excluding part of the population from the productive phase lowers average living standards for all. In addition, unemployment generally contributes to social problems—including crime, family separations, physical and psychological health issues—which have heavy economic repercussions. Moreover, the costs of unemployment tend to disproportionately affect disadvantaged social groups, such as young people, ethnic minorities, immigrants, individuals with disabilities and low levels of education.

The main criticism of the job guarantee proposal relates to the large amount of financial resources required, the excessive size and complexity of the programmes, the lack of incentives to seek employment, and the likely increase of labour cost in the private sector. The path to guaranteed employment requires significant public intervention, through direct hiring and financing of labour-intensive sectors. The risk is of excessive growth of the public administration and the semi-public sectors, with consequent high costs for public finances and low levels of efficiency. An alternative path is protecting existing jobs at any cost, for example through the introduction of stringent discipline on dismissals, of rules and taxation that slow down the spread of technology, of laws that foresee the obligation of humans to work side by side with machines (even when it is not necessary). In this scenario, the loss of flexibility in the labour market may significantly reduce competition.

The Third Path: Intelligent Cohabitation and Labour-Intensive Professions

There is also a "third path", based on the conviction that a better balance between growth and employment can be achieved through the intelligent coexistence between humans and machines.

In this scenario humans do not try to stop technological innovation, they do not surrender to the rise of machines, and they are not satisfied with the possibility of a job guarantee. None of these three paths is considered optimal. Obstructing the adoption of technology under the illusion of saving jobs is unrealistic. Accepting a massive replacement of workers by machines may generate economic and social problems, even when redistribution mechanisms are introduced to replace wages. Knowing that work is guaranteed may negatively affect productivity.

Intelligent coexistence can be achieved by partitioning of work activities: letting technology dominate those that are capital-intensive and investing heavily in those in which human labour continues to have a central role. This is the case of many professions in education and in health and social care. Other labour-intensive sectors are research and development, cultural heritage, landscaping and part of the green economy. In these activities technology may be useful but it cannot replace humans, because the reduction of human labour would be detrimental to the quality of service. As William

Baumol (1966) points out, in some activities replacing humans with technology to cut costs is counterproductive because the person is a fundamental prerequisite for the success of the activity and is therefore irreplaceable.[11]

In order to combat technological unemployment, Gallino (2015) suggests an industrial policy that governs a process of orderly transition from traditional sectors to those which are highly labour intensive. With reference to Italy, he suggests interventions to make schools safer, restructure hospitals, prevent hydrogeological instability and restore the artistic heritage.

One difficulty in implementing this proposal is that some of these occupations are often considered unattractive. Essentially for two reasons. The first is that the salary level is generally low. The second is that these are professions that have lost their social reputation over time. It is no coincidence that few young people want to be teachers or providers of basic personal care. Another limitation of this approach is that splitting the jobs between humans and machines may be considered as a defensive move dictated by a survival instinct rather than one inspired by a choice of collaboration.

The Third Path: Collaboration Between Humans and Machines

Intelligent coexistence can go beyond the macro-level partitioning of labour and pursue an actual day-to-day human–machine collaboration. The idea is that humans can create more value by interacting with machines than by working without technology or by letting machines operate on their own.

In some cases, partitioning is inevitable. There are tasks where it is more efficient to automate completely because they are particularly heavy or dangerous. Other tasks require exclusive human labour because they need a high level of creativity and flexibility. However, in the middle there are many activities that can benefit from a close interaction between humans and technology.

In many factories with complex production, collaborative robots and exoskeletons are becoming increasingly popular. The former operate alongside the workers—interacting with them in the same environment without any physical separation—and thereby increase efficiency and productivity.

---

[11] In *Performing Arts. The Economic Dilemma* (1966), the American economist explains the "cost disease"—also known as "Baumol effect"—using metaphors from the live performing arts: Puccini's *Turandot* cannot be staged with less than ten singers, a Vivaldi quartet cannot be performed live without at least four musicians and in less than an hour and a quarter. In some cases, replacing people with technology does not increase productivity but it rather decreases the quality of the result.

The latter are worn by workers and enhance their physical capabilities and performance. In operating theatres, robotics helps surgeons perform complex operations with less effort and with a higher level of precision. The combination of IoT, big data and computational capability allows the extraction of useful information to increase the productivity of human labour. In many industries, AI helps humans be more efficient by making better decisions in less time.

The human–machine combination can yield better results than either one alone. For this to happen, it is important that humans acquire the necessary skills to make the best use of technology. And that machines are not seen in opposition to humans, but rather as an opportunity to extend their skills.

Redistribution Mechanisms of Produced Wealth

The different alternatives analysed require financial resources and need new redistribution mechanisms that are independent of work.

The role of employment as a redistribution engine of produced wealth is relatively recent. The main economic activity in the past was agriculture, land was synonymous with wealth and the ruling class did not earn their economic status by working. In ancient Egypt the pharaoh owned everything by divine right. In the feudal system land was allocated in exchange for the obligation to serve the ruler militarily or on a hereditary basis.

The enlargement of the economy and the consequent reduction in the value of land have favoured the transition to a model in which it is the income earned with work that allows some redistribution of the wealth produced by the economy. Consumption, public spending and the welfare system, all largely depend on income from employment.

Today, the traditional redistribution mechanism based on employment income is undermined by an unprecedented wave of technological progress. As investment in technology grows, production is increasingly capital-intensive and the share of produced wealth that is allocated to workers declines. Moreover, the return on capital is often reinvested in more automation, producing further reductions in employment and in the total income from labour.

In a context where machines replace humans in most tasks, workers offering labour are in competition with each other, have little bargaining power and tend to impoverish. The result is an economic oligarchy where the masses work to produce luxury goods and futile services for a small group of very wealthy people. A scenario not so different from that of slaves in ancient Egypt and serfs in the feudal system, which can lead to serious social tensions.

The issue of resource allocation therefore becomes central. With a twofold objective: achieving fairness and supporting aggregate demand. Is it socially and politically sustainable that the benefits of progress go largely to the few with capital and less and less to labour? And, if innovation causes high rates of unemployment, who will buy the goods and services produced by machines? And again, who will ensure the sustainability of the social security system, largely financed by levies on labour income?

There are two possible answers to these questions, and they are not necessarily alternative to each other.

The first is a redistribution model based on "transfer of resources", in this case from the few who have high income and relevant assets to the many who have little or no income. The transfer can be direct, through subsidies, or indirect, through an expansion of social services. Resources to finance this plan may come from different sources depending on the underlying economic policy.

The second approach is based on "entitlement", i.e. the right to participate. Each individual would have to supplement income earned from work—which is declining and may disappear—with other income coming from participation in capital rather than from transfers. This mixed model is already a reality for workers who supplement, or replace, earned income with returns on their savings or who hold capital shares in their companies. The ongoing technological development, which is likely to produce a dramatic decline in employment, may make it necessary to increase the capital component of people's sources of income.

This scenario poses the problem of having to provide all citizens with a minimum amount of capital or assets that allow them to benefit from technological progress by receiving part of the produced wealth. A redistribution of the stock of existing assets is a politically difficult path to follow: the socialization of the means of production has had disastrous results in the course of history. The alternative is to draw either on public assets (assets owned by all, such as state property and other public resources), or on future assets (wealth that has yet to be generated).

Guaranteed Minimum Income and Negative Taxation

Universal basic income is often confused with guaranteed minimum income.[12] The former is paid to all members of a community regardless of their resources; the latter is a social protection benefit, selectively assigned to certain categories, at certain times and under certain conditions. Generally, minimum income is granted only to people of working age, until they remain in need or retire, with the condition that their disposable income be below a certain threshold considered to be poverty.

The main objective of minimum income is to support an individual in difficult circumstances, such as poverty, unemployment or underemployment. In this sense it can be an important tool to facilitate the transition of people who need to update their skills or to find a job. For this reason, the disbursement of minimum income can be conditioned to its utilization (e.g. for retraining) or even be paid directly in professional training hours rather than cash. Guaranteed minimum income can also have a redistributive function, with the aim of allocating at least part of the productivity gains generated by automation to those who lose their jobs due to automation itself. The beneficiaries of the guaranteed minimum income tend to spend it, thus increasing consumption and supporting aggregate demand.

The idea of guaranteed minimum income is not immune to criticism. While its main purpose is to facilitate the transition to a changed labour market, its weakness stems from the lack of empirical evidence of its effectiveness. Indeed, it may have a disincentive effect on job search. At the end of the eighteenth century, English magistrates decided to provide the inhabitants of a small town in Berkshire with a subsidy to supplement wages below a certain level. In studying the case, Karl Polanyi identified a tendency to prefer the subsidy to wages. As the Hungarian sociologist and anthropologist writes in *The Great Transformation* (1944) "in the long run the result was ghastly. Although it took some time till the self-respect of the common man sank to the low point where he preferred poor relief to wages, his wages which were subsidized from public funds were bound eventually to be bottomless, and to force him upon the rates. Little by little the people of the countryside were pauperized; the adage 'once on the rates, always on the rates' was a true saying".

---

[12] It is important to distinguish between guaranteed minimum income (GMI) and guaranteed minimum wage. The former is a form of welfare, independent of the existence of an employment relationship; the latter is the minimum remuneration—on an hourly, daily or monthly basis—that the employer must pay to employees by law.

Excessive income redistribution policies in advanced economies may also discourage entrepreneurship. In fact, sometimes the existence of economic and social inequalities may increase the propensity to take entrepreneurial risk. As with other redistributive measures, the minimum income proposal presents the issue of finding financial coverage.

To overcome some of these problems, Milton Friedman (1962) proposed the negative tax[13]: a personal income tax that below a certain threshold becomes a subsidy. The subsidy is equal to the difference between standard income (the minimum income that a person should receive) and actual family income, but it is always lower than the latter in order to discourage parasitic behaviour.

Like the guaranteed minimum income, the negative tax supports low-income individuals. However, while in the former case the benefit is payable to all taxpayers with the same characteristics—for example, a situation of involuntary unemployment—in the latter, the beneficiaries are only those who demonstrate that they have an income below a certain threshold. This should limit disbursements to those who really need help and reduce the administrative costs of running the programme. Moreover, this instrument of fiscal policy structured with two opposite monetary flows—the tax and the subsidy—makes it possible to link tax revenues and social expenditures, thus simultaneously pursuing two objectives: redistribution and containment of public expenditure.

Universal Dividend

The universal dividend is an unconditional distribution to all members of a political community of a dividend paid by a sovereign wealth fund owned by the community itself. The objective is the same as that of universal basic income, but unlike the latter the source of funding is defined and circumscribed and generally does not involve the introduction of new taxes.

A practical application is in Alaska, where since 1982 a dividend has been distributed to anyone who has been a resident for at least two years. The dividend is financed with the income received by the State for the private exploitation of oil wells and has helped to reduce economic inequality. Another example is Macao, a former Portuguese colony in China, which has

---

[13] The idea of a negative income tax was originally proposed by Juliet Rhys-Williams, a British writer and Liberal Party politician, in a government report (the Beveridge Report 1942) but it was popularized by Milton Friedman in the 1960s.

been redistributing gambling revenues since 2011.[14] In *Agathotopia* (1989), James Meade proposes a social dividend that, by guaranteeing everyone an income, spurs entrepreneurial risk-taking.

Yanis Varoufakis (2017) has suggested the introduction of a universal dividend at the European level with the aim of redistributing among citizens the productivity gains due to technological innovations. The proposal of the former finance minister of Greece is to create a common fund (*European Equity Depositary*) with the contribution of a share of the new equity issued by all companies (both in capital increase and new listing) of all sectors (because the technological revolution is transversal).[15] The fund thus becomes a shareholder of all companies and receives their dividends. In turn, the fund distributes its own dividend, in the same amount for all citizens.

The universal dividend in this case is financed by the returns on all fixed capital, whether it is robots, machinery or other productive investments. In other words, it is a socialization of the property rights of the income streams that are generated by invested capital. The main consequence is that, to the extent that automation improves productivity and profit-making capacity of firms, all citizens share in the benefits.

Varoufakis' proposal lends itself to some criticism. Firstly, the mechanism could damage the competitiveness of the geographical areas that introduce it by triggering a capital flight. Secondly, the obligation to contribute to the fund with shares issued for capital increase or new listing is essentially a corporate tax that overlaps with that already levied on profits. Furthermore, from a technical point of view the proposal should be refined: because it refers only to listed companies and because the income of the fund would be influenced not only by the profitability of the companies held but also by their dividend policy.

No Robotization Without Taxation

In a 2017 interview Bill Gates put forward the proposal to tax robots in order to finance measures to counter technological unemployment. The idea triggered a heated debate on the subject. The most authoritative contribution is that of Robert Shiller (2017), who sees the robot tax as a tool to cope with

---

[14] In recent years the dividend distributed in Alaska (750 thousand residents) has been between $1,000 and $2,000 per capita, including children; in Macau (650 thousand people) $1,200 per capita ($700 for non-permanent residents).

[15] Intellectual monopoly rights (such as copyrights, patents and trademarks) would also contribute to the fund in order to socialize some of the intellectual property.

the enormous changes in the labour market and, above all, to counter the increase in inequality.

The Nobel laureate points out that "a tax on robots [...] might slow the process [of replacing human labour with technology], at least temporarily, and provide revenues to finance adjustment, like retraining programs for displaced workers". According to the Yale economist, a modest tax contribution limited to a transition period would be sufficient, and "such a tax should be part of a broader plan to manage the consequences of the robotics revolution".

Shiller justifies the tax with two strong arguments. The first is that automation creates negative externalities. Not economic but social ones. And he quotes another Nobel Laureate—Edmund Phelps—who in his *Rewarding Work* (1999) points out that work also represents a "place in society, a calling" and that, when a large number of people cannot find work to support their families, "the functioning of the entire community may be impaired". Negative social externalities generated by robotization, therefore, justify public intervention.

The second argument is the need to fight rising inequality, which is in part caused by technology. Shiller admits that ideally the provision of a basic income should be funded by an increasing income tax progressivity. However, he notes that taxing robots is more politically acceptable and sustainable over time because it attracts wider popular support.

Shiller's arguments are very compelling and so is the summary of his final proposal. "A moderate tax on robots, even a temporary one [...], seems a natural component of a policy to address rising inequality. Revenue could be targeted towards wage insurance to help people replaced by new technology make the transition to a different career". Shiller points out that "this would accord with our natural sense of justice, and thus be likely to endure".

In spite of the authoritative and well-founded arguments, some strong doubts remain on the proposal of a robot tax. First of all, from a technical point of view, the ambiguity of the word "robot" and the difficulty of defining which technologies it includes make it difficult to precisely determine the taxable base. Second, there is an issue of double taxation because both the machines and the profits they allow the company to obtain are hit.

There are two other risks that are worth mentioning. The risk that companies using robots transfer the tax burden to the final consumers. And the risk of distortionary effects on the sectors in which robots are most used. Finally, it is important to remember that in a global economy a tax introduced in one country can encourage the flight of economic activity. Even in the case of an internationally agreed decision, a tax on technology would have the effect of undermining investment in innovation and slowing down technological development, with negative consequences on economic growth and employment. If personal computers and software had been taxed in the 1980s, this would probably have significantly slowed down the development of the computer industry (as well as the growth of Bill Gates' Microsoft!).

Web Tax

The issue of taxation of multinational companies operating on the web is highly topical. The web tax—or digital tax—is not talked about so much as a source to finance redistribution (as in the case of the robot tax) but rather for matters of tax fairness and free competition.

The digital giants, also called *over-the-top*,[16] operate in many states without having permanent establishments of means and employees in each of them. This "incorporeality" allows them to pay taxes in the countries where they are headquartered—that often have a very favourable fiscal system—and largely circumvent taxation in those where the income is actually produced.

The spread of multi-sided platforms makes it easier to conceal part of the tax base, especially revenues from the sale of advertising space, data transfer and intermediation activities between users and businesses. Indeed, it is easy for online transactions to avoid the taxation regime of the countries where the goods or services sold are used and where revenues are generated. As Public Economics expert Mauro Marè (2019) points out, the decisive aspect is that of intangible assets—such as patents, intellectual property, algorithms, big data—which eliminate the reference to physical presence.

This creates a problem of tax fairness but also one of unfair competition since, according to an estimate of former European Commissioner for Economic and Monetary Affairs Pierre Moscovici (2018), on average "digital companies are taxed at 9% and traditional ones at 23%". The risk is that OTTs acquire dominant positions and threaten free competition. Thanks to very high growth rates and margins, in just a few years innovative start-ups have become multinationals with the financial capacity to acquire major competitors, dominant positions in various sectors and access

---

[16] OTT are companies that sell products (such as Amazon and Alibaba), content and services (such as Netflix and Apple through Apple TV and iTunes) or advertising space (such as Google, Facebook and Twitter) over the Internet.

to unprecedented amounts of personal data—the management of which further increases their competitive advantage.[17]

Many have been the attempts to deal with this situation. The OECD (2013, 2019) has long been working on the definition of a "common consolidated tax base" to tax global companies.[18] The European Commission presented two proposals for a directive in March 2018: the first envisages a digital service tax of 3% on the turnover of certain services of digital companies, whose revenues would be shared among states according to the number of users; the second introduces the concept of "significant digital presence" in the definition of permanent establishment, and then allocates profits to the various states according to criteria such as value of digital services, number of users and contracts.

In a historic decision, in June 2021 the group of seven advanced economies (G7) agreed on the principle of a global minimum rate ensuring that multinationals pay tax of at least 15% in each country they operate. A few weeks later the decision was endorsed by the G20. In the light of this broader agreement, the EU has announced it would suspend its plans to tax online tech giants.

There are several critical aspects of the web tax. First of all, it is not easy to distinguish between digital and non-digital economy. Moreover, in order to be effective the tax must be international. Otherwise, companies that are resident in countries applying a web tax would be penalized. Double taxation, of both profits and revenues, is also a potential issue. Lastly, there is the risk that the web tax is passed on to consumers.

Digital Dividend: The Value of Data

In early 2019, the Governor of California—Democrat Gavin Newsom—proposed to distribute a "dividend" to (Californian) citizens in return for giving up their personal data. The rationale was that since the processing of personal data underpins the profit of many of Silicon Valley's giants, some of it should go back to users. "Companies that make billions of dollars collecting, curating and monetizing our personal data have a duty to protect

---

[17] In addition to issues of tax fairness and free competition, the digital economy raises concerns regarding privacy, copyright protection and, ultimately, the proper functioning of democracy.

[18] The reference is to two ongoing initiatives: AEOI (*Automatic Exchange of Information*), an exchange of financial information between tax authorities concerning non-resident citizens to reduce international tax evasion, and BEPS (*Base Erosion and Profit Shifting*), a package of measures to combat tax avoidance by international groups.

it", the new elected Governor said in his first State of the State speech. There-fore, he continued, "California's consumers should also be able to share in the wealth that is created from their data".

Newsom used the word "dividend", a term that has a positive meaning for citizens, but the core of his proposal rather seems to be a tax or fee to be paid for the purchase of data. While the robot tax affects automation with the goal of distributing the wealth produced by machines and the web tax aims to encourage free competition and reduce tax avoidance by commercial activities carried out on digital platforms, the digital dividend focuses on data and its value.

Newsom's proposal raises several reservations, including the difficulty of implementation. It is complex to measure the value of the data provided by each user. Moreover, data move as much as and more than capital: if a tax is imposed in California, companies will easily collect data elsewhere. However, the proposal is politically strategic because it simultaneously touches on three hot-button issues: the use of personal data and respect for privacy by OTT companies, the growth of economic inequality related to the rapid develop-ment of information technology and the rise of technological unemployment. More importantly, it contributes to the public debate on the value of data.

The importance of data grows hand in hand with the dimensions of the knowledge economy, of which data are a fundamental resource. Data may be considered as the "oil" of the digital era because its extraction and use make it possible to accumulate profits, influence and power. Extending this analogy, it might be interesting to remember that when the economic potential of oil was discovered, oil was taxed and oil companies were regulated by antitrust laws.

Public Research: Collective Risk and Private Profit

Many successful products and services are based on the use of personal data. Many others are commercial applications of public investment in research and development. A significant example is the iPhone, as its underlying tech-nologies were designed and developed thanks to research financed with public money. Very often research is initially funded for military purposes. As in the case of the Internet and the GPS system, from which countless commer-cial applications have originated. Even exoskeletons and drones are the result of military projects, and many Israeli start-ups are the offspring of military spending.

In *Entrepreneurial State* (2003) economist Mariana Mazzucato shows that in the past the state—much more than private companies—has funded the research that has produced the most revolutionary technologies. Still today, the state plays an essential role in funding the research of many innovative sectors—such as telecommunications, pharmaceuticals, green economy, nanotechnologies—and bears the initial investment risk of many of the new technologies. Mazzucato wonders why, when these efforts translate into commercial activities, "the profits from a collective risk end up in private hands". Some economists believe that, in such cases, a portion of the benefits should be somehow shared.

The strong link between public research and innovation is undeniable. However, an ex-post taxation of companies—proposed by some—is highly questionable. Because it is a double taxation and because it is difficult to quantify how much of the value is generated by the publicly funded research and how much comes from the private sector's ability to translate it into commercial success. More realistic is the possibility of the state giving up the rights to use public research in exchange for a share of the companies' equity, so as to benefit from any future value creation.

* * *

Many are the ideas for addressing the changes in the labour market, and specifically the challenge to employment coming from the spread of innovations. Some proposals are more realistic than others and all of them need financial backing. The good news is that the way forward still depends largely on human beings and their choices. But it is more urgent than ever to make choices.

Bibliography

W. Baumol, W. Bowen, *Performing Arts, The Economic Dilemma*, Twentieth Century Fund, New York 1966.

W. Beveridge, *Social Insurance and Allied Services*, British Library, 1942.

G. Brockell, *That Time America Almost Had a 30-Hour Work Week*, "The Washington Post", 7 September 2021.

F. Caffè, *La dignità del lavoro*, Castelvecchi, Rome 2013.

CQ Researcher, *The Thirty-Hour Week*, "CQ Press Archives", https://library.cqpress.com/cqresearcher/document.php?id=cqresrre1936011700

D. De Masi, *Lavorare gratis, lavorare tutti*, Rizzoli, Milano 2017.

L. Einaudi, *La crisi e le ore di lavoro*, "La Riforma Sociale", pp. 1–20, gennaio-febbraio 1933.

L. Einaudi, *Scritti economici storici e civili*, Mondadori, Milan 1983.

European Commission, Commission Staff Working Document, *Impact Assessment* (Accompanying the document Proposals for a Council Directive on a Common Corporate Tax Base and a Common Consolidated Corporate Tax Base), 2016.

M. Friedman (assisted by R. Friedman), *Capitalism and Freedom*, University of Chicago Press, 1962.

L. Gallino, *Il denaro, il debito e la doppia crisi. Spiegati ai nostri nipoti*, Einaudi, Turin 2015.

W. Gates, Interview by Kevin J. Delaney for QUARTZ, 17 February 2017.

G20, *Taxation*, OECD, Retrieved 1 May 2018, https://www.oecd.org/g20/topics/taxation/

J. Haskel, S. Westlake, *Capitalism Without Capital: The Rise of the Intangible Economy*, Princeton University Press, Princeton 2018.

P. Ichino, *Il lavoro e il mercato*, Mondadori, Milan 1996.

M. Magnani, *Privacy, mercato e colossi da regolare*, "IlSole24Ore", 22 March 2018.

M. Marè, *Web tax: ma qui l'Europa rinuncia alla caccia*, "Corriere della Sera", 25 March 2019.

K. Marx, *Grundrisse der Kritik der politischen Ökonomie*, 1857.

M. Mazzucato, *The Entrepreneurial State*, Penguin, London 2003.

J. E. Meade, *Agathotopia. The Economy of Partnership*, Feltrinelli, Milan 1989 (Aberdeen University Press).

H. P. Minsky, *Ending Poverty: Jobs Not Welfare*, Levy Economic Institute, New York 2013.

P. Moscovici, Interview by Jorge Valero for Euractiv, 30 January 2018.

G. Newsom, *California State of the State Speech*, February 2019.

OECD, *Action Plan on Base Erosion and Profit Shifting*, OECD Publishing, Paris 2013.

OECD, *Using Bank Deposit Data to Assess the Impact of Exchange of Information*, 2019.

T. Paine, "La giustizia agrarian", in *I diritti dell'uomo e altri scritti politici*, Editori Riuniti, pp. 341–361, Rome 1978 [Philadelphia 1795].

T. Paine, "Agrarian Justice", printed by R. Folwell for Benjamin Franklin Bache, Philadelphia 1797.

E. S. Phelps, *Rewarding Work: How to Restore Participation and Self-Support to Free Enterprise*, Harvard University Press, Cambridge, MA 1999.

K. Polanyi, *The Great Transformation*, Farrar & Rinehart, New York 1944.

D. Ricardo, "On machinery", in *On the Principles of Political Economy and Taxation*, John Murray, London 1821.

B. Russell, *The Conquest of Happiness*, TEA, Milan 2003 [New York 1930].

A. Sen, *On Economic Inequality*, Clarendon Press, Oxford 1973.

A. Sen, *Employment, Technology and Development*, Clarendon Press, Oxford 1975.

A. Sen, *The Economics of Life and Death*, "Scientific American", New York, May 1993.

A. Sen, *Rationality and Social Choice*, "American Economic Review" (Nashville, TN), 85, no. 1 (March), pp. 1–24, 1995.

A. Sen, *Inequality, Unemployment and Contemporary Europe*, "International Labour Review", 136, no. 2, International Labour Organization, 1997a.

A. Sen, *The Penalties of Unemployment*, Paper for the Bank of Italy (mimeo), 1997b.

R. J. Shiller, *Robotization Without Taxation?*, "Project Syndicate", 22 March 2017.

Y. Varoufakis, *A Tax on Robots?*, "Project Syndicate", 27 February 2017.

7

Human Beings at the Centre as "Shareholders" of Development

The revolution underway is not only limited to sustainability and technological innovations. It is also political, because it has consequences for the
economy, society and ethics. And it involves decisions about values that affect
present and future generations.

The first and most important choice is whether to prioritize *growth at
all costs* or to put *human beings at the centre*. Prioritizing growth without
worrying about sustainability and the impact of automation on employment
may be based on the assumption that the system will find a new point of
equilibrium on its own, as has happened in the past. However, this approach
may not be compatible with the many existing sustainability constraints. On
the other hand, favouring the centrality of human beings does not mean
rejecting progress. On the contrary, this choice requires people to interact
with technology without surrendering to machines, to pursue growth but in
a sustainable way, to increase the wealth produced but distribute it fairly, to
improve productivity but also the quality of life and work.

Putting human beings at the centre is the starting point that makes the
value system a compass to follow in order to find the right path and make
some unavoidable choices. Hence, compass in hand, we are going to formulate some proposals for dealing with a world revolutionized by innovation in
a way that is socially balanced and sustainable.

First of all, we need a new regulatory framework. One that deals with
certain critical issues—primarily legal, fiscal and ethical—relating to new
technologies and that incorporates the sustainability constraints into the

© The Author(s), under exclusive license to Springer Nature
Switzerland AG 2022
M. Magnani, *Making the Global Economy Work for Everyone*,
https://doi.org/10.1007/978-3-030-92084-5_7

economic growth model. We need an incentive system that makes sustainable behaviour economically advantageous and a labour policy that reconciles the protection of existing jobs with the creation of new ones. It is essential to invest in education and training and to improve collaboration between school and business in order to raise awareness of sustainability and to reduce the growing skills gap between what employers need and what employees offer. Finally, we need to address the issue of redistribution, to allow everyone to share in the benefits of technological progress and to reduce inequality and poverty.

These interventions are important and necessary but they are merely "defensive". And they definitely are not sufficient. While respecting the main sustainability constraints, it is also essential to strengthen the economic system. On three fronts. First: develop new labour-intensive activities, including those in traditional sectors. Second: sustain a high rate of innovation, investing in research and stimulating economic activities where the quality of human capital is central. Third: increase competitiveness vis-à-vis other territories, in order to attract innovative investments and high-skilled jobs.

Sustainability Goal: Scrapping or Adjusting the Traditional Growth Model?

According to Serge Latouche (2006, 2015), "we are aboard a pilotless fireball with no reverse gear and no brakes that is going to smash against the limits of the planet". The truth is that we are still in time to slow down. As long as we put human beings at the centre instead of pursuing growth at any cost. This does not mean scrapping and replacing the current growth model, as some are asking to do. To the ideological approach of "scrapping" it is preferable to adopt the pragmatic method of "adjustment", with the aim of incorporating the suggestions and stimuli emerging from the most constructive criticism. Moreover, among the various proposals for an alternative to the traditional model—although full of brilliant insights—none seems to be comprehensive enough to replace it entirely.

The liberal-capitalist system has clearly shown several fragilities. However, over the last two centuries it has proven to be better than other competing models from an economic and social standpoint and has also shown to be intimately linked to democracy. Furthermore, liberal-capitalism has demonstrated the ability to adapt and adjust itself to limit its flaws and excesses. Consider, for example, the introduction of labour protection regulations, social security and health welfare, antitrust laws. Finally, it should be noted that the adjustments to the model themselves can create new opportunities for growth.

Adjusting the traditional model is not easy. The fundamental challenge is to include a variable that takes into account the interests of future generations in a decision-making process aimed at maximizing the economic result in the present. The objective is to try to align—and not oppose—economic value with social value.

To this end, two aspects should be considered. The first is the *type* and *depth* of action required, which can vary from international to local, from public to private. When facing certain issues—such as climate change, deforestation, ocean pollution, world hunger and poverty, pandemics, management of migratory flows—globally coordinated actions are inevitable because, as Pope Francis reminds us in the encyclical *Laudato si'* (2015), "interdependence obliges us to think of one world with a common plan".[1] When dealing with other situations—such as pollution of cities, countryside and rivers, hydrogeological instability, land-use patterns, energy consumption, waste disposal and recycling, water management, food waste—the action required is at national and local level, involving the public sector, businesses and citizens.

The second aspect concerns *how* we intervene: whether through coercive measures and sanctions, incentives and disincentives, or persuasion. An additional option is pushing investments in research and development aimed at increasing sustainability.[2] In some situations, we need clear rules that prohibit unsustainable behaviour and provide for heavy and certain penalties in the event of non-compliance. These include rules on greenhouse gas emissions, reclamation and safety of contaminated sites, treatment of industrial waste and driving bans for specific categories of polluting vehicles. This approach, however, is not without weaknesses. First of all, highly regulated environments often generate excessive bureaucracy. Secondly, the perception of risk in the case of unlawful behaviour in this domain is very low, especially when compared with other types of crime. Finally, impositions and prohibitions are often determined without a proper cost-benefit analysis.

When it is difficult or useless to prohibit unsustainable behaviour, it is possible to discourage it through taxation that compensates—at least in

---

[1] The coronavirus pandemic has shown that, when facing global threats, a lack of international coordination (and cooperation) can result in dire consequences.

[2] The Green New Deal unveiled by the European Commission in July 2021 goes in this direction and has the ambition of becoming the cornerstone of E.U. policy. Its overarching objective is for the E.U. to become the first climate neutral continent by 2050, resulting in a cleaner environment, more affordable energy, smarter transport, new jobs and an overall better quality of life.

part—for the negative externalities that are generated. An example is the "green tax" in its various applications: carbon tax on energy sources that emit carbon dioxide into the atmosphere, tolls for urban transit, fees on plastic bags at the supermarket. Similar mechanisms can be devised to discourage unnecessary waste in the water, food and energy sectors. This approach can be very effective although it may sometimes raise problems of fairness. Let's see why.

Sometimes unsustainable behaviour—such as the exploitation of certain natural resources—is encouraged. In many countries there are subsidies on fossil fuels, agriculture, fisheries and water, even though these activities increase consumption of raw materials, greenhouse gas emissions and pollution. For example, fossil fuel subsidies—which are still granted in the hundreds of millions every year at the global level[3]—have the negative effect of reducing both the cost of virgin plastics and the competitiveness of recycled plastics. Why not abolish these subsidies and introduce fiscal disincentives and quotas to encourage circularity?

The matter is more complex than it may seem. Indeed, removing these subsidies may in some cases harm weaker individuals or countries. In other words, a policy that benefits the environment may trigger harmful social and political consequences. This is the case of many agriculture and transport subsidies—either paid directly or channelled through lower fuel taxes—that sometimes support economic activities (and related jobs) that are at the limits of survival. Similarly, aggressive energy transition policies may result in significant increase in the cost of utilities which, absent the appropriate countermesaures, would have regressive effects, penalizing low income individuals. As former editor-in-chief of "Corriere della Sera" Ferruccio de Bortoli (2019) points out, "if we want to create a different sensitivity [on sustainability], we must avoid the unpleasant division between those who can afford sustainability and those who can't".

Green taxes may cause other distortions too. If a carbon tax is introduced in one country and not at the international level, the result may be an increase in greenhouse gas emissions in other countries (carbon leakage). The consequence is that the country that has a strict climate policy loses competitiveness versus those that do not. To address the issue and encourage countries to introduce carbon taxes, a solution is to have *carbon border tax adjustments*

---

[3] According to the International Energy Agency (2021), global fossil-fuel consumption subsidies were $181 billion in 2020, $312 in 2019, $472 in 2018. From 2010 to 2020 subsidies for nearly 4.6 trillion have been granted. At the June 2021 summit in Cornwall, G7 leaders reaffirmed their commitment to eliminate inefficient fossil fuel subsidies by 2025 and called on all countries to join their undertaking.

to compensate for emissions attributable to imports from nations without a carbon price.

There are also circumstances in which, rather than punishing or taxing, it is more effective to introduce incentives that make it economically worthwhile for people to adopt a sustainable behaviour. The goal can be achieved in various ways: rewards for companies that convert their polluting behaviour or invest in green technologies, eco-bonuses and fiscal deductions on investments that allow energy savings, contributions for consumers that replace polluting vehicles or purchase electric cars, reward mechanisms for fishermen who bring to shore plastic and other waste caught in the sea,[4] bonuses for those who take care of private green areas, reduction of waste tax for businesses that donate food.

Attributing a positive economic dimension to sustainability can help change the behaviour of rational consumers, promote the conversion of industrial production cycles and raise awareness of sustainability issues. However, incentives and disincentives must be handled with caution. As a matter of fairness but also, sometimes, as one of effectiveness. In some cases, it might be preferable to direct those same resources towards investments in research aimed at the direct solution—rather than the containment— of problems. For example, in the case of plastic, it might be better to improve recycling technologies and develop alternative eco-sustainable materials, rather than taxing its use or giving bonuses to those who collect it. Research activity may also be financed by *ad hoc* bonds which, thanks to favourable tax treatment, could guarantee attractive returns to investors.

Finally, there are situations in which regulations, taxes or incentives are not necessary. *Behavioural economics*[5] shows that at times a strategy based on persuasion can be sufficient, and occasionally even more effective. According to the *nudge theory*, it is possible to improve people's well-being by guiding their decisions, without taking away their freedom of choice and without providing significant incentives.

No matter which mechanism is adopted to improve the traditional growth model, spreading a culture of sustainability is essential. And the adjustment of the model must be followed by the introduction of a new method of measuring results that gives weight to the many factors contributing to

---

[4] Prior to the introduction of the "Save the Sea" law in October 2019, in Italy those who brought plastic back ashore did not receive any reward and, in addition, were charged with committing an offence of illegal waste transportation and had to pay the disposal costs.

[5] Behavioural economics studies the decision-making process of people considering also notions of psychology and experimental analysis. Unlike traditional political economy, which is based on the assumption of rational consumer choice, behavioural economics analyses actual consumer decisions that may also be based on irrational motivations.

people's well-being. It is crucial to understand that economic growth and innovation are not the enemy of sustainability. On the contrary, they can be the best tools for pursuing it.

A Pragmatic Approach to Sustainability: The Cost–Benefit Analysis

"It is possible to injure yourself by driving along a road at too high a speed. But braking too abruptly can be just as risky". With this metaphor Francesco Ramella (2019) of the University of Turin warns about the risk of franticly adopting some measures to reduce environmental impact.

The reference is to William Nordhaus' (1993) studies. The Nobel economist argues that the adoption of policies aimed at reducing the negative impact of climate change should be evaluated considering not only the expected benefits but also the costs incurred, calculated in terms of the growth that is sacrificed to achieve them. In some scenarios, the latter are higher than the former. Nordhaus raises an issue of cost-effectiveness. Specifically, he criticizes the planned approach followed so far with the *a priori* definition of emission reduction targets—overall and for each economic sector—regardless of the costs to achieve them. According to Nordhaus, the optimal scheme to correct the emission of polluting gases is an internationally uniform carbon tax, which raises the social price of pollution and internalizes the external costs of economic activities. Alternatively, he proposes a system of *cap-and-trade*—tradable pollution permits—that would cap certain types of emissions and allow companies and countries to trade unused allowances of "permitted pollution". These approaches have the advantage of being pragmatic and unideological and, unlike subsidies for the transition to the green economy, they do not affect public spending, do not feed bureaucracy and are less subject to speculation and fraud.

In Nordhaus' view it is short-sighted to ignore the problem of polluting emissions. However, he thinks that overzealousness could also be counterproductive. Because a higher cost of energy would slow down the process of economic growth, which is ultimately what—combined with scientific progress—has made it possible for humankind to defend itself against the climate as never before in history.

A "Gentle Push" Towards Sustainability

Persuading and prodding can sometimes be more effective than imposing and sanctioning.

In *Nudge* (2008), Harvard Law School professor Cass Sunstein and Nobel laureate economist Richard Thaler explain that "positive reinforcement and indirect suggestions to encourage non-forced compliance can influence motives, incentives and decision-making at least as effectively as direct instruction, legislation, or enforcement". A nudge is not an imposition but "any aspect of the choice architecture that alters people's behaviour in a predictable way without forbidding any options or significantly changing their economic incentives".

Nudging can help sustainability—in its various dimensions—in many different ways. Japan's *Cool Biz* campaign in 2011, calling for people to go to work wearing light clothing, significantly reduced air conditioning consumption. A car odometer showing real-time fuel costs is likely to induce lower consumption. A different arrangement of healthy and unhealthy foods in schools' cafeterias affects students' dietary choices. During the pandemic, nudging has had an important role in some countries in complementing regulations about health measures (such as wearing masks and sanitizing hands), in making more acceptable social impositions (such as lockdowns or restrictions on restaurants and bar service) and, more importantly, in persuading vaccine holdouts to get shots and boost COVID immunization.

In all these cases, people's freedom of choice is not restricted. They are simply induced to make more sustainable choices, to behave virtuously. They don't receive any incentive but only a "gentle push". The nudge theory inspires policies that appeal to people's irrationality and positively exploit their cognitive errors.

Nudging can take many forms. We can group nudging practices into three broad categories: nudges that appeal to people's self-image, nudges that appeal to people's tendency to socially conform and nudges that re-set the default choice.

One way for stimulating individuals' virtuous behaviour is to leverage on their fundamental motivation of maintaining a positive self-image. People like to see themselves as good. Leveraging this motivation may nudge more environmentally friendly choices. This can be accomplished by simplifying the language used to describe the available options, to make it easier for consumers to recognize the environmental implications of their choices. It can also be achieved by increasing the importance and visibility of the environmental aspects of their choices. The idea is that increasing awareness of the environmental elements of a decision can influence consumers choice. An example of this kind of "green nudge" is eco-labelling. People buying a product in the supermarket with one of these labels tend to feel good about themselves and proud about their responsible lifestyle.

Another useful mechanism for stimulating virtuous behaviour is social comparison: if the message is conveyed that sustainable behaviour is the norm and not the exception, people tend to conform. Social pressure and willingness to conform to the group that is acting virtuously can lead to extraordinary results. The American firm Opower has achieved savings of between 2 and 6% simply by including in energy bills a comparison of the user consumption with the average utilization in the neighbourhood. Energy suppliers in several countries are adopting the same trick. In Italy, GSE (Gestore dei Servizi Energetici) has achieved similar results in maintenance and performance of photovoltaic systems. This method can be enhanced by giving people the opportunity to disclose their environmentally conscious behaviour, letting others know about their choice. This has positive effects on their reputation and helps them maintain a sense of belonging to the cultural groups that shape their identities.

Another mechanism is based on exploiting human tendency to inertia. People generally prefer to keep things the way they are if changing them requires effort or time. The default effect—or silent consent—explains the tendency for an individual to generally accept the default option in a strategic interaction. The default option is the course of action that the individual will automatically obtain absent the explicit choice of another option. Making an option a default increases the likelihood that such an option is chosen. Setting or changing defaults has been proposed and applied by firms as an effective way of influencing behaviour—for example, with respect to regulating air-conditioner temperature, giving consent to receive e-mail marketing, or automatic subscription renewals.

A study by Pichert and Katsikopoulos (2008) shows that a greater number of consumers choose the renewable energy options for electricity when it is offered as the default option. In some German communities, the introduction of "green defaults" for the use of renewables has resulted in more than 90% of the people signing up. Many hotels only change towels when the customer requests it explicitly by leaving them on the floor. That significantly decreases laundry's environmental impact. By introducing silent consent, Austria has increased organ donors to 99% (compared to 12% in a culturally similar country like Germany and to a European average of 17%). Some financial institutions have set up all clients as ethical investors: those wishing to make different investments must provide specific alternative instructions.

Nudging doesn't mandate behaviour but it helps decision-making. And it does so simply by making a certain choice easier, more palatable, or more socially acceptable than the available alternatives. A study by John Beshears (2017) of Harvard University has shown that policies based on persuasion are much less expensive and can be up to forty times more effective than economic bonuses and educational campaigns.

Moreover, a nudge is fairer than incentives and disincentives, which are generally non-progressive measures and therefore tend to penalize the weaker groups. For all these reasons, the governments of several countries—including the UK, Germany, Italy, the Netherlands, Australia and the United States—have created "nudge units".

Beyond Corporate Social Responsibility and New Consumer Awareness

Despite recent progress, sustainability is still struggling to enter the business world. Many companies only incorporate it into their communication without making concrete investments. Some even mislead customers and investors with "green washing", unjustly trying to promote practices, products and services as environmentally friendly through branding, mislabelling, packaging or public relations. The most forward-looking ones, however, adapt their business models to make sustainability a core part of their strategy and a competitive advantage.

The results are tangible: companies with sustainability programmes tend to be more productive and eco-friendly product lines generally perform better. The trend is strong in sectors such as the food and beverage, cosmetics and hygiene products, clothing and footwear.[6] It is growing in automotive, transport, retail, packaging, household appliances and consumer electronics. In addition to annual reports, the financial community is increasingly asking for sustainability reports. Several studies have shown that the most virtuous organizations tend to provide above-average returns in the long term. Finance is helping to reinforce the trend. Environmental, Social and Governance (ESG) factors are now decisive in the investment choices of many funds: according to the Global Sustainable Investment Alliance (2021), at the beginning of 2020 more than 35 trillion dollars (a 15% increase from 2018) were allocated to sustainable investments. That amounts to about one-third of global assets

---

[6] Sportwear giants Nike and Adidas recycle sneakers, Veneto-based textile manufacturer Bonotto uses recycled plastic to produce some of its high-quality fabrics, luxury fashion house Prada has replaced virgin nylon with yarn made from plastic waste recovered from the oceans.

under management. The growing attention paid to climate change by asset managers—and the diffusion of low carbon or carbon neutral funds—will push companies to adopt procedures to measure the pollution they generate.

An important tool in the hands of companies is eco-design: designing products and packaging with the goal of reducing the negative impact on the environment. For example, recycling is much easier if toxic additives are removed from plastics and common rules are adopted in packaging design.[7]

The decisive factor is to make it clear that socially responsible behaviour can become a competitive advantage for companies. Michael Porter and Mark Kramer (2011) propose a business management model focused on "shared value". The premise is that no company is a standalone entity and its success is influenced by the services and infrastructure it can use. Therefore, a firm should increase its competitiveness and—at the same time—improve the economic and social conditions of the community in which it operates, creating shared value.

In a previous essay I argued that when a company invests with intelligence and foresight in its "territory", it builds a competitive advantage and can gain a significant economic return. The concept of territory goes beyond the local geographical area where a company is located. It includes employees and managers, customers and suppliers, schools, universities and research centres, local institutions and communities. The support that a company gives to its territory—in its many dimensions—is an investment that creates both social and economic value. Because a healthy territory creates favourable conditions for business development.

The effort towards sustainability also concerns consumers and their lifestyles. A Unilever analysis (2016) regarding its products' value chain shows that as much as 70% of the negative environmental impact derives from end-use (25% from raw material procurement, only 3% from production and 2% from transport). Once again, technology can be of great help. It allows companies to produce in an eco-friendlier way and, in addition, it can influence consumer habits by enabling the creation of higher quality products. Unilever's study points out that while very few consumers—a mere 3%—are willing to spend more money for a product just because it is more

---

[7] An interesting case is that of plastic and aluminium polycoupled waste such as potato chip bags, beverage containers, biscuit packaging. Ecoplasteam, a firm based in Alessandria, Italy, has developed a technology that recycles and transforms such waste into *ecoallene*, a material that can be used to produce everyday objects. However, the impact of this innovation is still limited due to the heterogeneity in eco-design—for example thicknesses and quantities of aluminium—which hinders the recycling chain. Interestingly enough, the heterogeneity is not due to technical or economic reasons but rather to chance or habit. More coordination between manufacturing firms could start a virtuous circular economy behaviour.

environmentally friendly, the propensity to pay a premium increases when eco-sustainability is combined with improvements in product quality and performance.

The Human-Machine Relationship: Substitution or Collaboration?

According to the founder of Singularity University Raymond Kurzweil (2008), we are approaching the *singularity point*. This is when technological progress accelerates beyond the ability of human beings to understand it and predict it. The reality is that the future of the human-machine relationship still depends largely on our choices. However, these choices are complex, urgent and inescapable.

Humans can react in two different ways to the rise of machines. Choosing "growth at all costs" means favouring a *substitution approach* whereby humans accept to be replaced by machines without worrying about the consequences on employment. Putting "people at the centre", on the other hand, involves opting for a *collaborative approach* between humans and machines, using technology to enhance human work.

In a sense, the replacement approach implies accepting the superiority of machines in the name of productivity and efficiency. This is a scenario in which robots perform the work and increase productivity while humans engage in cultural and recreational activities thanks to universal basic income. Some consider this a desirable outcome. However, the downside is that it entails conceiving work only as a means of generating income and it implies giving up the pre-eminence of humans over machines.

With the collaborative approach, on the other hand, machines are at the service of humans, who continue to leverage the peculiarities that make them irreplaceable: critical thinking, exercising judgement, decision-making, empathy and creativity. Collaboration between humans and machines allows the former to expand their skills using the latter, to increase productivity without losing centrality and to improve the quality of life without letting technology prevail.

The substitution approach requires massive capital investment, may lead to unsustainable growth and significant unemployment, and requires a massive redistributive effort. The collaborative approach is more tortuous, as it requires labour market reforms, new employment policies and substantial investment in education and training. However, it has the advantage of allowing humans to retain control of development.

An Old Dilemma: Assembly-Line Worker or Thinking Professional?

The ongoing technological revolution makes a historical dilemma in the human-work relationship highly topical.

At the beginning of the last century, innovations in work organization and new production technologies revolutionized factories. In The *Scientific Organization of Work* (1911), Frederick Taylor sensed the efficiency advantages of centralized production and inspired the assembly line. The main objective was to increase productivity and, consequently, growth. However, in order to achieve these results, workers had to perform standardized, parcelled out and repetitive procedures. This is perfectly depicted in a memorable scene from Charlie Chaplin's *Modern Times* (1936) showing the worker with a passive role and the machine in control.[8]

In his 1933 essay *The Human Problems of an Industrial Civilization*, Elton Mayo demonstrated that workers' motivation derives largely from the social dimension, because relationships between people and an active participation in the work help improve productivity. According to the Australian psychologist, performance at work is closely linked to the individual's degree of satisfaction, psychological well-being, social recognition and sense of belonging. From this point of view, people are the real capital of a company. Therefore, submitting workers to machines, giving up their intelligence and centrality, is a huge mistake and has negative economic consequences.

As Magatti (2019) acutely observes, we are currently facing a dilemma similar to that of the assembly-line versus thinking workers. The only difference is that today the dilemma applies to society as a whole and not only to the factory. The mere substitution of humans by machines responds to "a neo-taylorist vision that limits itself to exalting the power of efficiency of the new technologies". In this perspective, "the improvement of results is obtained through the diffusion of simplified protocols and by training operators to perform without thinking [...]. This way, however, we end up impoverishing society, concentrating power and weakening democracy. Creating citizens-producers who are increasingly lonely and isolated, unable to understand (and therefore criticize) what is happening around them".

The alternative is to invest in education and training, to help workers and citizens grow. "With the aim"—suggests Magatti—"of developing a collective intelligence that [...] supports and spreads skills, abilities, autonomous

---

[8] According to Bauman (1989), who has extensively studied the relationship between modernity and totalitarianism, this organization of work contributed to the creation of a worker-citizen lacking autonomy and judgment. This was fertile ground for the spread of totalitarianism in the 1930s.

responsibilities" as well as helping to counter tendencies towards concentrated and authoritarian forms of power.

New Rules

New technologies offer enormous opportunities but conceal great risks. Much depends on how they are used. Robots can be programmed to do harm, digital technologies exploited to exert social control over individuals, an algorithm capable of learning can commit crimes. For this reason, successfully facing some of the new issues requires appropriate rules.

A first issue concerns the definition of the legal status of machines, with related rights and obligations. In 2017 Saudi Arabia granted citizenship—and therefore the status of legal person—to a humanoid robot. In the same year, an AI system with the *persona* of a seven-year-old boy was granted "residency" in Tokyo. The Estonian government has seriously considered attributing legal personality to machines.[9] Is this in the interest of society?[10]

Secondly, the emergence of new interactions—between humans and machines and between machines—requires regulating mechanisms and principles. Consider the issue of the responsibility. Who is responsible for Uber's driverless car that ran over and killed a forty-nine-year-old woman in a March 2019 test in Arizona? Who is liable for the mistakes made by a robot surgeon or for the stock market losses caused by an algorithm? Are machines responsible or are their developers? The question becomes particularly complex when dealing with machines capable of self-learning.

Another aspect concerns the use of data and AI to analyse consumer behaviour, make decisions, manage human resources, regulate relations with citizens. These are applications with great potential but considerable risks of different kind. Privacy risks, if data is acquired or transferred to third parties without permission, managed without guaranteeing anonymity, used and manipulated to exercise invasive and persuasive interventions in order

---

[9] In 2017, Estonia's national digital adviser proposed the adoption of a special AI law aimed at granting a legal personality to AI, with corresponding amendments to liability insurance legislation. However, a 2019 AI report of the Government of Estonia recommended adopting the same—more prudent—approach to a legal framework for AI as that of the E.U.

[10] The same question came up more than two centuries ago in relation to a company's legal status. The British Empire needed to confer to its colonial companies operating in India and America a certain legal status. Therefore, a private limited company was considered distinct from a person: while it hired human workers it had its own legal status. This decision was a source of significant disruption at that time. British parliamentarian Baron Thurlow rhetorically asked to his colleagues: "Did you ever expect a corporation to have a conscience, when it has no soul to be damned, and no body to be kicked?" (cited by Banerjee 2008). Today, we are facing similar issues regarding robots and AI.

to influence consumption or political decisions. Security risks, in the event of cyber-attacks or theft of digital identity. Competition risks, if data management gives some companies a disproportionate competitive advantage. Discrimination risks, if decision-making algorithms include biased socio-environmental factors or have been built and trained by biased people. Risks of authoritarianism, if technology is used to control or repress citizens.

There is also a tax issue. It is difficult to tax economic activities that operate worldwide without having permanent establishments in each country and whose main growth drivers are intangible assets. It is easy for these firms to conceal part of the tax base and largely avoid taxation. In this respect, it is important to set up mechanisms at the international level to bring tax revenues into line with the production of added value.

Finally, we cannot forget the ethical complexity posed by new technologies. Who can guarantee that they will not be used in a controversial way? What choice should be programmed into an autonomously driven car between hitting a pedestrian that walks across the street or avoiding him but risking falling into a slope and endangering the lives of the car passengers? Or between suffering a head-on collision with another car and swerving into a cycle lane used by children? Robots are trained by humans, who define their behaviour. It is essential that those who develop the technology have ethical training as well as technical expertise.

Legal status and responsibility of machines, protection of privacy, protection of free competition, prevention of discriminatory practices, appropriate tax treatment, definition of ethical principles, and rules guiding sustainable behaviour, are all urgent matters. An essential step in governing technological progress is rethinking the rules and building a new regulatory framework.

Employment Policies, Job Protection and New Welfare

The profound changes in the world of work due to technological progress make certain actions necessary and crucial.

Firstly, there is an urgent need for a drastic reduction in labour taxation, for both companies and workers. Secondly, employment policies must take into account how new technologies are changing the economy. Flexibility in the labour market should be increased, although without compromising workers' fundamental rights. Self-entrepreneurship should be supported, as it is an important potential source of new jobs.

We must encourage investment that generates skilled jobs linked to new technologies. At the same time, however, it is important to support unskilled workers, who are the most affected by innovation. In other words: while strengthening the locomotive-engine of growth and employment, we must also tend to the wagons at the back of the train in order to prevent them from breaking away. The first objective is pursued by creating fertile ground for innovation, including through tax incentives. The second goal can be achieved by promoting professional training and by eliminating bureaucracy and regulations that discourage hiring (as well as those preventing the dismissal of inefficient employees). From a geographic point of view, it is important to support employment in areas and communities that are lagging behind, because in the digital economy new jobs tend to concentrate in urban hubs, widening the gap between territories.

It is also important to redistribute employment time over people's life cycle, taking into account the many changes in the labour market. This should be done not by reducing working hours by law, but rather by increasing flexibility, in order to improve the well-being and productivity of workers, and by introducing periods of training in their work schedule.

Finally, we must update labour protection laws and design a modern welfare system. The current social protection is rooted in the industrial model of the last century, largely linked to the employer-worker relationship. Today's high mobility of labour requires that access to social protection be linked directly to the worker, following a person from one job to another and even across simultaneous occupations. In particular, there is a need to reconcile protections between employed and self-employed work, to achieve greater regulatory coherence between international and national governance regimes, and to reduce the differences between public and private sectors. It is important to dignify precarious work, casual performances and informal collaborations that do not fit into standard models. Labour protection also means having an adequate guaranteed minimum wage, introducing measures to increase compliance with safety laws and standards, and taking action to avoid excessive weakening of workers' bargaining power. Many forms of protection need to be extended to self-employed entrepreneurs, who often do the same job of employees but are not entitled to the same level of welfare.

We need to shift from traditional welfare to a new framework, in which standardized social rights are replaced by rights tailored to workers' actual needs, national contracts are substituted by decentralized agreements, health insurance is flanked by coverage for obsolescence of skills, and public welfare is integrated by corporate welfare.

Investing in Knowledge: School and Training to Reduce the Skills Gap

Living in the most innovation-intensive era in history, it is essential that people be equipped with the necessary tools and knowledge. Specifically, in the labour market—in addition to the typical skills of the industrial age—it is necessary to develop intellectual and personal skills that enable human beings to work alongside machines and, through collaboration, improve their professional performance. How? By investing in education and life-long training.

The formal education system—comprised of primary and secondary schools and universities—should aim at reducing the growing skills gap between what employers want and what employees offer. Technology has further widened this gap. Narrowing it involves investing in several areas: scientific and technical education, classical education, soft skills development and flexibility.

In the first place, greater emphasis should be placed on the teaching of technical and scientific subjects, enhancing the so-called STEM (Science, Technology, Engineering and Mathematics) education. These skills are in short supply and high demand in all sectors. Nevertheless, and this is the second area, it is also important to provide a solid classical and humanistic education—with basic knowledge of history, philosophy, art, theology, anthropology—to enable individuals to use technology without being overwhelmed by it and to face the complex ethical issues posed by progress. Adding an A that stands for Arts, STEM becomes STEAM. The convergence of scientific knowledge and humanistic skills—which we might call *industrial humanism*—is a trend taking place mostly at the highest levels of the educational system. At Harvard and Princeton, the boundary between technology and humanism is getting thinner. In Italy, Milan's Polytechnic and Humanitas University have launched Medtec School, the world's first university course in medicine and engineering. However, the crossover of skills should occur throughout the entire school curriculum.

The third crucial element is to enhance and strengthen the human characteristics that computers, software and algorithms cannot replace. The so-called soft skills include critical and creative thinking, ability to solve problems and make decisions, empathy and other dimensions of emotional intelligence, as well as relational, social and communication skills. From this perspective, the school system must rethink both teaching methodologies and assessment criteria. As far as the former are concerned, teaching has to leverage new technologies more and young people need to be educated to collaboration rather than competition. As for the latter, it is important to improve both IQ (intelligence quotient) and EQ (emotional intelligence quotient). A small, yet significant, example is the reversing trend in the use of personal computers and word processing in some schools in the United States and Canada, where teachers are forcing students to take notes by hand. Several studies show that handwriting stimulates abstract thinking, creativity and diversity, strengthens memory, facilitates the organization of information in specialized areas of the brain, increases language skills and, of course, improves overall manual dexterity.

Finally, it is vital to develop the skills needed to deal with change. Flexibility, adaptability and versatility are crucial to survive in a constantly changing labour market. Schools must teach how to learn. Teaching models themselves should become more flexible, as students with different skills and interests should not be forced into too rigid paths.[11]

Traditional education is very important but no longer sufficient to prepare for the labour market. It must be complemented by lifelong learning. Technology is making the career path changeable, fragmented and full of periods of inactivity. Hence, it is essential that training and skill-upgrading be available throughout the entire working life: to make it easier for those who lose their jobs to get back into the market and for those who are still employed to keep up to date.

Practically speaking, it is important to extend the right of workers to take study leaves, to introduce tax incentives for people and firms investing in training, to spread the use of technology to access life-long learning platforms, to provide targeted public interventions for the digital literacy of the weakest groups.[12] Training must expand skills of talented workers, but also take care of those who have fewer abilities. Unfortunately, today that is not always the case as professional training often tends to increase inequalities instead of reducing them. The OECD (2019) notes that the most qualified workers are three times more likely to receive training than those with fewer skills.

Continuing education is also useful in leadership roles and should include strategic topics (such as understanding international scenarios, macroeconomic framework, social responsibility) as well as frontier topics (such as

---

[11] To this end Floridi (2019) argues the importance of learning "languages", such as music, computer science, history, geography, chemistry. Only by mastering languages it is possible to use them to learn and build in a rapidly changing world.

[12] About half of the workers in OECD countries have low or no digital skills. To reverse this trend, a compulsory "digital licence" could be introduced for those entering the labour market, regardless of their function. It should also be noted that digital literacy and technology simplification could offer the elderly extraordinary job opportunities, with the additional benefit of increasing their social inclusion.

fin-tech, big data, blockchain). The goal is to add to the traditional manage-ment skills the ability to introduce innovation in organizations and make the best use of it.

Finally, while it is important for a country to invest in education, training and knowledge, it is crucial to retain and attract talent. The economic cost of a negative balance of intellectual mobility (the so-called "brain drain") is enormous.

Investing in Knowledge: The Role of Business in Training Human Capital

The success of a company depends largely on the quality of its workers and leaders. Among the most enlightened entrepreneurs, there is growing aware-ness that employee training is not a generous benefit granted to workers but a strategic investment that is essential for a firm to be competitive.

Companies undertake a large part of the effort of training human capital. This is because the extent and speed of change make it increasingly diffi-cult to find adequately prepared employees on the market. Hence, internal training and the ability to effectively manage the talent available inside the firm are strategic. This is a big incentive for companies to invest in upgrading and retaining skills. It is no coincidence that the use of corporate welfare is growing rapidly, increasing flexibility, internal mobility, involvement in decision-making and sharing of earnings.

An important feature for a successful firm is the ability to adopt inno-vations. Even more crucial is the aptitude to put them to use throughout the organization, sometimes replacing—but more often integrating—human work. This requires both a radical change in business models and the distri-bution of skills throughout the organization, with the aim of improving human capital. Companies that know how to use innovations to increase their human capital potential by reinventing processes and spreading skills will be at the forefront of their industries. Conversely, those that simply automate and concentrate knowledge among a few experts will likely have a workforce that is inadequate to deal with change in the long term.

Investing in continuing education and training is a necessary condition for successfully facing the challenges of innovation in the labour market. However, it may not be enough. As Larry Summers (2015) points out, "strengthening education is desirable [because] it will raise productivity and raise overall incomes in our society" but "it is not likely [...] to have large impact on inequality in any relevant horizon. Including the inequality that further concentration of machine ownership will instead worsen".

New Distribution (or Pre-Distribution) Model

In a machine-driven economy the production of wealth is increasingly independent of human work. Hence, the distribution of wealth is no longer largely based on work and on the taxation of its income, as it was in the past. In such a scenario the distribution of wealth should at least be supplemented, either by transfers or by allocation of rights to participate in capital ownership. Otherwise, the risk is that wealth be increasingly concentrated in the hands of the few who hold capital, with a consequent rise in inequality and contraction of aggregate demand.

My policy proposal is a combination of three measures, each supporting a specific stage of life: free and compulsory basic education (for the school term), universal loans (for university studies or for the vocational training phase) and endowment capital (for the working and retirement period).

This three-part proposal goes beyond the traditional mechanism to *re-distribute* produced wealth as it represents an attempt to *pre-distribute* the means that will produce the wealth. The goal is to provide everyone with an initial capital, in terms of education, knowledge, training and financial resources. This should allow everyone—or at least those who know how to exploit this endowment—to share in the benefits of technological progress. The basic idea is not very different from what parents and grandparents often do for their children and grandchildren: to provide for their education and training, giving them the initial help to buy a house or start a business.

This policy proposal does not claim to be an exhaustive solution, nor does it lack critical aspects. Its applicability depends on multiple variables, including demographic trends, economic and financial market outlook, flexibility in fiscal and monetary policy, and political vision. The ambition is to provide original ideas to contribute to a discussion on a topic of growing importance. This is the time when it is necessary to try to have a vision of a future that is marked, as never before, by innovations. That should not be done by giving in to unrealistic fantasies but neither by lazily relying on the tools and thinking framework of the past, which risk being inadequate. The best contribution is to circulate ideas, challenge priorities, venture hypotheses, raise proposals—sometimes even disruptive ones—and expose them to discussion and criticism.

Free and Compulsory Education

Education should be compulsory until the completion of high school and free for all, except for those whose families have high incomes or substantial assets. The field of study—vocational technical schools, classical studies, scientific studies—should be determined on the basis of students' interests but also of their academic performance. Gratuity should include school tuition and fees but also textbooks and teaching materials and, for children of low-income families, some extracurricular activities useful for multidisciplinary training. In some instances, families may be asked to contribute in part to expenses of the activities. Free education should be funded by a reallocation of current public expenditure, and financial resources should be directed mainly to upgrading teaching materials (including technology), remodelling classrooms and compensation of high performing teachers. The decline in the school population, due to the drop in the birth rate, should contribute to further increase the per capita investment. Additional resources could come from the proceeds of a web tax, ideally directed to fund digital education.

Universal Loan

After completing higher education, any young person who does not have sufficient financial resources may apply for a loan, at a subsidized rate and for a fixed period of time, to finance either the university education or professional training programmes. The loan should be disbursed by credit institutions and guaranteed by the State, which in turn can have recourse on the beneficiary's endowment capital (see paragraph below). Disbursement of the loan is conditional on the possession of merit and aptitude requirements (such as good high school grade point average and graduation mark, and a minimum score in university admission tests) and the achievement of intermediate objectives (for example in terms of university grades and attendance, number of hours and performance of in-company training, etc.). The loan repayment plan shall vary according to the income levels subsequently achieved by the beneficiary: faster pay back for those who earn well and a more flexible reimbursement schedule for those with financial hardships.

One of the advantages of this "honour loan" is that it is repayable and not an outright grant. Hence, it does not have an excessively negative impact on public spending. The possible critical points of this proposal—that partially emerged in the United Kingdom and the United States[13] where university student loans are widespread—are the fuelling of private debt "bubbles" and the risks of default. In addition to the introduction of a universal loan, strong tax incentives could be recognized to donors of non-profit organizations—such as schools, universities, hospitals, research centres—who allocate funds to merit-based scholarships or grants to the less well-off, as well as to companies that offer vocational training programmes jointly with schools and universities.

Endowment Capital

Each resident should receive an endowment in the form of an ownership stake of a fund that manages the capital invested in technological innovations. These investments in technology are the source of productivity gains and wealth increases but, at the same time, they are also the cause of job losses (due to machines replacing humans).

The proposed fund is structured on the model of sovereign wealth funds. The bestowals of the fund are a small equity stake of each economic activity of future constitution[14] and—at least at an initial stage—some liquid resources. The liquidity may come from different sources, such as international initiatives to recover evaded or eluded taxes,[15] a digital tax (on online transactions such as data transfer, sale of advertising space, and intermediation activities between users and business), inheritance taxes on high net worth, a partial reallocation of public spending.[16] The fund therefore holds stakes of many companies and is invested in all sectors of the economy. It should be noted that, over time, the increase in value of the capital shares of the economic activities contributed to the fund reduces—and eventually eliminates—the need for injections of liquidity.

---

[13] In the United States, student debt is about $1.6 trillion (second only to mortgage debt and higher than credit cards and auto loans) and involves about 44 million people.

[14] Only newly established activities contribute a stake to the fund because involving existing companies would represent an unfair and politically difficult ex-post change of the rules and would likely cause capital flight.

[15] The aforementioned (see Chapter 6) *Base Erosion and Profit Shifting* (BEPS) and *Automatic Exchange of Information* (AEOI), whose resources the OECD proposes to use to finance the *Transition Agenda for a Future that Works for All*. According to prudent estimates by the OECD, BEPS could generate between $100 and $240 billion. In addition, as of June 2018, voluntary compliance with the AEOI identified €93 billion in revenue between taxes, interest and penalties.

[16] Additional liquidity may come to the fund from resources related to technological innovation, such as issuing certificates of conformity for automation of production processes or issuing permits for the use of drones and unmanned vehicles.

From birth, each person should receive shares in the fund each year for twenty-five years and gradually build up an endowment capital. During this period, the fund reinvests the returns earned and the beneficiary cannot receive any dividends (nor can he dispose of the shares). After twenty-five years, the beneficiary starts receiving dividends from the fund (but still cannot dispose of the shares, which are reallocated to new-borns when the current beneficiary dies). This income from dividends supplements—or replaces in the event of unemployment—the beneficiary's work income, and at a later stage the revenue from social security. The end result is a diversification of people's income that mitigates the risks of increasing job insecurity. This mechanism could also become an incentive to start a self-owned business or to take entrepreneurial risks.[17]

In many cases, sovereign wealth funds are fuelled by revenues from natural resources: oil in Alaska and Norway, minerals in Wyoming, public land in some Texas' school and university funds. The "oil", "minerals" and "land" of the new digital and highly automated economy is the wealth produced through technological innovations and the use of data. This wealth comes from the appreciation over time of the capital shares of economic assets held by the fund. In many circumstances, sovereign wealth funds have purposes of intergenerational redistribution (that implies preserving part of the wealth for future generations) and of support to projects of public interest (such as education, infrastructures, pensions, social security). The objective of the proposed fund is to distribute part of the wealth produced to all, to broaden the spread of the benefits coming from innovation. This distribution of wealth takes place thanks to the returns from the fund paid out to beneficiaries in the form of dividends (and perhaps to the possibility of disposing part of the fund shares).

To be effective, the fund should be introduced on a transnational basis. This is because the ongoing technological revolution is global and cannot be contained or managed solely at the national level. The transnational approach provides more resources, reduces the risk of capital flight and—in the case of the Europe Union—it removes the proposal from the budgetary constraints imposed on individual countries.

---

[17] A variant could be envisioned such that, in the course of the beneficiary's life (upon reaching a certain age, or on the occurrence of particular needs for education, vocational training, health, welfare, or on the emergence of a business project), part of the fund's shares could be disposed. The only way to avoid having this measure burden public expenditure, is that the valuation and returns of the shares of the contributed economic assets are high enough that the contribution of liquid resources becomes unnecessary. In a scenario where the fund's shares can be disposed, the fund becomes a widely-owned capital vehicle with the State as a mere custodian.

The distributional objective of assigning an endowment capital could also be achieved in other ways. For example by using the same resources to provide a universal basic income. Or, more simply, each country with its own budgetary resources could repay its public debt, thereby reducing its per capita share. There are some differences, however, between these two alternatives and the assignment of an endowment capital.

The endowment capital proposal, although more complex, differs from the universal basic income because, unlike the latter, it is not a redistribution mechanism based on a mere transfer but an *entitlement* measure. That means it entitles the holder to own part of the capital and to enjoy its fruits. Rather than a *re-distribution* of produced wealth, it is therefore a *pre-distribution of* the means that will produce wealth in the future. Redistributing wealth through financial transfers can be divisive in the long term, as it creates social and political tension between those who give and those who receive. The risk is a polarization between those who are in favour of technological progress and those who would like to halt it. On the contrary, the sharing of part of the invested capital has a unifying effect, putting everyone on the same side. In this scenario, everybody favours innovation because everybody benefits from it due to the ownership of some of the invested capital. The result is a broad sense of belonging to the economic system and a direct participation in its progress. This translates into a stronger bond than that arising from receiving subsidies or social services. To better understand: it is one thing to own shares in a company, to attend its shareholders' meetings and participate in its decisions, to receive a dividend; it is quite another to receive that same sum as a philanthropic donation. Moreover, universal basic income is financed every year by public expenditure, while the life annuity generated by the assigned endowment capital is the continuous fruit of invested assets. The difference is similar to that between the grandparents who give some "pocket money" to their grandchild and those who, instead, periodically deposit sums in a savings book so that the grandchild can receive a stream of income, once an adult.

When compared to the public debt repayment option, assigning an endowment capital is also more appealing as it allows for a more equitable distribution. In the first case the benefit of each taxpayer is proportional to their income, while in the second case it is higher for those with lower income levels. Moreover, assigning an endowment capital is a strong signal to young people that there is a plan for their future. This fosters a sense of security and may even be an incentive for demographic growth.

The creation of a fund also provides the opportunity to direct part of the investments in support of strategic sectors of the economy, such as infrastructure or research and development activity, which require a long time to generate satisfactory returns.

The open questions about this tool regard the management of the fund, its investment criteria and the risk of political interference. However, these are issues that arise in any major economic policy initiative. There is also the problem of a long transitional phase, which is not easy to manage. The endowment capital mechanism has full effect twenty-five years after its introduction. This excludes current workers and unemployed people from the benefits. As a remedy, in the immediate term incentives could be introduced for workers to participate more in mutual funds or pension funds, which invest in companies in different sectors including the most technological ones. In addition, for those who are employed some rules could be introduced to encourage employees to participate in the employer's capital through reserved issues or stock options. Finally, for the unemployed a guaranteed minimum income could be envisaged: a mix of cash payments and hours of vocational training. One could also hypothesize an extraordinary provision to the fund in favour of individuals under twenty-five for the years remaining until their completion.

Strengthening the Economic System

Distributing the wealth produced is important. Actually producing it, however, is even more important.

For this to happen in a context of disruptive change, and with human labour maintaining a significant relevance, not only is it necessary for the economy to have an adequate supply of skills—hence the importance of education and training—but also that there is demand for these skills and for work in general. To this end, it is essential to strengthen the economic system. On three fronts. First: developing new labour-intensive activities, including those in traditional sectors. Second: sustaining a high rate of innovation, investing in research and stimulating economic activities in which the quality of human capital is central. Third: increasing competitiveness vis-à-vis other territories, in order to attract innovative investments and high-skilled jobs.

A first action must encourage the emergence of *new labour-intensive activities*. This does not mean hindering the adoption of technology, especially in areas where it increases productivity, but rather broadening the economy, investing in areas where automation is either not possible, too complex, or not economically viable. The aim is to diversify the sources of work and create new employment to compensate—at least in part—for the jobs lost elsewhere. In Italy, as in many other countries, opportunities of this kind are offered by territorial development, enhancement of the cultural and artistic heritage, urban modernization, education and training activities, social assistance, community services, safety aid services, cultural tourism and conventions, local and traditional crafts. Moreover, if sustainability becomes one of the variables for measuring well-being, the green economy can be a source of economic growth and new employment. An important contribution to employment can also come from the Third Sector—the economic sector consisting of non-governmental and other non-profit organizations—which is often rooted at the local level.

The second line of action is to support a *high rate of innovation* in the economic system. Innovative enterprises can generate the greatest employment gains because they are the only ones where human capital is more important than physical capital. Stimulating investment in research and opening the field to activities in which the quality of human capital is central means pursuing economic development driven by ideas and talent. This makes it possible to increase the rate of innovation, enlarge the economy and expand the demand from companies for skilled labour.

In terms of sectors, innovation is transversal. It is the catalyst for the creation of new businesses in frontier sectors—such as robotics, information technology, additive manufacturing, biotechnology, biomedicine, nanotechnology, new materials science, *green economy*—but it also helps existing firms in more traditional fields. According to Moretti (2012), "innovation is not limited to high technology" because it includes "any job that generates new ideas and new products [...] that cannot be easily replicated".

To strengthen the economic system, it is not enough to start new businesses: it is also necessary that the best ones survive and grow. Hence, start-up incubators should be flanked by *mentoring* initiatives to help transform brilliant ideas into more concrete business plans, the latter being decisive in finding financial resources. On the other hand, the exit from the market of companies that have exhausted their growth potential should be simple, quick and inexpensive. Promoting an efficient allocation of resources is more urgent today than it was in the past because technological progress shortens the life cycle of products and therefore that of companies themselves.

The third front is *territorial competitiveness*. In the global economy, local territories compete with each other to attract financial and human capital. All regions will suffer job losses due to automation, but not all of them have the necessary fertile ground to grow new activities and create new jobs. Creative, high value-added professions will concentrate in the most attractive places, turning them into hubs of skills and innovation that can supply the whole world. Other territories will be inevitably impoverished.

Moreover, the gap between winning and losing areas is growing over time and the coronavirus pandemic has further increased the mobility of intellectual labour. Areas with talented people and innovative businesses grow rapidly, attracting more human and financial capital and creating new activities and skilled jobs (which, in turn, generate a supply of lower-paid jobs linked to local services). Conversely, less attractive areas are likely to decline. For these reasons, the balance of migration of talented people is more important than the trade balance. And showing a surplus in intellectual mobility is an absolute priority.

Bibliography

S. B. Banerjee, *Corporate Social Responsibility: The Good, the Bad and the Ugly.* "Critical Sociology", 34, no. 1, pp. 51–79, 2008.

Z. Bauman, *Modernity and the Holocaust*, Cornell University Press, Ithaca, NY 1989.

J. Beshears et al., *Who Is Easier to Nudge?* NBER paper, 27 May 2016.

J. Beshears, K. Milkman, *Behavioral 'Nudges' Offer a Cost-Effective Policy Tool*, "Psychological Science", 8 June 2017

C. Chaplin, *Modern Times*, 1936.

A. D. Chandler, *The Visible Hand: The Managerial Revolution in American Business*, Harvard University Press, Cambridge, MA 1977.

O. Cuthbert, *Saudi Arabia Becomes First Country to Grant Citizenship to a Robot*, *Arab News*, 26 October 2017.

A Cuthbertson, *Artificial Intelligence ìBoy' Shibuya Mirai Becomes World's First AI Bot to Be Granted Residency*, Newsweek, 6 November 2017.

F. De Bortoli, *Ambiente che cosa si può fare*, "Corriere della Sera", 6 October 2019.

Estonia Government, *Estonian Artificial Intelligence: Report of the Expert Group of Development*, May 2019.

Estonia Library of Congress, *Estonia: Government Issues Artificial Intelligence Report*, National Library of Estonia, 31 July 2019.

M. Ferrera, *La società del Quinto Stato*, Laterza, Roma-Bari 2019.

L. Floridi, Discorso pronunciato durante l'inaugurazione dell'anno accademico 2018–2019 dell'Università del Piemonte Orientale, Vercelli, Teatro Civico, 12 febbraio 2019.

Pope Francis, *Laudato si'*, Encyclical Letter, 24 May 2015.

Investment Review 2020, Global Sustainable Investment Alliance, 2021.

M. King, *Public Policy and the Corporation*, Chapman and Hall, London 1977.

R. Kurzwell, *La singolarità è vicina*, Apogeo, Milano 2008.

S. Latouche, *Conference on Degrowth*, Greenrport, Lastra a Signa September 2006.

S. Latouche, *Breve trattato sulla decrescita serena-Come sopravvivere allo sviluppo*, Bollati Boringhieri, 2015.

M. Magatti, *L'era della digitalizzazione e la formazione che serve*, "Corriere della Sera", 3 January 2019.

M. Magnani, *Terra e Buoi dei Paesi Tuoi. Scuola, ricerca, ambiente, cultura, capitale umano: quando l'impresa investe nel territorio*, UTET, 2016.

E. Mayo, *The Human Problems of an Industrial Civilization*, Macmillan, New York 1933.

H. L. Mencken, *A New Dictionary of Quotations on Historical Principles form Ancient and Modern Sources*, A.A. Knopf, New York 27 June 1942.

E. Moretti, *The New Geography of Jobs*, Mariner Books, Boston 2012.

T. Muta et al., *Consumption Subsidies for Fossil Fuels Remain a Roadblock on the Way to a Clean Energy Future*, International Energy Agency, 21 June 2021.

W. D. Nordhaus, *Reflections on the Economics of Climate Change*, "The Journal of Economic Perspectives," 7, no. 4, pp. 11–25, 1993.

OECD, *Getting Skills Right. Engaging Low-Skilled Adults in Learning*, 2019.

D. Pichert, K. V. Katsikopoulos, *Green Defaults: Information Presentation and Pro-Environmental Behavior*, "Journal of Environmental Psychology", 28, no. 1, pp. 63–72, March 2008.

M. E. Porter, M. R. Kramer, *The Big Idea: Creating Shared Value*, "Harvard Business Review," January-February 89, 2011.

F. Ramella, *Catastrofismo e scienza: un approccio equilibrato*, "Aspenia", no. 86, p. 108, 2019.

Senato della Repubblica Italiana, *"Disposizioni per il recupero dei rifiuti in mare e nelle acque interne e per la promozione dell'economia circolare" ("legge SalvaMare")* (AS. 1571), Roma 2019.

L. Summers, *Robots Are Hurting Middle Class Workers*, "The Washington Post", 3 Mach 2015.

C. Sunstein, R. H. Thaler, *Nudge: Improving Decisions About Health, Wealth and Happiness*, Yale University Press, New Haven 2008.

C. Sunstein, R. H. Thaler et al., *Should Governments Invest More in Nudging?* Harvard Public Law Working Paper, 17–42, 2017.

F. W. Taylor, *The Principles of Scientific Management*, Harper & Brother, New York 1911.

B. Troczynski, *Estonia Plans the Boldest AI Regulations*, "Newtech.law", 23 October 2017.

Unilever, *Nuovo traguardo 'rifiuti zero'*, press release, 15 febbraio 2016.

8

Ye Were not Made to Live with the Virus: Lessons from the Pandemic

Black Swan or Foreseeable Event?

In 2020 and 2021, the world has been overwhelmed by a health emergency caused by the rapid spread of the COVID-19 pandemic (due to the new and deadly Sars-Cov-2 coronavirus). Many have referred to a "black swan", a metaphor introduced by the Lebanese-American mathematician and philosopher Nassim Taleb[1] to indicate a rare and unpredictable event with a disruptive and systemic impact at the international level. The black swan theory, however, is not entirely applicable to this pandemic. While on the one hand it is undeniable that the impact of the virus has been disruptive, systemic and global, on the other hand it is also obvious that this emergency was, to some extent, predictable. In fact, there had been recent disturbing precedents—albeit with much more limited consequences—such

---

[1] Nassim Nicholas Taleb is a scholar of the randomness that governs the world. He is the author of *The Black Swan: The Impact of the Highly Improbable*, Random House, London 2007.

Paraphrase of the famous verse from Dante Alighieri's Divina Commedia (Inferno, XXVI, 118–120): "Consider well the seed that gave you birth: you were not made to live as brutes, but to follow virtue and knowledge". These are the words used by Ulysses—who Dante places in Hell as guilty of fraudulent counsel—to urge his men to sail with him past the pillars of Hercules. Ulysses describes how he used his gift with words to convince his somewhat reluctant crew to continue their adventures together. As he recalls his words, Ulysses recognizes that his persuasiveness is a good part of why he is now in Hell, as he led his men to their deaths.

© The Author(s), under exclusive license to Springer Nature Switzerland AG 2022
M. Magnani, *Making the Global Economy Work for Everyone*,
https://doi.org/10.1007/978-3-030-92084-5_8

the SARS outbreak in 2002–2003, the "swine flu" in 2009–2010 and the "avian influenza" in 2016–2018. Moreover, in recent years several experts had stressed the risk of a global pandemic.

According to some historians, epidemics contributed to the fall of the Roman Empire. While Rome's decline was due to a number of different concurring factors, epidemics certainly weakened its army, economy and institutions. Around 165 A.D., the *Antonine* plague reduced manpower in vital sectors of the economy, causing production to collapse and prices to rise. And it decimated Marcus Aurelius' troops who were fighting against the Germans and Persians. A few centuries later—in 541 A.D.—the plague struck Constantinople and spread everywhere, undermining Justinian's military campaigns in the West aimed at rebuilding the empire. The COVID-19 outbreak has not caused the demise of empires, but in just a few weeks it revealed the lack of preparation of many governments, the inadequacy of several political leaders, the inefficiency of some international institutions and the fragility of an economic system heavily based on globalization.

This is not the first time that humanity has faced an epidemic. But the coronavirus has had different characteristics and consequences compared to the past. On the one hand, fortunately, medical and scientific progress has helped contain the number of deaths. The Black Death that struck Europe and Asia in the mid-1300s killed about 20 million people, one-third of the European population; the "Spanish flu" in 1918–1920 caused between 50 and 100 million deaths in a world population of about 2 billion. On the other hand, however, the current close interconnection between countries has caused both the viral and socio-economic contagions to spread much more rapidly than in the past.

Sailing in Uncharted Waters

The rapid spread of the virus and its negative consequences have brought to light the fragility of human beings and that of the economic system.

The impact of the pandemic on people has been very strong. The virus has reintroduced the feeling of fear, bringing death back as a central theme for mankind, after decades in which the exasperated consumerism and the enormous progress in the scientific and medical fields had almost removed it from our collective concerns. In addition, the pandemic has upset the relationship human beings have with time and space. Before the COVID-19 pandemic humans dominated space, thanks to technology that made travel easy and real-time communication possible. They were in a perpetual struggle against time, which was never enough. The lockdown has turned the situation upside down. On the one hand it has limited space to the perimeter of the homes where people were confined and from where they engaged in smart working. On the other hand it has increased the availability of time, mainly due to the collapse of travel and commuting. In addition, the rapid and unstoppable circulation of information—and sometimes of misinformation[2]—has contributed to increasing the level of collective anxiety. For all of these reasons managing emergencies in the age of knowledge and technology can be significantly more complex than in the past.

Shortly after affecting people, the contagion has spilled over to the global economy. The economic shock triggered by the virus is new from every point of view, starting with its origin. Indeed, it is not the consequence of a financial crisis, of an over-production not absorbed by the markets, nor of bad management of the economic system, but rather the result of an adverse and fortuitous natural phenomenon (although, as said, not entirely unpredictable). Also, the scale of the economic crisis is unprecedented. In 2008, the anti-crisis interventions in the Eurozone area were in the order of magnitude of a few hundred billion Euros; the unit of measure of fiscal and monetary policies adopted in response to the COVID-19 pandemic has become trillions.

An important consequence is that several established economic, social and political settings will be upset and even the geopolitical balance may be profoundly altered. The geography of production and the organization of work, trade relations between countries and the allocation of public and private investment, the psychology of investors and consumers' preference, are all likely to change. There will be an acceleration in the spread of technology in all areas, with benefits in terms of productivity but a negative impact on employment. The role of the state in the economy may be redefined, especially in Western economies. The risk of a further weakening of the middle class is high, as is the risk of increasing inequality.

Of course, new opportunities will also emerge. Some sectors—such as digital technologies and telecommunications, e-commerce and e-payments, logistics and shipping, pharmaceuticals and health care, education and distance learning—will see opportunities for accelerated growth. Provided

---

[2] According to the W.H.O. (2020), during the COVID-19 outbreak technology has enabled and amplified an "*infodemic*": an overabundance of information, both online and offline, that includes also deliberate attempts to disseminate wrong information. Infodemic has contributed to undermine the public health response and to jeopardize measures to control the pandemic, costing lives—because without the appropriate trust and correct information, diagnostic tests go unused and immunization campaigns do not meet their targets—and polarizing public debate on the topic.

there is a climate conducive to innovation and wide dissemination of cutting-edge technology.

The pandemic has triggered a domino effect in a number of areas. In some cases, the virus is the main source of change, in others it is merely an accelerator of trends already underway. The overall impact will be very significant and the long-term consequences only partly predictable. The situation of great uncertainty may be well described using the same words that Mario Draghi pronounced a few years ago with reference to the debt crisis in Greece. The then President of the European Central Bank pointed out the risk—had the situation degenerated—of entering "*uncharted waters*".[3] Today, more than ever, we are definitely navigating in uncharted waters.

Is It the End of Globalization?

For some decades globalization seemed unstoppable and with limited downsides. In recent years there has been a reversal of this trend with the emergence in many countries of populist movements that have tried to curb and neutralize it. The recent global health emergency seems to have achieved—at least in part—this objective. In a few weeks, a virus—an invisible biological structure—has blown up the global production system and brought the world economy to its knees. Borders were closed, immigration faced aggressive restrictions, tourist and business travel collapsed, imports and exports were frozen, and nation states once again became protagonists. Could all this lead over time to the end of globalization?

A modern economy is a complex network of interconnected parts. Workers and businesses, suppliers and consumers, banks and other financial institutions are links of a single chain that are connected by constraints and interdependencies. The breaking of just one of these links causes a domino effect that can cripple the whole system.

The pandemic has highlighted the limitations and risks implicit in the current configuration of international economy, revealing the vulnerability of the world production system. Firstly, many advanced economies have discovered that they are closely dependent on supplies of products (not only health related ones) from Asia, particularly China. And the excessive

---

[3] On 18 April 2015 at press conference outside the International Monetary Fund (IMF) meetings in Washington, D.C. Mario Draghi said "We are certainly entering into uncharted waters if the crisis were to precipitate".

concentration of suppliers in one country presents economic and geopolitical risks.[4] Moreover, the strong process of delocalization occurred in recent decades—aimed at containing costs and maximizing company profits—has led to excessive fragmentation of the production chain. With inevitable negative consequences on health controls and also on the environment, due to the very high volume of trade that produces pollution.

Riding the Wave of Change Without Being Overwhelmed by It

The crisis caused by the coronavirus raises personal and existential challenges. But also economic, social, political and ethical ones. No individual, business or country was adequately prepared to deal with the health crisis and its consequences. However, as I argue in a recent essay,[5] the key to directing change in a positive direction—to ride the wave of change without being overwhelmed—is its management. Once the emergency phase is over, three possible paths present themselves.

The first is to try to recreate the situation that existed before the crisis and to reconstruct the lost balance. This means using the mechanisms of the old socio-economic model—the one displaced by the pandemic—to recover points of gross domestic product and jobs. It is a long and tortuous path with a critical weakness: it does not leave much room to learn from the change that has taken place and to improve the system by adapting it to the new reality.

The second possibility is to completely replace—by "scrapping" it—the growth model of which the emergency has exposed the limits. Such a scenario is not inconceivable given the already widespread belief that the damages produced by globalization outweigh its benefits. The main consequence would be a surge of protectionist policies and economic nationalism. That would trigger a drastic reduction in international trade, a sudden reversal of delocalization processes and a return to bilateralism as a method of defining world balances. A situation not very different from that of the 1930s, which was fertile ground for the rise of totalitarian regimes and the outbreak of World War II.

---

[4] As Fernando de la Iglesia Viguiristi observes with reference to the origins of the European project, "European agricultural policy arose in the 1970s to ensure a vital supply of food [to all member countries] without triggering very dangerous dependencies" (*The Global Economic Crisis*, in "La Civiltà Cattolica," no. 4078, May 16, 2020).

[5] Marco Magnani, *L'onda perfetta. Cavalcare l'onda senza esserne travolti* (The Perfect Wave. Riding Change Without Being Overwhelmed), Luiss University Press, Rome 2020.

Between the two extremes—recreating the status quo that preceded the crisis and completely erasing the past—there is a middle way. That is trying to fully understand the fragility of the current model—from a health, economic and social standpoint—and making the most of it, rebuilding new and more stable balances taking into account the critical aspects of the past. The aim is to seize some opportunities, even while dealing with a crisis.

To successfully navigate this path, it is essential to be able to adapt to the new reality and learn from what has happened.

No Growth Without Health Sustainability

Several lessons have emerged from the pandemic. First, the coronavirus pandemic reminded us of the importance of sustainability: from a health, environmental and social perspective.

Never has it been clearer than today that without health sustainability there can be no economic growth. The difficulty in treating and containing the contagion—which has reached 188 countries around the world—has had immediate economic consequences: supply chain crises, factory closures, drastic reductions in the labour supply. The supply shock was followed by one on the demand side, with the collapse of household consumption and business investment. The result was a symmetrical recession.

The difficulty in efficiently managing the emergency was largely due to the inadequacy in many countries of the healthcare infrastructure, particularly the public one. According to several experts, it would have been relatively easy to curb the pandemic by systematically screening infected people from the beginning, tracking their movements, placing them in targeted quarantine, and massively distributing masks and other protective materials. These are all activities that a public health system—which is not seeking a short-term economic return—should be able to perform better than a private one. It is thanks to such a strategy that South Korea and Taiwan—strengthened by the experience of Sars in 2002—have contained both the contagion and the economic damage. Other countries have adopted—with worse results—the strategy of confinement,[6] isolating infected people while waiting for collective immunization. Sometimes mistakes were made for short-sightedness, but more often they were due to inadequacy of the public healthcare structure.

---

[6] As Gaël Giraud points out, confinement is an ancient strategy, since as early as 1347 Pierre de Damouzy—the physician of Margaret of France, Countess of Flanders—recommended confinement to the inhabitants of Reims to escape the Black Death.

Investing in strengthening public health care is therefore important to be able to respond efficiently to similar emergencies in the future. And it is a necessary condition for economic growth. Investing in making workplaces and social gathering places safer can also be a source of growth. Factories and warehouses, train stations and airports, public transport and shopping centres, banks and shops, theatres, cinemas and stadiums will have to be adapted—sometimes redesigned—to overcome the fear of workers and customers.

Strong investments in this direction can eliminate—or at least drastically reduce—the sense of uncertainty generated by the pandemic, which is a major obstacle to economic growth. Reducing the fear of a return of the contagion or the threat of a new one, helps restoring and reinforcing the sense of confidence necessary to stimulate investment and consumption.

The health emergency has reminded us that health is a global common good—as are the environment, biodiversity, education, culture—and must be managed as such. The aim is to help build a more resilient world, one that is better equipped to withstand future shocks.

A More Prudent Globalization

The second lesson of the pandemic is about the fragility of the global value chain. While it is certainly excessive to consider the epidemic a consequence of globalization, there is no doubt that the virus has shed light on its intrinsic weakness. Today there is stronger awareness that it is sufficient for a shock to hit one of the links in the value chain for the impact to become systemic.

The lesson to be learned—the opportunity to be seized—is that a transition towards new and more stable equilibria is necessary. This means being more prudent in taking decisions to offshore productions, building shorter supply chains that are less vulnerable and closer to end-markets, facilitating the reshoring of certain activities considered strategic—such as pharmaceuticals, technology and telecommunications—leveraging local territories more and making them a competitive advantage. This approach is not a refusal of the many benefits of international trade and economic relations, and it should not become an alibi to descend into economic nationalism, but just a stimulus to purse a more prudent globalization.

This crisis does not mark the end of globalization—a process that to a large extent is irreversible—but it can be helpful to understand its excesses and limits. And to pursue a more rational and sustainable growth.

Respect for the Environment and Sustainable Growth

Another lesson from the health emergency is that it has reaffirmed the importance of environmental sustainability.

The link between declining biodiversity—itself a consequence of deforestation, pollution and climate change—and the spread of animal viruses among humans is more evident than ever. It is also known that thawing permafrost can release viruses and pathogens that are dangerous to humans.

Humans have a great responsibility. The intense extraction and use of natural resources, the conversion of forests for agricultural exploitation, the spread of industrial fishing and intensive livestock breeding, are all activities that upset the ecological balance, reduce biodiversity and facilitate the diffusion of epidemics. It should also be noted that while humans have become throughout history the dominant species on Earth, they are also the best vehicle for pathogens.[7]

It is interesting to note that it is not the first time in recent years that a global epidemic has originated in China. This raises serious doubts about the sustainability of Beijing's strategy of pursuing exasperated expansionism, with the aim of bringing 1.4 billion people into the consumer economy in forced stages, making a reckless use of resources and disrupting the natural environment.

It is essential that economic growth takes into account the constraints of energy and environmental sustainability. Hence, it may be useful to reflect on the fall in pollution observed immediately after the spread of the coronavirus. This could be a stimulus to rethink some production and transport systems, showing more respect for the environment.

Greater awareness, attention and sensitivity to environmental issues can generate significant growth opportunities—through investments in the green economy, dissemination of virtuous practices of circular economy, rediscovery of values and resources of the territory.

---

[7] As Serge Morand, a researcher at CNRS-CIRAD, well explains, "in terms of biological evolution, it is much more effective for a virus to infect humans than the Arctic reindeer, which are already endangered by global warming. And this will be increasingly so because the ecological crisis will decimate other living species" (*Coronavirus: la disparition du monde sauvage facilite les épidémies*, interview given to the French weekly "Marianne" on 17 March 2020).

Solidarity Networks, the Role of the State in the Economy and International Cooperation

Crises tend to encourage individualism, in people and in nations. However—and this is another lesson from the pandemic—the coronavirus has highlighted the importance of solidarity networks. Families were the first solidarity cells to deal with closed schools, remote work and loss of employment. Many companies played a crucial role in supporting employees, their families and sometimes entire communities, through corporate welfare measures. States intervened massively to mitigate the negative economic and social impact of the virus. Mario Draghi's famous *"whatever it takes"* (2012) became the paradigm for action by central banks and governments.

This crisis offers a great opportunity to improve solidarity networks.[8] The health emergency has emphasized the importance of rethinking and adjusting certain institutions, starting with the international ones, which have proved inefficient. This will be possible by redefining their governance, introducing rules that favour cooperation, making them more effective in providing adequate responses to global emergencies. At the European level, the need has emerged to improve coordination in many areas—starting with health—and to introduce supranational economic policies. This is not an easy step because it requires individual states to give up part of their sovereignty, but it would represent a meaningful reversal in the decline of the European integration project. While the initial reaction of the EU to the pandemic was slow and confused, some of the actions taken to respond to the economic crises were very relevant and effective. At a global level, it has become apparent that some institutions need to be profoundly reformed, starting with the WHO.

More generally, the pandemic has made it clear that in the face of global problems—not only health crisis such as the coronavirus, but also other types of emergencies such as climate change and environmental sustainability, terrorism and cybersecurity, money laundering and drug or human trafficking, mass migration and world hunger—the only responses with a high probability of success can come from a strong political and technological collaboration at the international level.

---

[8] As Cardinal Jean-Claude Hollerich notes, "the post-World War II reconstruction was important for the formation of new networks of relations, such as the Western one, which brought the United States and a part of Europe closer together" (*Europe and the Virus*, in "La Civiltà Cattolica", no. 4076, April 18, 2020).

Innovation, Work and Social Sustainability

The coronavirus has also made social sustainability more topical. The pandemic has accelerated the spread of technological innovations, making many jobs redundant. The economic downturn that followed the health emergency has weakened the middle class and further increased inequality.

The technologies to replace human labour already existed and the trend was underway. However, in the post-coronavirus economy the rise of machines will proceed more rapidly than in the past and will touch new areas. For at least three reasons. Firstly, the economic crisis is pushing companies to cut costs and staff reduction is generally the first and most immediate source of savings. Secondly, to reduce the risk of contagion in case of future pandemics: robots do not catch the virus, smart working and distance education protect workers and students, virtual fairs and showrooms avoid dangerous gatherings. Finally, by forcing companies and individuals to use new technologies, COVID-19 has made them familiar and in common use, overcoming pre-existing cultural barriers to their adoption.

The higher penetration rate of innovations will lead to productivity gains, provide new investment opportunities and stimulate the creation of new jobs. But it will also require the sacrifice of many traditional jobs, putting a strain on social sustainability. Moreover, a scenario with less work and more precarious and lower paid jobs weakens aggregate demand, with negative implications for growth and welfare.

It is therefore more urgent than ever to rethink the human-machine relationship. One option is to passively wait for the *singularity point*—the moment when, according to some, machines will overtake humans—and lazily delegate most jobs to robots and AI. The alternative is to maintain a function of pre-eminence of humans over machines that allows mankind to put technology at its service, using it to increase productivity but also to improve the quality of life.

An example is to exploit the sudden and forced spread of distance education to improve teaching methods and to broaden access to instruction. Another example is to take advantage of the diffusion of smart working to reduce the negative impact on the environment due to commuting, improve the quality of work and—more in general—the lives of individuals and families. Moreover, there is an opportunity for companies to leverage on work in remote to access a wider talent pool, increase employees' attraction and retention rates, and enhance diversity.[9]

Putting *humans at the centre* means focusing on the future of work, investing in education and training to prepare people for new professions (or to use technology to perform current jobs in a different way), introducing new ways of redistribution. Alternatively, as I have suggested in this essay, introducing a mechanism of *pre-distribution* that rather than just transferring income aims to put people in a position to generate it. Finally, the pre-eminence of humans over machines means rethinking the right to privacy and personal freedom of citizens at a time when technology is a very useful tool, but at the same time a possible means—for companies and governments—of surveillance and mass control.

What's Past Is Prologue

The coronavirus pandemic marked the beginning of a long and difficult journey through uncharted, largely stormy waters full of perilous and treacherous currents. Confidence and vision are essential to tackle it successfully.

Trust is key in trying to turn threats into opportunities, to have the courage to change course and start a new path. "What's past is prologue" says Antonio to Sebastian in William Shakespeare's *Tempest*.[10] Accepting the past is crucial to overcoming it and moving forward. The end of something can be the beginning of something else.

The pandemic and subsequent crisis offer an opportunity to build a more sober and sustainable society that respects the limits of nature, and a more equitable economy that is resilient to future shocks (not just health ones). The goal is to build a growth model that is a little less efficient than the pre-virus one but a lot more resilient. Resilience, after all, means efficiency in the long term. The way to seize this opportunity is to make some adjustments to the current growth model, enhancing health, environmental and social sustainability.

---

[9] The COVID-19 outbreak has pushed many companies to rethink the workplace and change policies regarding smart working, allowing employees to work in remote even post-pandemic. This is becoming a strong trend, particularly in the Tech sector.

[10] The full verse from *The Tempest* (Act Two, Scene One, 253–254) is "Whereof what's past is prologue; what to come / in yours and my discharge" also translated as "...the past is prologue and the future / lies in your hands and mine". It suggests that what has happened up until now only sets the stage for the future, and that we are the creators of our own lives and the authors of our own story.

Trust is the wind that makes it possible to navigate uncharted waters. However, wind on its own is not enough to survive the storm and reach a safe harbour. What is also necessary is to know in which direction to go, to have a detailed navigation plan and a clear destination to reach. In addition to the wind of confidence in our sails, we need a compass of vision, a long-term perspective. Because, as Seneca points out, "if one does not know to which port one is sailing, no wind is favourable".[11]

* * *

After the health emergency caused by the coronavirus, and the subsequent economic and social upheaval, it will be very difficult to turn back. This sudden and unexpected change inexorably throws us into a different era. The pandemic has accelerated a revolution that was already underway, involving sustainability and technological innovations, with disruptive consequences on the economy, society, politics and ethics. Redefining new equilibria and eliminating the economic and social contagion generated by the pandemic will take much longer than the creation of the vaccine.

Our future largely depends on our ability to manage this difficult transition, learning from the past and adapting to the new reality.

Bibliography

D. Alighieri, Inferno, *Divine Comedy*.

F. de la Iglesia Viguiristi, *The Global Economic Crisis*, in "La Civiltà Cattolica," no. 4078, 16 May 2020.

M. Draghi, Global Investment Conference, London 26 July 2012.

M. Draghi, press conference, IMF meetings, Washington, DC, 18 April 2015.

Pope Francis, *Fratelli tutti*, Encyclical Letter, 3 October 2020.

G. Giraud, *Per ripartire dopo l'emergenza Covid-19*, in "La Civiltà Cattolica", no. 4075, 4 April 2020.

J. C. Hollerich, *Europe and the Virus*, in "La Civiltà Cattolica", no. 4076, 18 April 2020.

M. Magnani, *L'onda perfetta. Cavalcare l'onda senza esserne travolti*, Luiss University Press, Rome 2020.

S. Morand, *Coronavirus: la disparition du monde sauvage facilite les épidémies*, interview given to "Marianne", 17 March 2020.

Seneca, *Letters to Lucilius*, letter 71.

W. Shakespeare, *The Tempest*, Act Two, Scene One (253–254), 1610–1611.

---

[11] "*Ignoranti quem portum petat nullus suus ventus est*" (Seneca, Letters to Lucilius, letter 71).

N. T. Taleb, *The Black Swan: The Impact of the Highly Improbable*, Random House, London 2007.

W.H.O., *Managing the COVID-19 Infodemic: Promoting Healthy Behaviours and Mitigating the Harm from Misinformation and Disinformation*, 23 September 2020.

Conclusions:
With Great Power Comes Great Responsibility

The wave of innovations that characterize our age is a source of risk but it also offers unique opportunities. Think of the unprecedented progress in medicine and science and the extraordinary improvements in the quality of life. Or the creation of economic wealth through technological development. Humanity will change more in the upcoming decades than it has in many centuries.

The challenge we are facing is unprecedented. It calls for complex and urgent choices that require courage and long-term vision. The objective is to manage this disruptive process to mitigate the negative consequences and contain the risks, to seize the extraordinary opportunities that emerge and to ensure sustainable growth and a fair distribution of the fruits of progress.

The temptation to postpone these difficult choices to the next generation is strong, especially for a short-sighted ruling class focused almost solely on immediate results. However, the enormous potential offered by technological innovations must be a stimulus to face the challenge, because—as Peter Parker acknowledges when he discovers he has Spider-Man superpowers—"with great power comes great responsibility".

Mankind can govern this epochal change and positively influence its outcome. There are two conditions for this to happen. First, it must not renounce its own centrality and understand how to ride the wave of technological progress instead of being overwhelmed by it. Second, it must have a long-term vision and the courage to take on great responsibility, making the bold and difficult choices that will turn that vision into a reality.

M. Magnani, *Making the Global Economy Work for Everyone*, https://doi.org/10.1007/978-3-030-92084-5

Bibliography

S. Lee, S. Ditko, *Amazing Fantasy—Spider Man #15, Marvel Comics*, 1 August 1962.

Index

© The Editor(s) (if applicable) and The Author(s), under exclusive
license to Springer Nature Switzerland AG 2022
M. Magnani, *Making the Global Economy Work for Everyone*,
https://doi.org/10.1007/978-3-030-92084-5

195

CPSIA information can be obtained
at www.ICGtesting.com
Printed in the USA
LVHW012058101022
730381LV00008B/346